# people skills
## for the salon professional

Robert J. Wright

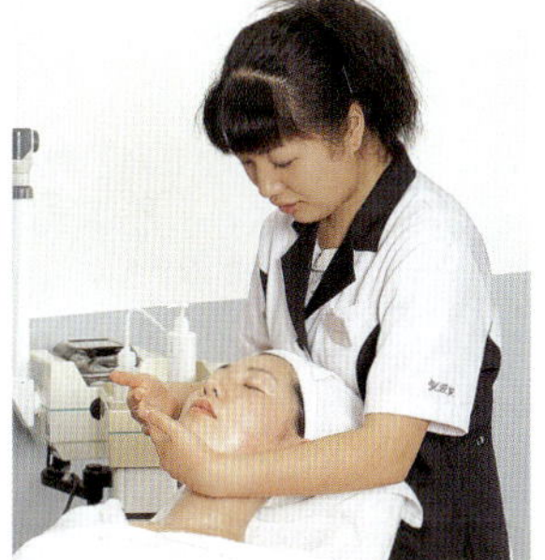

**Part One:**
**Relating with CARE**

**Part Two:**
**Serving with CARE**

ISBN 0-9715610-1-X

Fifth printing March 2005

Pivot Point International, Inc.
1560 Sherman Avenue, Suite 700
Evanston, Illinois 60201
1.847.866.0500
www.pivot-point.com

# A Message from Leo Passage, Founder of Pivot Point International

Every day we interact with people, personally and professionally, taking for granted the people skills that cause each interaction to be successful—or not successful.

In our business, these skills are vitally important. Expert use of people skills, and learning to understand their components enables us, as salon professionals, to realize our potential as business people—to make each encounter with clients, co-workers, or supervisors a progressive step up our career ladder.

Experts believe that as much as 80 percent of your success depends on your ability to deal effectively with people. Only 20 percent of your success is dependent on technical ability.

Those statistics make a powerful statement!

Increasingly, in today's high-tech and often impersonal world, caring, individualized service is important to our clients. And of course, good client relationships not only assure our financial success but help us feel good about ourselves and our work environment.

Learning about and practicing people skills awaits you in the coming pages. It is up to you to learn to use the simple and effective techniques we offer.

Author Robert Wright, co-founder of The School of Exceptional Living in Chicago, is an expert at teaching others how to build relationships. He has worked with Pivot Point and in the beauty industry since the early 1980s. In *People Skills*, he shares his insights on the importance of understanding ourselves and our clients so that we can provide excellent service.

I, along with everyone at Pivot Point, wish you a rewarding career, full of success with people skills. Good luck!

*Leo Passage*

Leo Passage
Chairman
Pivot Point International

Robert Wright
Author
*People Skills*

# Part One: Relating With CARE

## Unit 3: Relating: Analysis



## Unit 4: Relating: Application

## Part Two: Serving with CARE

### Unit 5: Serving: Introduction



### Unit 6: Serving: Fundamentals



### Unit 7: The Service Cycle

HAIR - DRE
PEOPLES HAIR-DRESSING ROOM
YOU'VE COME A LONG WAY, BABY
$12.50
MEERSCHAUM
OPEN
FROM
7 AM To 9 PM
ATURDAY T. 11

**BEFORE 1970:**
**Beauty Parlors**
**Beauticians**
**Wash & Set Styles**
**Barber Shops**

**1970s:**
**Unisex Salons**
**Wash & Wear Styles**
**Precision Cuts**

**1980s:**
**Franchises**
**Liquid Tools**
**Computers**
**Full-Service Salons**
**Specialty Licenses**

**1990s:**
**People Skills**
**High-Tech Salons**
**Day Spas**
**More Male Clients**

**NEW MILLENNIUM:**
**Color Explosion**
**Texture Fusion**
**Health & Wellness**
***What's Next?***

# EXTRA: A Look at the Changing Salon Scene

The salon industry is booming—busy and exciting! Salon professionals have never been in so much demand. You are stepping into a bright picture. To help you make the most of your opportunities, we want to help you understand the historic context surrounding your new career and, along the way, meet the owners, managers, and clients who you join in this glowing picture.

You are joining an industry that has been expanding and changing rapidly for some 30 years. Before 1970, salons were known as "beauty parlors" and served women, whereas "barber shops" served men. The hair care industry was largely small-town, friendly and composed of independently owned businesses. Clients were loyal to "their" beauticians and barbers. As a result, clients developed close relationships with their hair experts.

The '70s saw a new trend sweep the salon industry. Cut and blow dry replaced wash and set. Weekly comb-outs became a thing of the past. You may be familiar with some of the terms from those days: precision haircutting, wash-and-wear hair, and unisex.

Hair and beauty education began to change to meet the demand created by new techniques and lifestyles.

Clients began to visit the salon less frequently—every four to six weeks for a cut—caring for their own hair on a daily basis. Bathrooms began to feature blow dryers, electric rollers, curling irons and styling aids. The shakeup inside the industry was impacted by another far-reaching trend—women entering the workforce by the millions—with less time available for hair, nail and skin care. The industry itself changed as specialty shops for nail care and makeup opened up.

You've come a long way, baby!
*Clockwise from above are beauty advertisements from 1924, 1952, and 1932, respectively. Historical photos are courtesy of: Tony Kendall, Wild Hair Museum, French Lick, IN.*

## Management by the Numbers

With all these various changes (skyrocketing costs, client turnover, competitive advertising, rapid technology changes, more franchises) it is obvious that salon operations today are very different from operations even a few years ago.

Management must pay closer attention to the numbers: dollars (sales), number of clients, percentage of returning clients (client retention rate), stylist productivity, and the soaring expenses of being in business.

Success is about managing costs—and retaining clients. Attracting new clients is expensive! Losing one, an avoidable tragedy! Practicing people skills maintains client relationships.

## The Average Salon Client

The profile of the average salon client in the U.S.A. has definitely changed over the years. Today, the average client is a man or woman between the ages of 30 and 45. (This is the average because more salon clients fit this particular profile than any other, according to research statistics.) He or she is a college graduate; married; works full-time in a professional, technical, management, or service occupation; owns a home; has one or more children living in that home; and generally has two income earners in the family.

The typical client visits a salon once every four to six weeks for a haircut and style. He or she changes salons every two years.

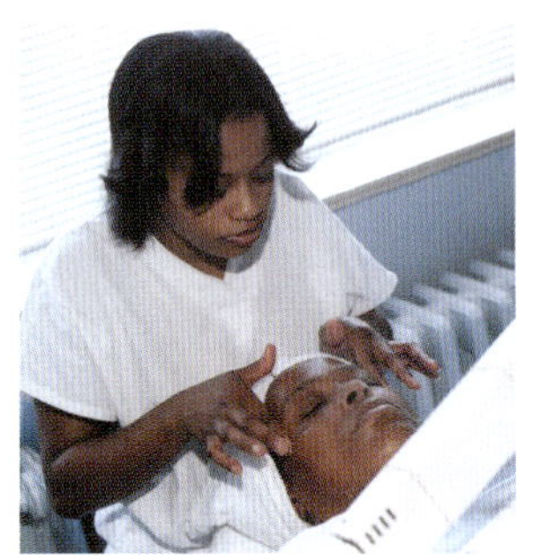

Take a moment to consider everything you know about average American salon clients. What do you see?

You will generally see very busy people. Good grooming and physical image are crucial to their demanding lifestyle, personal well-being, and career success.

This means you can make a positive difference in their life. Whether your clients are bankers, film stars, cab drivers, attorneys, homemakers, or carpenters—they all want to look their best and feel good about it. With your people skills, you'll be better able to help them present their best image.

The *People Skills* program will help you learn to recognize tension and anxiety in your clients. You will know just how to communicate with those clients, ease their tensions, and make their salon visit one of the most enjoyable, fulfilling parts of their day.

Your reputation, income and career success will be boosted daily on the foundation of your outstanding people skills.

In conclusion, keep this changing picture of the salon, and the salon client, in mind. Realize that each person has different needs and motivations—and that by using people skills, your perception of clients will expand and in many cases even help elevate their self-perception.

To be successful in your career and in your relationships, practice people skills!

## The Importance of People Skills

The hair, skin and nail business is primarily a people business. Yes, you must learn technical skills. But as technical skills are only one aspect of your success, you also need to become an expert at applying people skills. Some say managing both the technical side and the people side is an art. First, of course, you need the basics.

When you cut hair, apply makeup, and care for nails, you are creating, designing, and somehow altering a person's physical presentation. That requires an understanding of the person underneath the image—his or her personality style, lifestyle, work style, likes, and dislikes.

Mastery of people skills provides a key tool in achieving success. It helps you know more about yourself, know more about others, and therefore communicate more effectively. Only then will you be able to better realize your full potential, as well as your clients' full potential.

In the following example, meet Madison, who is technically above average, but lacks people skills.

### In the Salon. . .

Madison had limitless creativity and executed fantastic hair designs. While in school, she competed and won numerous awards. This winning attitude helped her to land a position in an exclusive salon with affluent and slightly conservative clients.

Madison was exhilarated thinking of all the clients that would be coming to her for her highly regarded expertise. She took pride in the fact that she was always current on the latest trends and imagined that this was truly the career of her dreams.

Soon, the salon manager took Madison aside and told her to learn more about the clients' personal preferences before deciding on the appropriate styles—that some clients had complained that her hair designs were a little too flamboyant. Madison took offense to this, and began to feel suffocated, unable to express her creativity and expertise. She quit in search of the salon that would allow her to express herself. Her failure in realizing that her creativity needed to be adjusted—to meet the needs of her clients and not just herself —cost her a wonderful career opportunity.

Madison's story is too often repeated. Her difficulties could have been overcome had she known about and practiced the *People Skills* program. But instead, she relied only on her creativity and technical mastery.

In an easy-to-use format, the *People Skills* program shows not only the concepts of people skills, but how you can apply the concepts.

## How to Use This Book

This book is designed with individual educational units in a sequential format. It takes you through the basics, step-by-step, to help you acquire and polish your skills with people. This course is divided into two parts: *Relating with CARE* and *Serving with CARE*. In *Relating with CARE*, we get to know ourselves and others more deeply to strengthen our relationships. *Serving with CARE* teaches us how to master the cycles of service for greater success and profit. Each part is divided into four units, as follows:

## Part 1: Relating with CARE

### Unit 1: Relating: Fundamentals

The light blue section provides an overview of the key *People Skills* concepts used throughout the course.

### Unit 2: Relating: Observation

The purple section introduces you to the characteristics of the four personality styles. You learn how to identify individuals' styles and distinguish the styles by noticing differences in behavior and preferences.

### Unit 3: Relating: Analysis

Indicated by gold, this section shows you how to analyze the interaction of different personality styles. You learn how each style complements and clashes with the others—and what to do about it.

### Unit 4: Relating: Application

Indicated by blue, in this section you practice using your new people skills. You will identify the personality styles of others and learn to shift your own actions to better communicate with a style preference that is different from your own.

## Part 2: Serving with CARE

### Unit 5: Serving: Introduction

The light blue section provides an overview of service, an introduction to the Service Cycle, and a review of people skills concepts from *Relating with CARE*.

### Unit 6: Serving: Fundamentals

The purple section introduces you to the  skills used throughout the Service Cycle. Mastering these concepts and skills will give you the foundation to provide excellent service.

### Unit 7: The Service Cycle

The gold section explains each phase of the Service Cycle. You learn the goals of each phase and the techniques for success.

### Unit 8: Service Development

In the blue section, you learn how your service skills help you build your business. You learn how to evaluate your progress with clients and set service standards for your development as a salon professional.

While it may sound like a lot to learn, practicing people skills will eventually become second nature. Your enhanced skills can be used all the time—at home, out shopping, with friends or co-workers and with supervisors and employees.

But what's really rewarding is when you see the positive results of people skills in the salon, as your clients return time and time again.

Even when something goes technically wrong, your people skills can turn the situation around, and will help you keep your client comfortable. Clients will more likely trust you to meet their hair, skin, and nail needs.

## How to Use the Lessons

The format of each lesson is sequential. This makes it easier to take advantage of the information in the course. First, you will learn the reason behind each skill or concept. Then, you learn actions required to bring each skill into your work. Finally, the text defines the outcomes you can expect once you practice the skill or concept.

The *People Skills* lessons are divided into several sections. To help you navigate the sections, we organized the information into a special format introduced on the following pages.

### Units of Learning

*Relating with CARE* and *Serving with CARE* are structured into eight units of learning. Each unit begins with an introductory vision page.

### The Vision

This section appears at the beginning of each unit. It shows you a progression of how your people skills will develop over time so you know what to expect regarding your skill, Novice, Professional or Master.

Relating: Analysis

Unit 3:

## Relating: Analysis

### THE VISION

In Unit 1, you explored the transitions of a salon career over time through the stages of Novice, Professional, and Master. We hope you use these opportunities to develop a rich personal vision of the many opportunities the salon industry has to offer. Remember that in Unit 2 you learned the personality styles—observing the major types of behaviors that characterize each style. We'll now take a look at how salon professionals in each stage begin to apply their understanding of personality styles by looking at strengths, weaknesses, differences, and similarities. This will help you further to learn and envision what to expect for yourself, and the clients you serve.

**Novice**

Novices tend to judge people quickly. Novices have not usually grasped how the strengths, weaknesses, similarities and differences of the personality styles can enhance relationships. Instead, they may use the style preference concept to pigeonhole clients into neat boxes as an easy way to label differences. The Novices are still firming up their technical basics and can feel more easily frustrated by more challenging personalities. They often need the guidance of a Professional or Master salon professional to learn to analyze, rather than judge clients. Being challenged by and focused on the technical side of the business, the adventure of interpersonal interactions awaits.

**Professional**

Professionals are able to step back and look at people-problems objectively. They are able to analyze style preferences and the interactions of the personal styles. Salon professionals at the Professional level understand the strengths and weaknesses of each personality style, as well as similarities and differences, and use that knowledge to improve relationships when confronted with problems. However, they are still likely to wait until a problem presents itself and then accurately assess and fix the situation. They are beginning to use these skills as a matter of course and have a great deal of room for growth.

**Master**

Masters are quick to analyze personalities encountered. They use their knowledge as a matter of course, without thinking about it. To Masters, every new interaction is

85

### Guide on the Side

Guidance from a salon expert in *People Skills*—along with summaries and overview of the main points in the lessons.

### Objectives

Lesson objectives—what you will be able to do when you've completed the lesson.

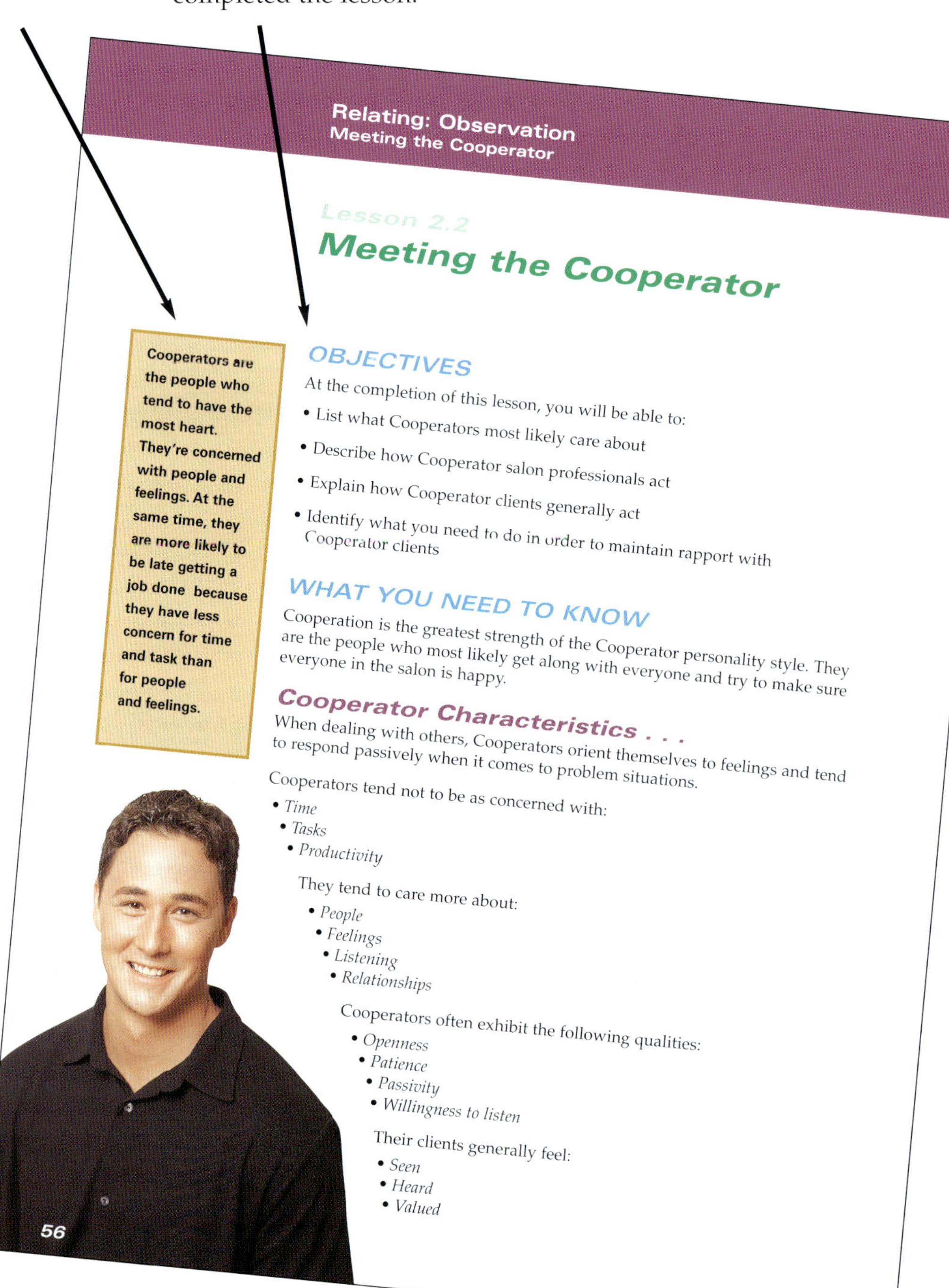

Relating: Observation
Meeting the Cooperator

Lesson 2.2

## Meeting the Cooperator

**Cooperators are the people who tend to have the most heart. They're concerned with people and feelings. At the same time, they are more likely to be late getting a job done because they have less concern for time and task than for people and feelings.**

### OBJECTIVES

At the completion of this lesson, you will be able to:

- List what Cooperators most likely care about
- Describe how Cooperator salon professionals act
- Explain how Cooperator clients generally act
- Identify what you need to do in order to maintain rapport with Cooperator clients

### WHAT YOU NEED TO KNOW

Cooperation is the greatest strength of the Cooperator personality style. They are the people who most likely get along with everyone and try to make sure everyone in the salon is happy.

### Cooperator Characteristics . . .

When dealing with others, Cooperators orient themselves to feelings and tend to respond passively when it comes to problem situations.

Cooperators tend not to be as concerned with:

- *Time*
- *Tasks*
- *Productivity*

They tend to care more about:

- *People*
- *Feelings*
- *Listening*
- *Relationships*

Cooperators often exhibit the following qualities:

- *Openness*
- *Patience*
- *Passivity*
- *Willingness to listen*

Their clients generally feel:

- *Seen*
- *Heard*
- *Valued*

56

Relating with CARE

### *In the Salon ...*

Stories from salon professionals and clients—showing the direct impact of your people skills on the job. The *Serving with CARE* part also features Salon Calimité—stories showing how *not* to serve clients.

### *Remember*

An idea from a past lesson that provides insight into a concept in the current one.

### *Review*

Tables that organize information into bite-size pieces—so you can review main points.

### *Exercises*

Chances to practice the skills and concepts—so you can enhance your abilities.

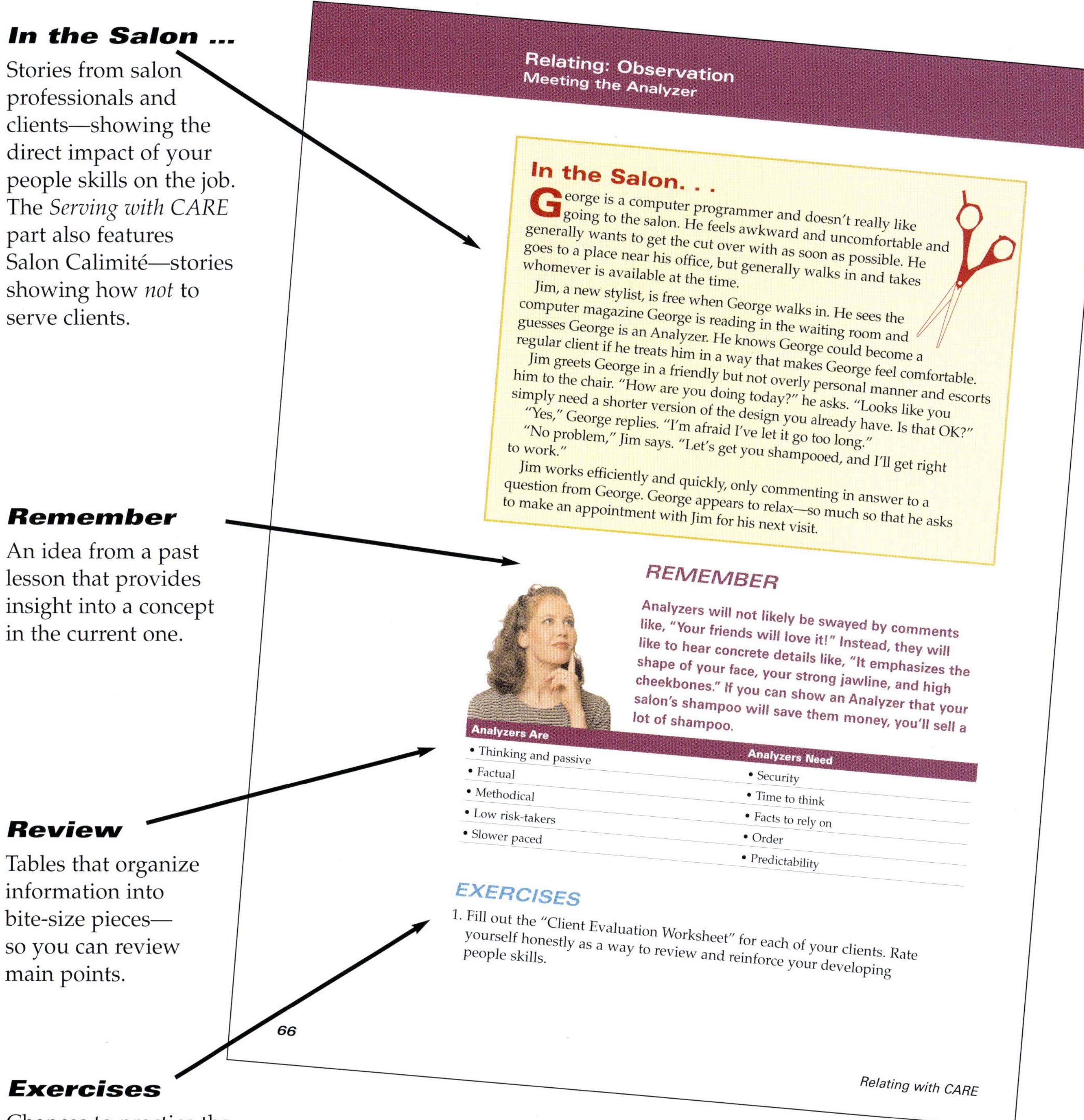

Relating: Observation
Meeting the Analyzer

**In the Salon. . .**

George is a computer programmer and doesn't really like going to the salon. He feels awkward and uncomfortable and generally wants to get the cut over with as soon as possible. He goes to a place near his office, but generally walks in and takes whomever is available at the time.

Jim, a new stylist, is free when George walks in. He sees the computer magazine George is reading in the waiting room and guesses George is an Analyzer. He knows George could become a regular client if he treats him in a way that makes George feel comfortable.

Jim greets George in a friendly but not overly personal manner and escorts him to the chair. "How are you doing today?" he asks. "Looks like you simply need a shorter version of the design you already have. Is that OK?"

"Yes," George replies. "I'm afraid I've let it go too long."

"No problem," Jim says. "Let's get you shampooed, and I'll get right to work."

Jim works efficiently and quickly, only commenting in answer to a question from George. George appears to relax—so much so that he asks to make an appointment with Jim for his next visit.

REMEMBER

Analyzers will not likely be swayed by comments like, "Your friends will love it!" Instead, they will like to hear concrete details like, "It emphasizes the shape of your face, your strong jawline, and high cheekbones." If you can show an Analyzer that your salon's shampoo will save them money, you'll sell a lot of shampoo.

| Analyzers Are | Analyzers Need |
|---|---|
| • Thinking and passive | • Security |
| • Factual | • Time to think |
| • Methodical | • Facts to rely on |
| • Low risk-takers | • Order |
| • Slower paced | • Predictability |

EXERCISES

1. Fill out the "Client Evaluation Worksheet" for each of your clients. Rate yourself honestly as a way to review and reinforce your developing people skills.

66

Relating with CARE

**Main Point Summary**
These are the most important concepts. They identify what you most need to retain from each section.

**Self-Test/ Review**
These are opportunities to check your knowledge—highlighting what you learned and what you need to review.

Relating: Observation
Meeting the Analyzer

## MAIN POINT SUMMARY

With Analyzers, salon professionals will do best to focus on consistency, facts and methods. But don't expect them to be forthcoming.

They tend not to be fashion-oriented clients and generally don't take risks. You'll also need to make sure your Analyzer clients and colleagues feel secure, and that means with consistency and sameness.

If you are an Analyzer salon professional, you'll likely do best where precision counts, like duplicating a style, mixing color or applying nail polish with precision.

## SELF-TEST/REVIEW

1. Place an "X" in the blank before each answer that accurately completes the following sentence. There should be four X's for the answer.

Analyzers tend to be:

___ Thinkers

___ Doers

___ Slow to make decisions

___ Slow to change

___ Party animals

___ Dependable

2. When an Analyzer is given a choice, he or she will most likely:

A. Be willing to take a risk

B. Choose quickly

C. Think it over and ask for more information

3. What are Analyzers most concerned with?

_______________________________________________

_______________________________________________

4. A client who is an Analyzer will never try a new style. Circle One:

True or False

68

Relating with CARE

# Part One:
# Relating with CARE

**C** ooperator

**A** analyzer

**R** regulator

**E** energizer

# Part One:
# Relating with CARE

## Unit 1
## Relating: Fundamentals

## Unit 2
## Relating: Observation

## Unit 3
## Relating: Analysis

## Unit 4
## Relating: Application

## Unit 1
# Relating: Fundamentals

## THE VISION

It is useful to think of a salon career as a journey of personal and professional development over time. For example, you begin as a Novice. Then, after a period of time, your technical and people skills develop, and you become a full-fledged Professional. Finally, with conscientious learning and experience, you develop increased abilities and you become a Master.

This concept can be applied to many skills and professions. And, when it comes to your career as a salon professional, it is helpful to identify your place on this continuum. That way you, your co-workers, and your managers know what to expect as you progress through each skill level.

### Novice

Novices tend to focus more on the challenges of applying technical skills and are less likely to apply people skills. Novices generally are focused on developing new skills and are unaware of how much they do not know.

When the Novice turns his or her attention to personality interactions, it is generally to solve a problem, or because they are directed to do so by a Professional. If they are conscientious, they take continuing education courses beyond those required, and they request feedback about their progress, seeking out Professionals and Masters to expand and validate their own observations.

### Professional

Professionals have basic technical skills down cold. Technical challenges are in the realm of creativity and strengthening weaker areas. They spend time consciously applying their people skills—to avoid and resolve people problems as well as operate more effectively with clients. They are often able to identify areas in which they are skilled in relating to people in addition to areas in which they are not yet skilled.

Because technical skills are no longer an overriding concern, Professionals increasingly turn their attention to people skills. They understand what it means to be in rapport with their clients and seek ways to deepen their relationships.

Professionals also seek to understand and then to overcome the relationship barriers they experience with some people. They use both their understanding of themselves and their relationships with other salon professionals, to work through people problems.

### Master

Masters are highly proficient in both the creative and technical skill areas as well as with people skills. They are so adept that they are most often unaware of their skills. They easily establish rapport with a wide range of people. They know that all people are not the same, and they enjoy learning and appreciating the differences between individual clients, co-workers, bosses, and vendors. Master salon professionals experiment freely with relationships, learning and growing through all that they do.

## What's Ahead . . .

The lessons in this unit are designed to introduce you to the two fundamentals of the *People Skills* program: Rapport and the CARE Profile. The salon business is based on building relationships, and Rapport is the key skill in building long-lasting and mutually satisfying ones.

The CARE Profile is the main tool used throughout the *People Skills* program. Understanding yourself and others in terms of the CARE Profile gives you a method of deepening rapport.

In this unit of *Relating with CARE*, you will learn the fundamental skills of rapport. Then you will complete the CARE Profile to determine your personality style. After completing this unit of the *Relating with CARE* program, you will:

- Understand what it means to build rapport with your clients, family, and friends.
- Learn the barriers to rapport and how to overcome them.
- Complete and score the CARE Profile Questionnaire.
- Determine your primary and secondary personality styles.

### Unit 1: Relating Fundamentals, consists of two lessons:

### Lesson 1.1: Building Rapport

### Lesson 1.2: Discovering Your Personal Style

Lesson 1.1

# Building Rapport

Establishing rapport with your clients allows you to develop lasting relationships with them. This leads to both personal satisfaction and financial success.

## OBJECTIVES

At the completion of this lesson, you will be able to:

- Define rapport
- Discuss the benefits of establishing rapport
- Describe dis-rapport
- List five barriers to rapport
- Practice rapport skills

## WHAT YOU NEED TO KNOW

The skills you learn in this program teach you to build better rapport, or relationships with others. The focus is on developing positive communication skills.

### Defining and Establishing Rapport

A successful "people business," like the salon industry, depends on your ability to manage relationships. The rapport skills you learn can be applied to clients, co-workers, and friends—leading to increased career and personal success.

Once you understand yourself and others, not only will your opportunities increase, but your income potential will be higher. Once you have established rapport with a client, you can:

- Communicate better
- Foster stronger relationships
- Achieve more success because of the new client bonds you have formed

Rapport is defined as a close relationship with harmony and agreement. Establishing rapport is creating the harmony that enables you to get along better with people. People who establish harmony can generally put themselves in someone else's shoes. When you have established rapport, others feel understood, and are drawn to you.

**Rapport is a feeling. It's also a skill you can learn. First you need to understand the barriers to rapport and then how to overcome them.**

Rapport is an **abstraction**. You can't touch or measure it, but you know that it is there, and can sense when it is not. It varies on different days, and with different people in different circumstances.

Establishing rapport is something you can learn how to do. It's a simple, two-step process:

1. Understand the differences or barriers that exist between you and others

2. Learn how to overcome the barriers

## In the Salon . . .

Jordan met Bob at her sister's wedding. While conversing, she discovered that he had done the hair and makeup for the entire wedding party. When Jordan shared with Bob that she was unhappy with her hair, he made some suggestions that appealed to her. She called the salon and booked an appointment. When Jordan arrived at the salon, she was informed that Bob was running a little late. Jordan waited for 30 minutes without any further acknowledgement.

During the consultation and throughout the service, Bob was constantly interrupted to take calls. Jordan was uncomfortable with the situation, but gave him another chance by booking another appointment. Again Bob was late for her appointment and seemed to pay more attention to others than to her service. Jordan did not feel comfortable confronting Bob, and simply decided not to go to that salon again.

By running late (valuing conversation and a relaxed pace over timeliness), Bob lost the opportunity to establish the rapport that could have led to a successful service for Jordan. He and the salon not only lost a client, but future referrals, too, ultimately because Bob wasn't able to place a higher value on the client currently sitting in his chair.

Bob's failure to establish rapport with Jordan left him with no cushion for problems. He had taken unfair advantage of her trust when she was willing to give it—and received none when he needed it.

When you learn to create and nurture rapport, you succeed in establishing and maintaining good client relationships.

***Trouble brewing:*** *A client waits impatiently because salon personnel did not make an attempt to establish rapport.*

**When you learn how to establish rapport, you can relate to a wide range of clients, as Nicole does in the example at the right.**

## In the Salon . . .

Nicole is a highly skilled Master Designer who treats each client as an individual. She handles each situation based on what she knows about her clients.

Emily, her first client, has just lost her job. With her, Nicole is gentle and understanding. She listens carefully and offers her opinion only when asked.

As Emily is leaving, she hesitates to make her next appointment because of financial concerns. Nicole reminds Emily that she will be going on job interviews, making her appearance more important than ever—and that feeling good about herself will build self-esteem. Emily makes her next appointment and leaves the salon feeling more positive about the future.

A few minutes later Nicole's next client, McKenna, arrives at the salon. McKenna helps herself to coffee and calls out a boisterous greeting to Nicole across the salon. Nicole responds in kind, with an exuberant greeting of her own. As McKenna sits in Nicole's chair, the two of them chat comfortably for a few minutes about McKenna's hair, then spend the rest of the service time teasing and joking back and forth. At the end of the service, they hug and McKenna books her next appointment before leaving the salon. Nicole was sensitive enough to her clients' needs on an individual basis and was also able to style shift to meet those needs.

You've just met two stylists and their clients, with different personalities and in different circumstances. Bob abandoned rapport for creativity. Nicole's rapport-building flexibility is evident—she met each client on their own ground. Nicole maintained rapport by using the creativity of good people skills.

## EXERCISE

Think of someone (friend, relative, or co-worker) with whom you have experienced a relationship of harmony and agreement. Now think of one word that describes that relationship.

Write it here: ______________________________.

Now compare your response with the words used by other salon professionals, listed below:

| | | |
|---|---|---|
| *playful* | *respectful* | *carefree* |
| *adoring* | *moving* | *outrageous* |
| *togetherness* | *exciting* | *easy* |
| *warm* | *caring* | *challenging* |
| *mutual* | *trusting* | *timeless* |
| *fun* | *tender* | *accepting* |

**There are five main barriers to rapport that you can learn to overcome:**

1. **Personality differences**
2. **Blame, judgment, righteousness**
3. **Cultural, gender, generational, and sexual-orientation differences**
4. **Different goals, expectations**
5. **Technical problems**

Was there a match? Do these words fit your experiences of rapport? You probably noticed that some of the words seem contradictory, like "easy" and "challenging" or "playful" and "respectful." That's because rapport is a very personal experience. The *People Skills* program is built around research on salon professionals. The salon professionals interviewed knew a great deal about clients, but some lacked a systematic way to organize and use that knowledge more powerfully to establish high-quality rapport with the widest range of clients.

## Understanding Dis-rapport

You will begin to see hair, skin, and nails differently when you understand and acquire your professional skills. In the same way, you see relationships differently when you understand and acquire the skills of rapport.

Like styling, some people have a natural ability for people skills—and others require more practice to gain competence.

When you know how to recognize rapport, you also know how to recognize when you are out of it. In the *People Skills* program, this situation is called "dis-rapport."

Dis-rapport has the same effect on rapport as a sour note in music—it's just "off-key."

You may have heard of a stone that is called fool's gold—it looks like gold but is worthless. Fool's rapport is equally worthless. It seems like the real thing but in reality is false. In fool's rapport, you are pretending to be in rapport. *People Skills* teaches you to recognize when this happens.

Remember that only a few dissatisfied clients take the time and effort to explain when something is wrong. Most people feel too uncomfortable—and simply don't come back. Instead, they search for the salon and salon professional who understands them and gives them what they want.

A salon professional who learns to distinguish between real and fool's rapport generally won't lose clients without knowing why. If you have true rapport with your client, you will see and feel when something isn't right.

In addition, a client will be comfortable enough with you to put his or her dissatisfaction into words. Then you have a chance to correct the situation before it is too late.

## Five Barriers to Rapport

At this point, you may still be asking, "Exactly what is rapport and how do I start building it?" Remember, rapport is a notion, thought or generalization. It is sometimes easier to recognize when you do not have rapport than when you do. Rapport is a feeling.

However, it's easy to learn how to build rapport by:

- Identifying what gets in the way
- Overcoming those barriers

You may want to eliminate rapport barriers from your personality, but you can't. They are just part of human nature. Instead, look at the barriers and learn how to work around them. That's why we say "overcome" barriers.

Everyone experiences rapport barriers. It's important to know that you will not eliminate all the barriers to rapport. They are a part of human nature. They represent the challenges on your journey. By understanding the barriers, however, you can learn to work around or overcome them.

Barriers to rapport can stop you from establishing good relationships with clients, co-workers, and bosses. In salons, at any given moment you can find some or all of these five barriers in operation.

Learn to recognize and overcome each one of these barriers, and you will enjoy your career even more.

### Barrier 1: Personality Differences

Different people, as you know, have different personality styles. The *People Skills* program suggests that everyone's style falls into one or two of four basic styles. This program teaches you how to recognize and successfully relate to each style.

Barrier 1 identifies that overcoming personality differences requires greater understanding of personalities. Recognizing your own and your clients' personality styles:

- Gives you ways to communicate your ideas to your clients in a way that suits their style
- Helps you understand the various needs and perceptions of the different personality styles and their preferences
- Allows you to do a host of simple things to help intentionally create rapport

Responding to each individual style is equivalent to speaking a different "language" with each.

By decreasing the differences between you and your client, you create the necessary environment for a strong salon professional-to-client relationship.

### Barrier 2: Blame, Judgment, Jealousy, and Righteousness

Any one of the above attitudes can create a big barrier to rapport. Overcoming them requires expanding your tolerance, and maybe even your acceptance.

Judging others harshly, blaming people, feeling jealous, and being righteous about and acting upon your opinions guarantees a life filled with continual disharmony and low-quality rapport with others.

More tolerance and style flexibility means that you are able to appreciate and get along with a greater range of personalities. Review the next example to see how Olivia developed the skill of rapport.

## In the Salon . . .

Olivia, a successful salon professional for nine years, got along with most people. However, one client, Madeline, drove her crazy. Madeline would come into the salon and playfully tease Olivia, saying things like, "Wow, your blouse is such a bright color, I can see you a mile away!" Olivia felt hurt and decided that Madeline simply enjoyed being rude. In other words, she judged Madeline.

After studying *People Skills*, however, Olivia saw that Madeline simply had a different personality style and, as a result, a different perception of rapport. If Olivia wanted to enjoy herself with Madeline, she had to relate differently to her.

Upon observing Olivia's boldly patterned jeans on her next visit, Madeline said, "You won't be able to get lost in a crowd with those jeans!"

Olivia replied, "I wore these just for you. I wanted to make sure that you didn't miss me when you came in."

Madeline laughed in delighted surprise. Olivia had won the day with her people skills. She had shifted her style of introduction.

By meeting Madeline on her own ground, Olivia had made life easier for herself and for Madeline. In this case, learning to match Madeline's assertive humor helped Olivia build rapport. The *People Skills* program helps you understand differences instead of judging. As you take responsibility instead of blaming, your success will reduce your righteousness. You learn that the less you judge and blame others, the more you will enjoy life.

### *Barrier 3: Cultural, Generational, Gender and Sexual-Orientation Differences*

Cultural, generational, gender and sexual-orientation differences stem from people's diverse personalities, customs, and beliefs that are part of the different cultures in which people are born and raised. Knowing how to treat clients who may be different from you is a critical rapport skill.

Once again, overcoming these barriers requires working on tolerance and acceptance skills.

No matter what someone is like, or how they behave, they want to be respected for who they are and how they act.

Look at the next *In the Salon* example to see how not recognizing the culture of your client might affect your success.

## In the Salon . . .

Florence is an esthetician who some people might call a "liberated woman." She arrived at work early one morning as a special favor for a new client. The appointment was booked by the client's husband, Ali. He requested an earlier time when no other men were in the salon.

Her new client, Khadia, dressed in the traditional long dress and veil of the Muslim faith, arrived at the salon with her husband for an eyebrow waxing. Florence was beginning to wonder what the customs of the faith were and wasn't sure how best to perform the salon service. Ali asked and answered all questions Florence asked Khadia, which made Florence angry. He allowed no conversation with his wife. When the eyebrow waxing was complete, Florence asked Khadia if she would like a makeup lesson, since there were still no men in the salon at the time. Ali became visibly angered.

Ali abruptly told Khadia to leave the room. Florence and Ali argued, eventually drawing the attention of the manager and the entire salon.

Florence's lack of awareness about her client's culture represented her lack of understanding and tolerance. Acceptance and understanding were the problems. When faced with people from a different culture, she failed to acknowledge the validity of their differences and judged them through the lens of her own experiences and attitudes.

By being aware and accepting cultural differences, Florence could have been aware of how this acceptance could lead to overcoming rapport barriers. She could have:

1. Been more sensitive to Ali's request and asked to understand why they wanted no men in the salon.

2. Continued discussion with Ali as soon as she recognized it was not part of the Muslim custom to talk directly to a man's wife.

3. Proposed additional services directly to Ali, instead of addressing Khadia, once she saw that they had preferred this method of communication.

### Barrier 4: Different Goals and Expectations

Sometimes clients are dissatisfied because some aspect of the style they received is not the style they expected. Though the style may suit them, it does not fit their expectation or self-perceived image.

To overcome this barrier, make sure you understand and respect your clients' goals.

As professionals, our goals and desires are to receive positive responses from our clients. We want our tastes and preferences to be respected, just as we want respect from the clients.

In order to manage our own expectation of receiving a positive response to our work, we must work with our clients to understand their point of view and share ours. The burden of harmony rests with us.

### Barrier 5: Technical Problems

Even the best salon professionals make mistakes and experience problems beyond their control—such as allergic reactions or chemicals that fail to process properly. When you have built rapport with the client, problems can be resolved to the client's satisfaction much more easily.

Overcoming the barrier of technical problems requires honesty more than anything else. If something goes wrong, be honest about the problem and offer alternatives.

## The Ins and Outs of Rapport

Remember—rapport is a skill you can learn. The key to learning rapport skills is recognizing when you are in rapport and when you are out of rapport—when you have overcome a barrier and when you are up against one.

Your **behavior** and **feelings** tell you whether you are in rapport or dis-rapport, whether you are creating or breaking rapport.

You build rapport with your clients by understanding, respecting, and relating to them on their terms while overcoming your personal judgments. In fact, you begin to see your clients as they really are, rather than through your own biased lens.

Your older clients, for instance, may want to be referred to as Mr. or Mrs., rather than by first name. When you are in rapport, you will be able to match their preference easily.

The behaviors and feelings outlined in this table provide examples.

| You are in rapport when ... | You are out of rapport when ... |
|---|---|
| You feel close to the person | You feel distance between the client and yourself |
| You work easily together on easy tasks | You each do your own thing |
| You work cooperatively together on harder tasks | You pull in opposite directions |
| You ask questions and understand what the other person is saying | You talk to someone else instead of with that person |
| You want the person with you | You want to get away |

One thing that may surprise you about rapport is that you don't need to say anything to be in rapport. In fact, 80 percent of rapport is non-verbal and only 20 percent is verbal. Notice in this table how you can create or break rapport non-verbally.

| You are more likely to create rapport when ... | You break rapport when ... |
|---|---|
| You notice the client's values and styles and adapt | You do whatever you feel without monitoring |
| You hold eye contact with the client | You look away when the client talks to you |
| You mirror his/her language and posture | You take an opposing posture |
| You listen carefully | You are easily distracted |
| You understand, even if you don't agree | You abruptly change the subject |

Rapport is the thread that runs throughout the *People Skills* program. Throughout the rest of *Relating with CARE*, you will learn three skills necessary for establishing and enhancing rapport:

1. Understanding your personality style.

2. Understanding your client's personality style.

3. Managing relationships using personality styles as a guide.

With those three skills, you will be able to build rapport with just about anyone. And that will lead you to success as a salon professional.

You will learn how to understand yourself in Lesson 1.2, *Discovering Your Personal Style.*

## EXERCISES

1. Identify a relationship in which you have good rapport with the other person. Talk with that individual about the relationship and the reasons you are in rapport. List the words that describe the relationship. Then list the reasons here:

___

___

___

2. Identify a relationship in which you are in dis-rapport with another person. Acknowledge the situation and approach the other individual, explaining that you are trying to improve your relationships with people. Ask for the other person's views on why there is disharmony. List the reasons for not being in rapport:

___

___

___

___

3. Analyze the rapport skills of another salon professional or someone else taking this course. Write a list of his/her strengths and weaknesses. Ask someone else to evaluate your rapport skills.

   - Strengths of ______________'s (name of other person) rapport skills:

   ___

   ___

   ___

   - Weaknesses:

   ___

   ___

   ___

4. Dedicate a day to observing interactions between people. Make mental (or written, if possible) notes of any barriers to rapport that you notice.

____________________________________________

____________________________________________

____________________________________________

____________________________________________

## MAIN POINT SUMMARY

Rapport is a condition of getting along harmoniously. You need to have good rapport in order to get along with clients, which leads to increased personal and professional success.

Rapport is a skill you can learn by knowing the barriers to rapport and creating strategies for yourself to overcome them.

The five barriers to rapport are:

1. Personality differences
2. Blame, judgment, jealousy, and righteousness
3. Cultural, generational, gender, and sexual-orientation differences
4. Different goals and expectations
5. Technical problems

Your behavior and feelings give you clues about whether you are in or out of rapport, and whether you are creating or breaking rapport.

## SELF-TEST/REVIEW

1. List three benefits of establishing and maintaining rapport.

   1. ____________________________________________

   2. ____________________________________________

   3. ____________________________________________

2. Give another word that means the same thing as:

A. Rapport
B. Being out of rapport

A. ______________________________________

B. ______________________________________

3. Which of the following is *not* a barrier to rapport?

_____A. Personality differences
_____B. Blame, judgment, jealousy, and righteousness
_____C. Respect for all religions
_____D. Different goals and expectations
_____E. Technical problems

4. What does "abstraction" mean? Why is rapport an abstraction?

______________________________________

______________________________________

______________________________________

______________________________________

5. What is dis-rapport?

______________________________________

______________________________________

______________________________________

______________________________________

Lesson 1.2

# Discovering Your Personality Style

In this lesson you identify and learn about your own personality and preferences. Through the CARE Profile, you'll learn about the four personality styles and apply the concepts to your own individual personality makeup.

## OBJECTIVES

At the completion of this lesson, you should be able to:

- Complete the CARE Profile Questionnaire
- Score your CARE Profile Questionnaire
- Graph your CARE Profile
- Interpret your CARE Profile and discover your personality style preferences

## WHAT YOU NEED TO KNOW

The CARE Profile is a systematic way of helping you understand yourself and others so that you can be more effective in communicating and meeting the needs of others. Applying the concepts will provide a way for you to sort out your personal tastes, behaviors, and beliefs from those of others. Ultimately, this will help you manage your judgments and interpersonal differences. This is a basic technique for improving your rapport skills.

The CARE Profile is not a test. There are no right or wrong answers. There are no good or bad **personality styles**. In fact, each has areas of strength, and each has areas of challenge.

### Completing the CARE Profile Questionnaire

The CARE Profile Questionnaire contains 51 questions. Each question asks you to select from two or more responses. You must choose the one that best describes how you actually feel or act most of the time—not how you would *like* to feel or act. Answer honestly and openly.

If you tend to react differently in different circumstances, choose the reaction you would have with clients and co-workers.

If you are not sure of an answer, move on and come back to it.

Work as quickly as you can. Answer each question. Take about 20 minutes to complete the questionnaire. Relax and have fun.

You will find three types of questions, as illustrated by the following examples:

### Type I

Multiple choice, where you circle the one response that matches the way you tend to feel or act most closely.

*Example:*

Q. When starting something new, it is important to . . .

A. Organize
B. Be careful
C. Understand the power structure
D. Be enthusiastic

### Type II

Word pairs, where you circle the one response that matches the way you tend to feel or act most closely.

*Example:*

A. Outgoing OR B. Shy

### Type III

Statement pairs, where you circle the one response that matches the way you tend to feel or act most closely.

*Example:*

A. It is important to consider the feelings of others in a relationship.

OR

B. Objectivity is the most important ingredient for maintaining a relationship.

Again, answer the questions as quickly as you can. In most cases, first impressions are the best.

*An example of a few questions of each type appears on the next page.*

Relating: Fundamentals
Discovering Your Personality Style

## Sample CARE Profile Questionnaire

**Type I**

### Part I

**Complete the following sentences with the choice that best describes you. Circle the letter of your choice.**

1. When I first meet someone new, I most often feel . . .
   A. Excited B. Cautious
   C. Interested D. Indifferent

2. I most like people who . . .
   A. Know what they want B. Are considerate and listen
   C. Listen and do as I say D. Think before they speak

3. I most like working with people who . . .
   A. Are friendly and talkative B. Appreciate my ideas
   C. Listen and do what I say D. Leave me alone and let me do my job

**Type II**

### Part II

**Circle the letter to the left of the word in each pair that best describes you.**

14. A. Outgoing B. Shy
15. A. Sensitive B. Logical
16. A. Act B. React
17. A. Caring B. Effective
18. A. Obedient B. Dominant

**Type III**

### Part III

**Choose the one phrase from the two choices given that most describes you or your behavior. Circle the letter of your choice.**

34. A. I am sexually appealing B. I am faithful
35. In responding to other people, I usually follow . . .
    A. My heart B. My head
36. A. I need to belong B. I don't care whether I belong
37. I would rather my friends refer to me as . . .
    A. Sensitive B. Reasonable

38

Relating with CARE

## The CARE Profile Questionnaire

This is not a test. Answer all questions in terms of your actual behavior or feelings, not in terms of how you would like to be. That way you will have a tool that can help you better understand yourself, your clients, and co-workers.

**Remember that the CARE Profile Questionnaire is not a test. Answer as accurately and honestly as you can, and you'll get a good picture of your preferences in relationship to others.**

### Part I

**Complete the following sentences with the choice that best describes you. Circle the letter of your choice.**

1. When I first meet someone new, I most often feel . . .
   A. Excited
   B. Cautious
   C. Interested
   D. Indifferent

2. I most like people who . . .
   A. Know what they want
   B. Are considerate and listen
   C. Listen and do as I say
   D. Think before they speak

3. I most like working with people who . . .
   A. Are friendly and talkative
   B. Appreciate my ideas
   C. Listen and do what I say
   D. Leave me alone and let me do my job

4. It is most important to me that things be . . .
   A. Effective
   B. Accurate
   C. Interesting
   D. Personal

5. In making decisions, I most often prefer to . . .
   A. Have all the facts
   B. Follow my feelings
   C. Have someone do it with me
   D. Do it myself

6. When considering a new project, I most like to . . .
   A. Consider all the alternatives
   B. Follow my feelings
   C. Try the most exciting alternative
   D. Find a project most useful for my purposes

7. The most important trait for me in a leader is . . .
   A. Accuracy
   B. Being a fact-finder
   C. Control
   D. Caring

8. I am . . .
   A. Sensitive
   B. A fact-finder
   C. A problem-solver
   D. A good listener

9. I most often get what I want by . . .
   A. Proving my point
   B. Using logic
   C. Inspiring people
   D. Being patient

10. When working with others, I mostly . . .
    A. Feel concern about their feelings
    B. Want to avoid mistakes
    C. Want them to be enthused
    D. Want them to respect me

11. In my job, I most need . . .
    A. Stability
    B. Excitement
    C. To be in charge
    D. Appreciation

12. At work, I am most often . . .
    A. Confident
    B. Enthusiastic
    C. Precise
    D. Warm

13. At work, I most fear . . .
    A. Making mistakes
    B. Being controlled
    C. Rejection
    D. Being ignored

### Part II

**Circle the letter to the left of the word in each pair that best describes you.**

14. A. Outgoing — B. Shy

15. A. Sensitive — B. Logical

16. A. Act — B. React

17. A. Caring — B. Effective

18. A. Obedient — B. Dominant

19. A. Aggressive — B. Passive

20. A. Warm — B. Precise

21. A. Intellectual — B. Emotional

22. A. Express — B. Analyze

23. A. Order — B. Obey

24. A. Follower — B. Leader

25. A. Sympathetic — B. Reasonable

26. A. Steady — B. Enthusiastic

27. A. Demanding — B. Appealing

28. A. Risk-taker — B. Security-seeker

29. A. Liked B. Respected

30. A. Cautious B. Spontaneous

31. A. Feeling B. Factual

32. A. Reserved B. Expressive

33. A. Fight B. Avoid

## *Part III*

**Choose the one phrase from the two choices given that most describes you or your behavior. Circle the letter of your choice.**

34. A. I am sexually appealing B. I am faithful

35. In responding to other people, I usually follow . . .
A. My heart B. My head

36. A. I need to belong B. I don't care whether I belong

37. I would rather my friends refer to me as . . .
A. Sensitive B. Reasonable

38. I would rather my friends refer to me as . . .
A. Rebellious B. Someone who likes structure

39. In delivering services, I place a higher value on . . .
A. Feeling and creativity B. Precision and planning

40. A. I positively like to be different from others.
B. Being different from others makes me uncomfortable.

41. I least like working with people who are . . .
A. Unsympathetic B. Unreasonable

42. A. I am difficult to please B. I like to do favors

43. The trait I most want in my manager is . . .
A. Caring B. Fairness

44. A. I need someone in whom I can confide completely.
B. I am selfish

45. I have the most difficulty working with people who are . . .
A. Too emotional B. Not emotional

46. A. I play fair B. I am an individualist

47. I most want my co-workers to respect my . . .
    A. Feelings    B. Rights

48. A. I am independent.    B. I am loyal.

49. My favorite people are usually. . .
    A. Reserved    B. Enthusiastic

50. A. There are people I admire so much that I would not question their opinions
    B. I do not admire anyone that much

51. I like being known for . . .
    A. Being sensitive    B. Being technically expert

**Now you'll score the questionnaire and build your CARE Profile.**

## Building Your CARE Profile

Building your CARE Profile is a three-step process:

1. Transfer your answers from the questionnaire to the CARE Profile Answer Sheet which appears on page 43. An example appears on the next page.
2. Score your CARE Profile by calculating the totals on page 43.
3. Graph the results to see your CARE Profile on the CARE Profile Graph, page 47. An example appears on page 46.

### 1. Transferring Your CARE Profile Answers

**'C', 'A', 'R', and 'E' are the first letters of the four personality styles. To find out which style fits you, start by transferring your answers to the CARE Profile Answer Sheet.**

When you have completed this questionnaire, transfer your responses to the CARE Profile Answer Sheet. Circle the letters in each row on the Answer Sheet that correspond to your answer on that number of the questionnaire.

Note that on every line, each letter appears twice. In lines 1 through 13 of the Answer Sheet, the letters are together in pairs. So, if you circled 'A' in response to question 1, circle 'AA' on line 1 of the Answer Sheet, and so on through line 13.

On lines 14 through 51, there are two A's and two B's on each line. If your answer was A, make sure you circle the A in both places it appears on the line. The same applies to your B answers.

This was not done to confuse you! It is an important device in scoring and developing your CARE Profile Graph—the next step in this lesson.

Following is a sample CARE Profile Answer Sheet.

## Sample CARE Profile Answer Sheet

Relating: Fundamentals
Discovering Your Personality Style

### CARE Profile Answer Sheet

**Answer Block A**

1. Circle your answers to questions 1-13 in the space below and total each column. Each answer is worth two points.

| | | | | |
|---|---|---|---|---|
| 1. | BB | DD | CC | AA |
| 2. | BB | DD | AA | CC |
| 3. | AA | DD | CC | BB |
| 4. | DD | BB | AA | CC |
| 5. | CC | AA | DD | BB |
| 6. | BB | AA | DD | CC |
| 7. | DD | AA | CC | BB |
| 8. | DD | BB | CC | AA |
| 9. | DD | BB | AA | CC |
| 10. | AA | BB | DD | CC |
| 11. | DD | AA | CC | BB |
| 12. | DD | AA | CC | BB |
| 13. | CC | AA | BB | DD |
| | 4 | 6 | 4 | 12 |
| | A1 | A2 | A3 | A4 |

**Subtotal should equal 26 points.**

**Answer Block B**

2. Circle your answers to questions 14-51 in the space below. Circle each answer in both columns and total each column. Each answer is worth one point.

| | | | | |
|---|---|---|---|---|
| 14. | B | B | A | A |
| 15. | A | B | B | A |
| 16. | A | A | B | B |
| 17. | A | B | B | A |
| 18. | A | A | B | B |
| 19. | B | B | A | A |
| 20. | A | B | B | A |
| 21. | B | A | A | B |
| 22. | A | B | B | A |
| 23. | B | B | A | A |
| 24. | A | A | B | B |
| 25. | A | B | B | A |
| 26. | B | A | A | B |
| 27. | B | B | A | A |
| 28. | B | B | A | A |
| 29. | A | A | B | B |
| 30. | B | A | A | B |
| 31. | A | B | B | A |
| 32. | B | A | A | B |
| 33. | B | B | A | A |
| 34. | B | B | A | A |
| 35. | A | B | B | A |
| 36. | A | A | B | B |
| 37. | A | B | B | A |
| 38. | B | B | A | A |
| 39. | A | B | B | A |
| 40. | B | B | A | A |
| 41. | A | B | B | A |
| 42. | B | B | A | A |
| 43. | A | B | B | A |
| 44. | A | A | B | B |
| 45. | B | A | A | B |
| 46. | A | A | B | B |
| 47. | A | B | B | A |
| 48. | B | B | A | A |
| 49. | B | A | A | B |
| 50. | A | A | B | B |
| 51. | A | B | B | A |
| | 14 | 25 | 24 | 13 |
| | B1 | B2 | B3 | B4 |

**Subtotal should equal 76 points**

**Total**

3. Add the results of each column in Answer Block A in Step 1 to the results of each column in Answer Block B in Step 2. The Grand Total should equal 102 points. Graph the sums of each column on page 27.

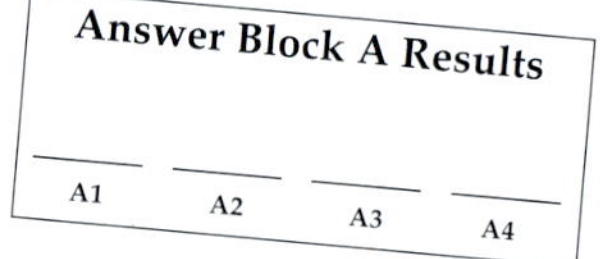

**Answer Block A Results**

A1 A2 A3 A4

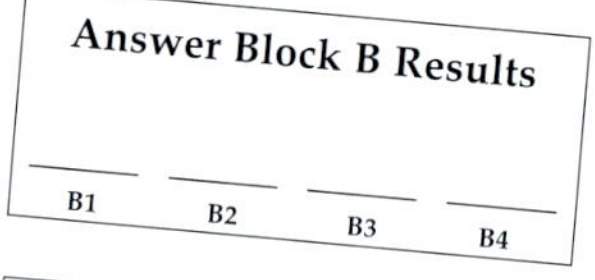

**Answer Block B Results**

B1 B2 B3 B4

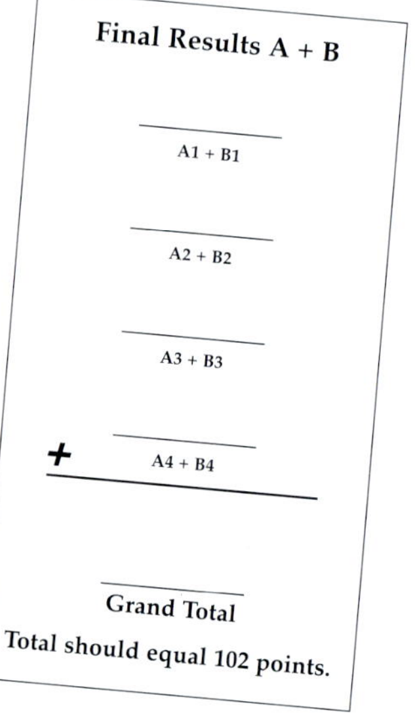

**Final Results A + B**

A1 + B1

A2 + B2

A3 + B3

\+ A4 + B4

Grand Total

**Total should equal 102 points.**

*Relating with CARE*

43

## CARE Profile Answer Sheet

### Answer Block A

1. Circle your answers to questions 1-13 in the space below and total each column. Each answer is worth two points.

| | | | | |
|---|---|---|---|---|
| 1. | BB | DD | CC | AA |
| 2. | BB | DD | AA | CC |
| 3. | AA | DD | CC | BB |
| 4. | DD | BB | AA | CC |
| 5. | CC | AA | DD | BB |
| 6. | BB | AA | DD | CC |
| 7. | DD | AA | CC | BB |
| 8. | DD | BB | CC | AA |
| 9. | DD | BB | AA | CC |
| 10. | AA | BB | DD | CC |
| 11. | DD | AA | CC | BB |
| 12. | DD | AA | CC | BB |
| 13. | CC | AA | BB | DD |
| | ____ | ____ | ____ | ____ |
| | A1 | A2 | A3 | A4 |

**Subtotal should equal 26 points.**

### Answer Block B

2. Circle your answers to questions 14-51 in the space below. Circle each answer in both columns and total each column. Each answer is worth one point.

| | | | | |
|---|---|---|---|---|
| 14. | B | B | A | A |
| 15. | A | B | B | A |
| 16. | A | A | B | B |
| 17. | A | B | B | A |
| 18. | A | A | B | B |
| 19. | B | B | A | A |
| 20. | A | B | B | A |
| 21. | B | A | A | B |
| 22. | A | B | B | A |
| 23. | B | B | A | A |
| 24. | A | A | B | B |
| 25. | A | B | B | A |
| 26. | B | A | A | B |
| 27. | B | B | A | A |
| 28. | B | B | A | A |
| 29. | A | A | B | B |
| 30. | B | A | A | B |
| 31. | A | B | B | A |
| 32. | B | A | A | B |
| 33. | B | B | A | A |
| 34. | B | B | A | A |
| 35. | A | B | B | A |
| 36. | A | A | B | B |
| 37. | A | B | B | A |
| 38. | B | B | A | A |
| 39. | A | B | B | A |
| 40. | B | B | A | A |
| 41. | A | B | B | A |
| 42. | B | B | A | A |
| 43. | A | B | B | A |
| 44. | A | A | B | B |
| 45. | B | A | A | B |
| 46. | A | A | B | B |
| 47. | A | B | B | A |
| 48. | B | B | A | A |
| 49. | B | A | A | B |
| 50. | A | A | B | B |
| 51. | A | B | B | A |
| | ____ | ____ | ____ | ____ |
| | B1 | B2 | B3 | B4 |

**Subtotal should equal 76 points**

### Total

3. Add the results of each column in Answer Block A in Step 1 to the results of each column in Answer Block B in Step 2. The Grand Total should equal 102 points. Graph the sums of each column on page 27.

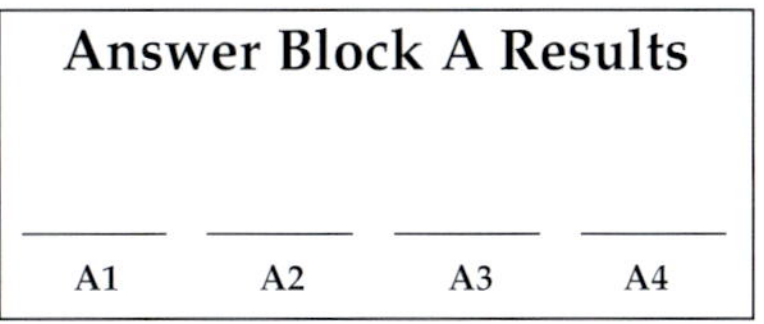


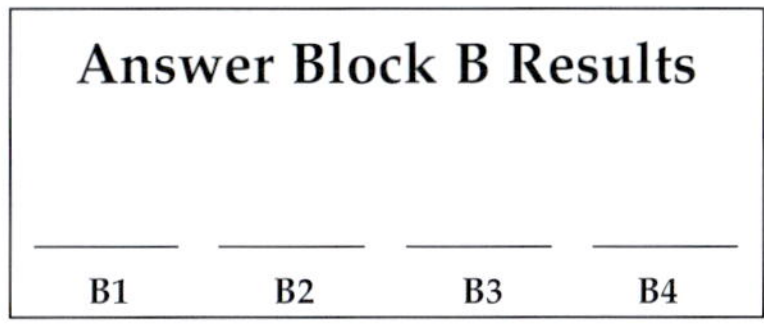


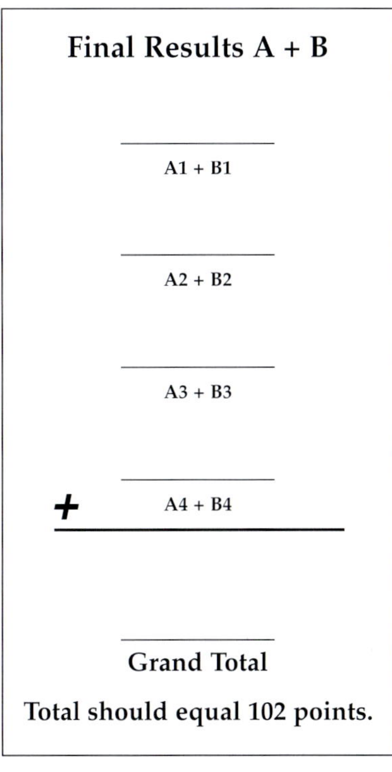

**Once you've transferred your answers, total your score for each column. Then total all the column scores to make sure they add up to 102.**

## *2. Scoring Your CARE Profile*

Once you have transferred all your answers to the CARE Profile Answer Sheet by circling all the appropriate letters, total the letters circled in each column and put your totals at the bottom of each column.

*Note*: Double letters count as **two**. When you have finished totaling all four columns, add your scores across. The result should be 102. If it is not, go back and check first to make sure you counted properly. (Remember to count each double letter answer in lines 1 through 13 as two answers.) If you did, then check each line on the Answer Sheet to make sure you circled two letters on each line for questions 14 through 51.

Scoring your CARE Profile is a four-step process:

1. Total the scores of each column in questions 1-13.
2. Total the scores of each column for questions 14-51.
3. Total the scores of the columns in both answer blocks, as indicated on the CARE Profile Answer Sheet.
4. Verify that the total of the four numbers in the Final Results block is 102.

*See the sample scored CARE Profile Answer Sheet on the next page.*

## Sample Scored CARE Profile Answer Sheet

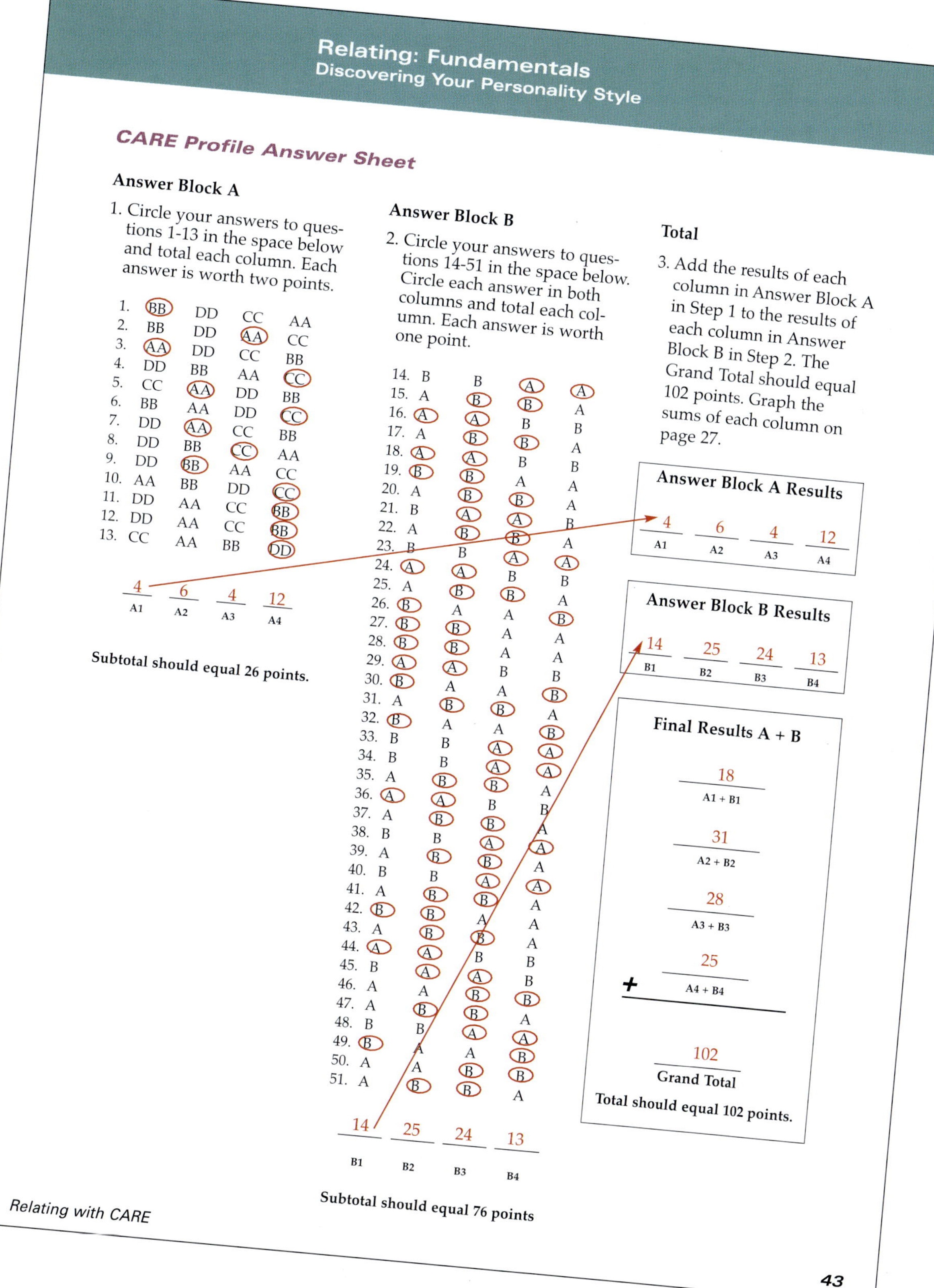

Relating: Fundamentals
Discovering Your Personality Style

### CARE Profile Answer Sheet

**Answer Block A**

1. Circle your answers to questions 1-13 in the space below and total each column. Each answer is worth two points.

| | | | | |
|---|---|---|---|---|
| 1. | BB | DD | CC | AA |
| 2. | BB | DD | AA | CC |
| 3. | AA | DD | CC | BB |
| 4. | DD | BB | AA | CC |
| 5. | CC | AA | DD | BB |
| 6. | BB | AA | DD | CC |
| 7. | DD | AA | CC | BB |
| 8. | DD | BB | CC | AA |
| 9. | DD | BB | AA | CC |
| 10. | AA | BB | DD | CC |
| 11. | DD | AA | CC | BB |
| 12. | DD | AA | CC | BB |
| 13. | CC | AA | BB | DD |
| | 4 | 6 | 4 | 12 |
| | A1 | A2 | A3 | A4 |

Subtotal should equal 26 points.

**Answer Block B**

2. Circle your answers to questions 14-51 in the space below. Circle each answer in both columns and total each column. Each answer is worth one point.

| | | | | |
|---|---|---|---|---|
| 14. | B | B | A | A |
| 15. | A | B | B | A |
| 16. | A | A | B | B |
| 17. | A | B | B | A |
| 18. | A | A | B | B |
| 19. | B | B | A | A |
| 20. | A | B | B | A |
| 21. | B | A | A | B |
| 22. | A | B | B | A |
| 23. | B | B | A | A |
| 24. | A | A | B | B |
| 25. | A | B | B | A |
| 26. | B | A | A | B |
| 27. | B | B | A | A |
| 28. | B | B | A | A |
| 29. | A | A | B | B |
| 30. | B | A | A | B |
| 31. | A | B | B | A |
| 32. | B | A | A | B |
| 33. | B | B | A | A |
| 34. | B | B | A | A |
| 35. | A | B | B | A |
| 36. | A | A | B | B |
| 37. | A | B | B | A |
| 38. | B | B | A | A |
| 39. | A | B | B | A |
| 40. | B | B | A | A |
| 41. | A | B | B | A |
| 42. | B | B | A | A |
| 43. | A | B | B | A |
| 44. | A | A | B | B |
| 45. | B | A | A | B |
| 46. | A | A | B | B |
| 47. | A | B | B | A |
| 48. | B | B | A | A |
| 49. | B | A | A | B |
| 50. | A | A | B | B |
| 51. | A | B | B | A |
| | 14 | 25 | 24 | 13 |
| | B1 | B2 | B3 | B4 |

Subtotal should equal 76 points

**Total**

3. Add the results of each column in Answer Block A in Step 1 to the results of each column in Answer Block B in Step 2. The Grand Total should equal 102 points. Graph the sums of each column on page 27.

**Answer Block A Results**

| A1 | A2 | A3 | A4 |
|---|---|---|---|
| 4 | 6 | 4 | 12 |

**Answer Block B Results**

| B1 | B2 | B3 | B4 |
|---|---|---|---|
| 14 | 25 | 24 | 13 |

**Final Results A + B**

18
A1 + B1

31
A2 + B2

28
A3 + B3

\+ 25
A4 + B4

102
Grand Total

Total should equal 102 points.

Relating with CARE

43

**Now plot the results in a graph so you can better see the mix of personality styles in yourself.**

### 3. Graphing Your CARE Profile

With the grid completed and the total score equaling 102, it is time to turn to the CARE Profile Graph. In this case, "graph" means "picture,"—you are about to draw a picture of your personality. Graphing your CARE Profile Graph is a five-step process:

1. In the Final Results block of the CARE Profile Answer Sheet, find your total score in the first column.
2. On the first or "C" column of the graph, find the number that corresponds to your score. Plot that number by darkening the circle.
3. Plot your scores from columns 2, 3 and 4 of the Answer Sheet on "A," "R," and "E" of the CARE Profile Graph.
4. Connect the dots to see your CARE Profile. A sample graph is completed for you, below.

### Sample CARE Profile Graph

C COOPERATOR — A ANALYZER — R REGULATOR — E ENERGIZER

51 50 49 48 47 46 45 44 43 42 41 40 39 38 37 36 35 34 33 32 31 30 29 28 27 26 25 24 23 22 21 20 19 18

## Your CARE Profile Graph

| | C COOPERATOR | A ANALYZER | R REGULATOR | E ENERGIZER | |
|---|---|---|---|---|---|
| 51 | | | | | 51 |
| 50 | | | | | 50 |
| 49 | | | | | 49 |
| 48 | | | | | 48 |
| 47 | | | | | 47 |
| 46 | | | | | 46 |
| 45 | | | | | 45 |
| 44 | | | | | 44 |
| 43 | | | | | 43 |
| 42 | | | | | 42 |
| 41 | | | | | 41 |
| 40 | | | | | 40 |
| 39 | | | | | 39 |
| 38 | | | | | 38 |
| 37 | | | | | 37 |
| 36 | | | | | 36 |
| 35 | | | | | 35 |
| 34 | | | | | 34 |
| 33 | | | | | 33 |
| 32 | | | | | 32 |
| 31 | | | | | 31 |
| 30 | | | | | 30 |
| 29 | | | | | 29 |
| 28 | | | | | 28 |
| 27 | | | | | 27 |
| 26 | | | | | 26 |
| 25 | | | | | 25 |
| 24 | | | | | 24 |
| 23 | | | | | 23 |
| 22 | | | | | 22 |
| 21 | | | | | 21 |
| 20 | | | | | 20 |
| 19 | | | | | 19 |
| 18 | | | | | 18 |
| 17 | | | | | 17 |
| 16 | | | | | 16 |
| 15 | | | | | 15 |
| 14 | | | | | 14 |
| 13 | | | | | 13 |
| 12 | | | | | 12 |
| 11 | | | | | 11 |
| 10 | | | | | 10 |
| 9 | | | | | 9 |
| 8 | | | | | 8 |
| 7 | | | | | 7 |
| 6 | | | | | 6 |
| 5 | | | | | 5 |
| 4 | | | | | 4 |
| 3 | | | | | 3 |
| 2 | | | | | 2 |
| 1 | | | | | 1 |

### *Interpreting Your CARE Profile Graph*

Now that you've built your CARE Profile, you can look more closely at your personality style, its traits, and how it tends to interact with other personality styles.

To find your style, simply look at the graph you created.

As you've most likely discovered, each column in the CARE Profile Graph represents one of the four personality styles:

**C**ooperator

**A**nalyzer

**R**egulator

**E**nergizer

The highest peak on the graph represents your primary personality style, while the second highest peak represents your secondary personality style. You now have a picture showing the relative "weight" of each personality type within your individual personality profile.

The relative weight is important because it's your unique mix of styles that helps to make you one of a kind. Nobody has a pure single-note personality style. In fact, everybody is a mix of all four styles.

In Lesson 2.1, *Understanding Personality Styles,* you will learn the basic differences of the four personality styles.

## *MAIN POINT SUMMARY*

You've filled out the CARE Profile Questionnaire, scored it, and graphed the results on the CARE Profile Graph.

Now you're ready to find out more about the four styles: Cooperator, Analyzer, Regulator, and Energizer.

Remember that nobody is a purely one style. That's why you look at a primary style and a secondary style. But even then you have traits of all four styles.

To show you what you can do by knowing your style, it is important that you spend some time getting to know each of the four styles in some detail, starting with some more information on how to interpret your CARE Profile.

## Unit 2
# Relating: Observation

## THE VISION

In Unit 1, you learned about rapport, the fundamental skill in building relationships, and how to overcome the barriers that can get in the way of building or maintaining rapport. You also completed the CARE Profile and determined your primary and secondary personality styles. We'll now take a closer look at the four CARE personality styles and define the major characteristics of each. You'll see the major types of behavior that characterize each style and learn some of the traits that make each style "tick." This will help you learn more about yourself and the way you think and act, which will lead to greater understanding of how you relate to clients, friends, and family members.

### Novice

Novices are learning the behaviors and traits that make up their primary and secondary personality styles and are becoming aware of how they exhibit those behaviors and traits in their daily lives. They are starting to become aware of the characteristics of each personality style in their friends and family and may be able to see the differences between their personality style and others.

At this stage, the Novice is learning how to observe behaviors and traits in themselves and others and categorize them into the four CARE styles. They see the importance of understanding personality styles and can imagine how that knowledge will improve their relationships and lead to greater rapport.

### Professional

Professionals understand each of the four personality styles without having to think about what traits and behaviors make up each personality style. They are in the habit of observing others and understand how their own personality style influences their relationships and rapport.

When Professionals are not sure of a personality style, they focus on obtaining more information. They rely on both their own intuition and their colleagues to help them understand others. Professionals constantly observe themselves and are increasingly aware of the effect of their own behavior upon different personality styles. They use new experiences to increase their self-knowledge about their motivation and how to achieve better relationships with others.

### Master

Masters understand personality styles so well that they generally do not think in terms of labeling clients by personality style any longer. Their observation of others is automatic, as is their knowledge of how a person's traits and behaviors influence their personalities. Masters are aware of their own personality style and can easily assess situations and identify how they are likely to interact with others. Because they understand their own interpersonal chemistry, they have very few people problems and face challenges with confidence.

## What's Ahead. . .

Each lesson in this unit is designed to further your competence and acquisition of skills in the area of rapport. Your competence should grow in the same way your career develops through the levels of Novice, Professional, and Master.

In this unit of *Relating with CARE*, you will be introduced to the basic characteristics of the four personality styles, and you will learn to observe these characteristics in yourself and others. After completing this unit of *Relating with CARE*, you will:

- Understand the four personality styles in the CARE Profile and what makes them tick.
- Begin to learn the service opportunities and challenges that each personality style presents to the salon professional.
- Begin to imagine new ways of relating to people intentionally in order to be more effective.
- Learn more about yourself and what motivates you so that you can start to shift your behavior in order to build better relationships.

**Unit 2: Relating: Observation, consists of five lessons:**

**Lesson 2.1: Understanding Personality Styles**

**Lesson 2.2: Meeting the Cooperator**

**Lesson 2.3: Meeting the Analyzer**

**Lesson 2.4: Meeting the Regulator**

**Lesson 2.5: Meeting the Energizer**

Lesson 2.1

# Understanding Personality Styles

**Knowing your personality style is a key to managing good relationships. If you know that you may have difficulty with certain personality styles, you are better able to shift your behavior and are more likely to avoid judgments and conflicts. This is what Professional and Master salon professionals do.**

## OBJECTIVES

At the completion of this lesson, you will be able to:

- Discuss the basic behavior patterns of the four personality styles
- Describe the basic differences of the four personality styles

## WHAT YOU NEED TO KNOW

Your personality style and unique preferences, as defined in the CARE Profile, provide a perspective on how you are likely to think and act in relationships both in and out of the salon. That's what observation is all about. What if you scored equally high in two areas? Then, both styles dominate your personality. The good news is you will have an increased ability to shift from one style to another.

After you complete the lessons in this part of the *People Skills* module, you may find that you identify with one style more than another. You may also find that the style you identify with may change, depending on the situation. In any case, these are important aspects of your personality makeup.

### Using CARE in the Salon

But what makes the CARE Profile important to salon professionals? Why understand your style and the styles of your clients?

Communication experts say that any live message between people is, at most, 30 percent content (words) and, at least, 70 percent feeling, action and body language. Non-verbal signals, such as tone of voice, eye movement and body posture communicate as much as what people actually say.

The CARE Profile provides a way for you to identify how different people communicate in words versus feelings and behaviors so that you can communicate with more people in even more rewarding ways.

Remember that people really aren't as simple as the CARE Profile makes them out to be. The CARE Profile is, to some extent, an exaggeration, because it only measures a few traits. By looking at the exaggeration, we make the behaviors stand out so we can recognize the subtleties in real people. That's part of observation.

Anyone who wants to excel in a service environment such as ours is wise to learn to monitor and shift his or her use of **both** parts of any communication where appropriate. The two parts of communication are:

- **Content**
- **Feeling**

Different people give various emphasis to each of these aspects depending on their preferences. Similarly, some people are more active or assertive, where others are passive.

## *Understanding Areas of Behavior*

The CARE Profile provides a good tool to understand content, feeling and the degree that different personality styles emphasize one or the other. It also examines assertiveness.

To do that, the CARE Profile contrasts two main behavior variables along two intersecting lines or axes:

1. Thinking vs. Feeling

2. Passive vs. Assertive

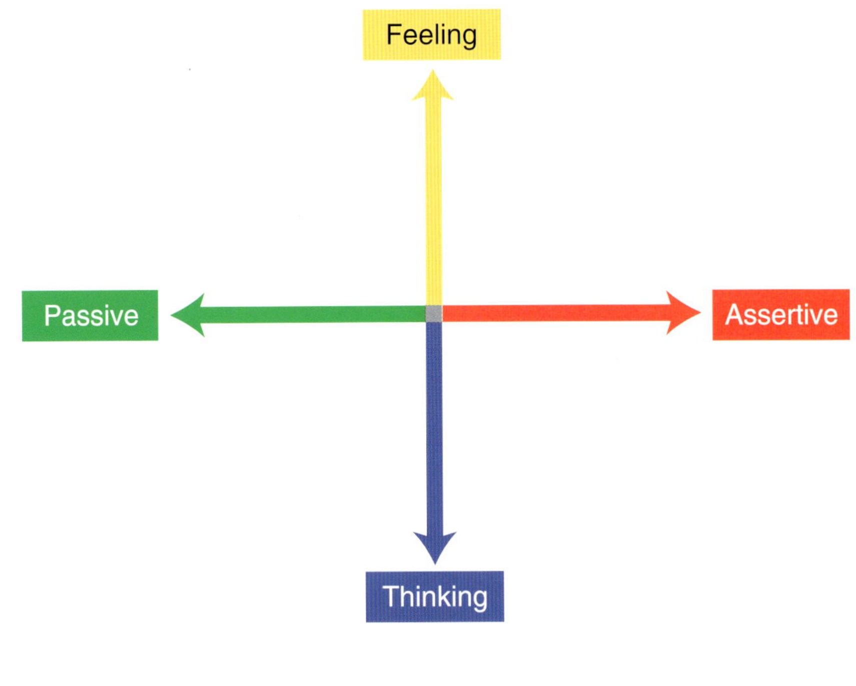


The four areas of behavior match in four combinations. Each of those combinations, in turn, determines the primary behavioral characteristics of the four personality styles.

### Thinking vs. Feeling

For a variety of reasons, much like tastes in food, people tend to prefer thinking and feeling in different proportions. Some use thinking almost to the exclusion of feeling in relating, while others go to the opposite extreme, preferring feeling, while still others mix and match according to taste in between.

**Thinking-oriented people generally:**

- Keep to themselves
- Are less verbal
- Value thought over emotion

**Feeling-oriented people generally:**

- Act more sociable
- Relate more than act
- Value emotion over thought

### Passive vs. Assertive

People use passivity and assertiveness in much the same variation they use thinking and feeling. There are virtually exclusive extremes and a rich variation of mixtures in between.

**Passive people tend to act:**

- Shy
- Submissive
- Compliant
- Indirect

**Assertive people tend to act:**

- Forthright
- Dominant
- Direct
- Assured

## Matching Areas of Behavior to the Styles

The following chart shows the basic behaviors of the four CARE personality styles:

### Personality Styles and Behavior Matches

| | Thinking/Feeling | Passive/Assertive |
|---|---|---|
| • Cooperator | Feeling-oriented | Passive |
| • Analyzer | Thinking-oriented | Passive |
| • Regulator | Thinking-oriented | Assertive |
| • Energizer | Feeling-oriented | Assertive |

You can begin to see how the styles are similar and dissimilar. Both the Analyzer and Regulator are thinking-oriented, for instance, but the Analyzer is more likely to be passive, while the Regulator is generally more assertive.

The degree of passive or assertive, outgoing or reserved behaviors are key variables that account for the differences among people. However, just because you have an Analyzer preference does not mean you will always act in a certain way. The styles serve as guides to personality; they are not personalities in and of themselves. They can and do inform behaviors.

In Lesson 2.2, *Meeting the Cooperator*, you will learn about the "C" personality in CARE.

## EXERCISE

Think about a person you know. Circle below whether that person is thinking or feeling, and passive or assertive. Write the person's name in the space below and identify what style you think that person is. Discuss your reasoning in class.

Thinking or Feeling    Assertive or Passive

Name: ______________________________

Style: ______________________________

Keep that person in mind and apply new information to him or her as you continue through the *People Skills* program.

## MAIN POINT SUMMARY

The key basic behaviors of the CARE Profile are:

- Passive or assertive
- Thinking or feeling

The different degrees of those traits make for an unlimited variety of people.

*People Skills* looks at primary and secondary personality styles to "round out" a person's personality and show how the combination of behavioral traits makes for unique individuals.

Understanding the basics of your personality gives you important clues in how you can relate well to other people. Good interpersonal relations are critical to feeling satisfied in the salon business. Most salon professionals feel better when their clients are happy with them and their work.

You'll find that your relationships with everyone will improve. To make that a reality, we'll meet the styles in more detail.

## SELF-TEST/REVIEW

1. Communication between persons is at most 30 percent ____________________

   and at least 70 percent ____________________________.

2. The main behaviors contrasted in the *People Skills* program are:

   __________________________ and __________________________

   __________________________ and __________________________

3. What are the main characteristics of thinking-oriented people?

   ______________________________________________________________________

   ______________________________________________________________________

   ______________________________________________________________________

4. What are the main characteristics of feeling-oriented people?

   ______________________________________________________________________

   ______________________________________________________________________

   ______________________________________________________________________

5. What are the main characteristics of passive people?

   ______________________________________________________________________

   ______________________________________________________________________

   ______________________________________________________________________

6. What are the main characteristics of assertive people?

   ______________________________________________________________________

   ______________________________________________________________________

   ______________________________________________________________________

Lesson 2.2

# Meeting the Cooperator

Cooperators are the people who tend to have the most heart. They're concerned with people and feelings. At the same time, they are more likely to be late getting a job done because they have less concern for time and task than for people and feelings.

## OBJECTIVES

At the completion of this lesson, you will be able to:

- List what Cooperators most likely care about
- Describe how Cooperator salon professionals act
- Explain how Cooperator clients generally act
- Identify what you need to do in order to maintain rapport with Cooperator clients

## WHAT YOU NEED TO KNOW

Cooperation is the greatest strength of the Cooperator personality style. They are the people who most likely get along with everyone and try to make sure everyone in the salon is happy.

### Cooperator Characteristics . . .

When dealing with others, Cooperators orient themselves to feelings and tend to respond passively when it comes to problem situations.

Cooperators tend not to be as concerned with:

- *Time*
- *Tasks*
- *Productivity*

They tend to care more about:

- *People*
- *Feelings*
- *Listening*
- *Relationships*

Cooperators often exhibit the following qualities:

- *Openness*
- *Patience*
- *Passivity*
- *Willingness to listen*

Their clients generally feel:

- *Seen*
- *Heard*
- *Valued*

## Cooperator Professionals . . .

The Cooperator's friendly and warm nature may foster team spirit, but not always teamwork—teamwork requires a focus on task achievement. This tends not to be the Cooperator's main concern. Cooperators will likely make clients feel valued.

## Cooperator

Cooperators tend to:

*Smile*
*Seldom criticize*
*Chat easily*
*Remember your last conversation*
*Listen*

At the same time, Cooperator professionals are not likely to take risks. They don't want to make anyone angry.

**Cooperators are the clients that likely make you feel the best about yourself and your work. They also can have a hard time making up their minds and stating their preferences.**

## *Cooperator Clients . . .*

Cooperator clients are generally friendly and personable, unless they are painfully shy. They may make sure that you feel special when they are in your chair. And you may find yourself frustrated at times because they can be so indecisive.

Cooperator clients tend to:

- *Smile*
- *Criticize seldom*
- *Chat easily*
- *Remember your last conversation*
- *Listen*

Cooperator clients may be:

- *Passive*
- *Low risk-takers*
- *Indecisive*

Cooperators may experience difficulty when making a decision about their hairstyle.

### In the Salon. . .

Grace, a steady client of the salon for many years, is a Cooperator. Her regular stylist has moved out of the area, and Grace has been switched to a new salon professional, Greg. Grace has no thought of changing styles, but Greg suggests a new style at their first appointment.

Greg suggests cutting Grace's long hair to the top of her shoulders and adding some soft layering around her face. "I'm not sure," Grace replies. "My husband likes me to wear my hair long. I've worn my hair long for so many years, I'm not sure I could handle something different."

Greg senses that Grace's husbands' opinion is very important to her, and the thought of making a major change makes her uncomfortable. So he shifts and suggests adding a few longer layers around her face to soften her look, rather than cutting her hair shorter. The layers could be left long enough that she could pull her hair back or wear it down to frame her face.

Greg assures her that her layers will be long, and if she decides at a later date that she would like to go shorter, they would always have that option. Grace relaxes and agrees to the long layers around her face.

Greg listened to Grace and acknowledged her reluctance to making a major change. As a result, Grace realizes that Greg cares about her wishes and feels more comfortable returning to him for future services.

As a salon professional, you may feel challenged because:

- You may need to help Cooperators put their feelings about their image into words.
- It may be a challenge to introduce Cooperators to new styles because they don't tend to take risks.

**Cooperators base their behaviors on their tendency toward feeling and passivity.**

### When Serving Cooperators . . .

- Remember to move slowly and maintain rapport.
- Take into account their desire for acceptance.
- Remember the importance they place on feelings.
- Keep in mind their desire to project warmth and caring.
- You may need to move them to decisions respectfully without making them feel rushed or pressured.

Be careful. Like Grace, Cooperators may go along with an idea even if they question the action. Don't use the force of your personality to get them to change. Be sure your suggestions are for their style, not yours. When you give them information and reassurance, they are better able to make decisions that truly fit their needs.

## REMEMBER

**Cooperators are less likely to tell you if they don't like the style you want to create. Instead, they will more likely show their disappointment by simply not re-booking or canceling before their next appointment.**

| Cooperators Are | Cooperators Need |
|---|---|
| • Feeling and passive | • To be accepted |
| • Concerned about people | • To be liked |
| • Concerned about feelings | • To get along |
| • Patient | • Cooperation |
| • Good listeners | • Feelings |
| • Not time-oriented | • More measured movement |
| • Not risk-takers | |

As demonstrated in the chart above, you can meet the needs of Cooperators by first understanding what qualities make up the "C" in CARE. In Lesson 2.3, *Meeting the Analyzer*, you will learn about the "A" personality in CARE.

## EXERCISES

1. Write the names of television or movie characters (past or present) whose primary personality patterns can best be described as a Cooperator. Write your reason for believing this in the space provided.

**Character** **Reason**

2. Circle the character in the *"Wizard of Oz"* that is most like a Cooperator. Why?

| | | |
|---|---|---|
| Dorothy | The Scarecrow | The Good Witch |
| The Tin Man | The Lion | The Wizard |

## MAIN POINT SUMMARY

Cooperators are great people to be around, as long as time isn't a concern. You may find that you feel the warmest toward your Cooperator clients.

At the same time, Cooperators are not likely to be the ones you experiment on. They tend not to be risk-takers. You'll also need to make sure your Cooperator clients and colleagues feel accepted and liked.

If you are a Cooperator salon professional, you'll likely need help with staying on schedule. Getting the job done on time isn't a Cooperator's strong point.

## SELF-TEST/REVIEW

1. Place an "X" in the blank before each answer that accurately completes the following sentence. There should be four X's for the answer.

   Cooperators are:

   ____ Chatty

   ____ Listeners

   ____ Caring

   ____ Always on time

   ____ Supportive of salon programs

   ____ Likely to take over and run things

   ____ Patient

2. As a salon professional, your strength as a Cooperator is that you:

   A. Foster teamwork

   B. Make your client feel valued

   C. Can take risks with others

3. What are Cooperators most concerned with?

   ______________________________________________

   ______________________________________________

4. You can depend on a Cooperator to tell you when he is dissatisfied. Circle One:

True or False

5. What are main characteristics of a Cooperator client?

___

___

___

6. What challenges do Cooperator clients present to salon professionals?

___

___

___

7. How should you approach styling Cooperator clients?

___

___

___

## Lesson 2.3
# Meeting the Analyzer

**Analyzers are factual, precise, and methodical people. They tend more toward thinking than doing. Left to their own style, they generally don't like change. And they are less likely to chit-chat during service delivery.**

## OBJECTIVES

At the completion of this lesson, you will be able to:

- List what Analyzers most likely care about
- Describe how Analyzer salon professionals generally act
- Explain how Analyzer clients generally act
- Identify what you need to do in order to maintain rapport with Analyzer clients

## WHAT YOU NEED TO KNOW

Organization and accuracy are the greatest strengths of the Analyzer personality style. Analyzers are the people who organize the work well and understand the facts of a situation.

### Analyzer Characteristics . . .

They are oriented toward **thinking** in their approach to people, and **passive** and methodical in responding to problems.

Analyzers tend not to be as concerned with:

- *Speed*
- *Feelings*
- *Friends*

They tend to care more about:

- *Accuracy*
- *Perfection*
- *Precision*
- *Security*

Analyzers often exhibit the following characteristics:

- *Focus*
- *Hesitancy*
- *Neatness*
- *Shyness*

## *Analyzer Professionals . . .*

Analyzers tend to be quiet. They may work intently, though slowly, throughout their entire shift. Analyzers can be counted on to duplicate techniques precisely and follow the directions to the letter.

**Analyzer**

Analyzers will likely:

*Deal in facts*
*Worry about the time*
*Focus on concrete details*
*Listen intently and respond after reflection*

Their clients tend to feel:

- *Secure*
- *Distant*
- *Safe*

Finally, Analyzers are not socializers. They can appear cold and distant to their clients.

**Analyzer clients generally want the same thing every time. Though less interested in style changes, they can be very steady clients if they like how you work with them.**

## Analyzer Clients . . .

Analyzer clients are less likely to chat. When it comes to styles, they care about ease. You may feel frustrated that they only want "the usual" or do not articulate what they want.

Analyzers will likely:

- *Deal in facts*
- *Worry about the time*
- *Focus on concrete details*
- *Listen intently and respond after reflection*

Analyzers tend to be:

- *Factual*
- *Slow*
- *Precise*
- *Passive*
- *Methodical*
- *Low risk-takers*

Analyzers are less likely to talk about fashion or their appearance. They seem to be the client you are least likely to convince to try a new hairstyle.

As a salon professional, you may feel challenged because it's more difficult:

- To explain things to Analyzers who want all the facts
- For Analyzers to call attention to themselves and their appearance
- To get Analyzers to tell you what they want and how they like your work

**Analyzers base their behaviors on their tendency toward thinking and low-risk.**

### When Serving Analyzers . . .

- Be factual and give concrete details
- Give them time to make decisions
- Use concrete information and facts in your conversation
- Respect those who lack interest in conversation

## In the Salon. . .

George is a computer programmer and doesn't really like going to the salon. He feels awkward and uncomfortable and generally wants to get the cut over with as soon as possible. He goes to a place near his office, but generally walks in and takes whomever is available at the time.

Jim, a new stylist, is free when George walks in. He sees the computer magazine George is reading in the waiting room and guesses George is an Analyzer. He knows George could become a regular client if he treats him in a way that makes George feel comfortable.

Jim greets George in a friendly but not overly personal manner and escorts him to the chair. "How are you doing today?" he asks. "Looks like you simply need a shorter version of the design you already have. Is that OK?"

"Yes," George replies. "I'm afraid I've let it go too long."

"No problem," Jim says. "Let's get you shampooed, and I'll get right to work."

Jim works efficiently and quickly, only commenting in answer to a question from George. George appears to relax—so much so that he asks to make an appointment with Jim for his next visit.

## REMEMBER

**Analyzers will not likely be swayed by comments like, "Your friends will love it!" Instead, they will like to hear concrete details like, "It emphasizes the shape of your face, your strong jawline, and high cheekbones." If you can show an Analyzer that your salon's shampoo will save them money, you'll sell a lot of shampoo.**

| Analyzers Are | Analyzers Need |
|---|---|
| • Thinking and passive | • Security |
| • Factual | • Time to think |
| • Methodical | • Facts to rely on |
| • Low risk-takers | • Order |
| • Slower paced | • Predictability |

You can see in the chart above that the "A" in CARE represents a much different personality style than the "C,"which was outlined in the previous lesson. Next, we'll look at the "R" in CARE—the Regulator—in Lesson 2.3, *Meeting the Regulator*.

## EXERCISES

1. Write the names of television or movie characters (past or present) whose primary personality patterns can best be described as an Analyzer. Write your reason in the space provided.

| **Character** | **Reason** |
|---|---|
| ______________ | ______________________________ |
| | ______________________________ |
| | ______________________________ |
| | ______________________________ |
| ______________ | ______________________________ |
| | ______________________________ |
| | ______________________________ |
| | ______________________________ |
| ______________ | ______________________________ |
| | ______________________________ |
| | ______________________________ |
| | ______________________________ |
| ______________ | ______________________________ |
| | ______________________________ |
| | ______________________________ |
| | ______________________________ |

2. Circle the character in the *"Wizard of Oz"* that is most like an Analyzer. Why?

| | | |
|---|---|---|
| Dorothy | The Scarecrow | The Good Witch |
| The Tin Man | The Lion | The Wizard |

______________________________________________

______________________________________________

## MAIN POINT SUMMARY

With Analyzers, salon professionals will do best to focus on consistency, facts and methods. But don't expect them to be forthcoming.

They tend not to be fashion-oriented clients and generally don't take risks. You'll also need to make sure your Analyzer clients and colleagues feel secure, and that means with consistency and sameness.

If you are an Analyzer salon professional, you'll likely do best where precision counts, like duplicating a style, mixing color or applying nail polish with precision.

## SELF-TEST/REVIEW

1. Place an "X" in the blank before each answer that accurately completes the following sentence. There should be four X's for the answer.

   Analyzers tend to be:

   ____ Thinkers

   ____ Doers

   ____ Slow to make decisions

   ____ Slow to change

   ____ Party animals

   ____ Dependable

2. When an Analyzer is given a choice, he or she will most likely:

   A. Be willing to take a risk

   B. Choose quickly

   C. Think it over and ask for more information

3. What are Analyzers most concerned with?

   ______________________________________________

   ______________________________________________

4. A client who is an Analyzer is least likely to try a new style. Circle One:

   True or False

5. What are main characteristics of an Analyzer client?

______________________________________________

______________________________________________

______________________________________________

6. What challenges do Analyzer clients present to salon professionals?

______________________________________________

______________________________________________

______________________________________________

7. How should you approach styling Analyzer clients?

______________________________________________

______________________________________________

______________________________________________

Lesson 2.4

# Meeting the Regulator

Regulators tend to be the leaders of the world. They're doers, and very goal-oriented. They keep salon professionals on their toes by expecting and demanding great service, delivered on time.

## OBJECTIVES

At the completion of this lesson, you will be able to:

- List what Regulators most likely care about
- Describe how Regulator salon professionals act
- Explain how Regulator clients generally act
- Identify what you need to do in order to maintain rapport with Regulator clients

## WHAT YOU NEED TO KNOW

Getting things done is the greatest strength of the Regulator personality style. Regulators tend to be people who take charge and make things happen. The Regulator likes to organize and lead, and does it well.

### Regulator Characteristics . . .

Regulators are more thinking-oriented when dealing with people and generally respond assertively to problems and situations.

Regulators tend not to be as concerned with:

- *Feelings*
- *Analysis*
- *Approval*
- *Others*

They tend to care more about:

- *Doing*
- *Achieving*
- *Action*
- *Leading*

Regulators often exhibit the following characteristics:

- *Independence*
- *Assertiveness*
- *Purposefulness*
- *Leadership*

## *Regulator Professionals . . .*

Regulator salon professionals often deal with clients efficiently and effectively. Regulators can be counted on to serve clients in a timely, professional manner, and to reflect the salon's best in any project they take on.

## *Regulator*

Regulators will usually:

*Be direct*
*Feel wary if you hesitate*
*Be to the point*
*Direct you without hesitation*
*Speak their minds*

Their clients may feel:

- *Served*
- *Satisfied*

or they might feel dispatched.

However, Regulators can seem unfriendly. They may also seem to provide an authority against which others may wish to rebel.

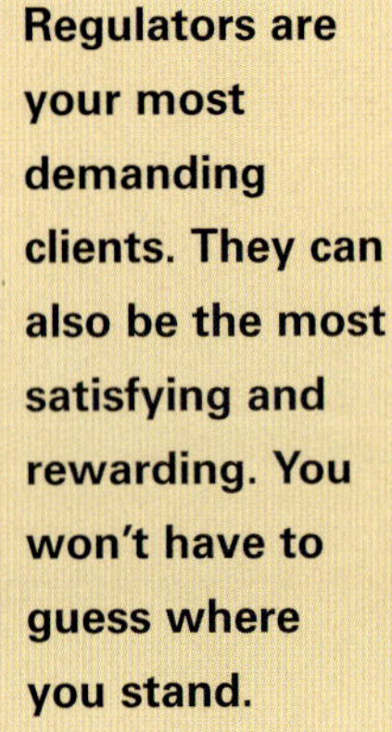

**Regulators are your most demanding clients. They can also be the most satisfying and rewarding. You won't have to guess where you stand.**

## *Regulator Clients . . .*

Regulator clients can be both your most challenging and most rewarding. They will expect you to be on time, accurate, and effective in your service delivery. If you are not, they will let you know directly and immediately.

Regulators will usually:

- *Be direct*
- *Feel wary if you hesitate*
- *Be to the point*
- *Direct you without hesitation*
- *Speak their minds*

Regulators are largely:

- *Decisive*
- *Goal-Oriented*
- *Independent*
- *Dominant*

Regulators feel more comfortable when in control of decisions regarding their hairstyle and image.

As a salon professional, you may feel challenged because it's difficult:

- For Regulators to just accept your view and leave decisions to you.
- To introduce Regulators to new hairstyles without good reasons, because they need to see the advantage.

**Regulators base their behaviors on a tendency toward thinking and assertion.**

### *When Serving Regulators . . .*

- Focus on the task.
- Provide confident, logical, and professional advice.
- Leave final decisions to the client.
- Start on time, work quickly and without hesitation.
- Remember they prefer goal-oriented, purposeful conversation.
- Provide options for re-booking or waiting if you are late.

## In the Salon. . .

Allison rushes to her salon for a facial. A corporate attorney, she's smartly and conservatively dressed. She's running totally on schedule and needs to make sure she's out of the salon exactly on time in order to pick up her children from school. She knew she was cutting it close, but felt the facial would relieve the stress she's been under and help her health more than anything else.

Lois, the salon's esthetician, knows the situation because Allison has had her secretary call ahead. As soon as she sees Allison, Lois snaps into action.

"Hi, Allison," Lois says, with a crisp yet friendly snap in her voice. "I know you're cutting it close today, so let's get started right away."

Allison leads the way, feeling relieved that Lois is following right behind and they are getting right down to business. "Thanks," she says. "I am in a hurry but can use a few minutes of quiet."

Lois makes sure her touch is firm and her actions are quick—she wants to make sure Allison knows she's not wasting time. She finishes up so Allison can get out exactly on schedule.

As she's leaving, Allison thanks Lois for her speed and efficiency. "I'll tell my associates that an appointment with you is the best way to find time for yourself," she says.

### *REMEMBER*

**Regulators will be most likely to tell you if they are upset, but you may not hear they are happy in so many words. Instead, you will see it in the form of tips and, perhaps, client referrals.**

| Regulators Are | Regulators Need |
|---|---|
| • Thinking and assertive | • To feel things are well-run |
| • Independent | • Challenge |
| • Cool and in-control | • To win |
| • Take-charge types | • To see a purpose |
| • Doers | • Reasons without too much detail |

Review the chart above and notice how Regulators' needs differ from the needs of Cooperators and Analyzers you studied in the two previous lessons. Next, we'll look at the "E" in CARE—the Energizer—in Lesson 2.5, *Meeting the Energizer*.

## EXERCISES

1. Write the names of television or movie characters (past or present) whose primary personality patterns can best be described as a Regulator. Write your reason in the space provided.

| Character | Reason |
|---|---|
| | |

2. Circle the character in the *"Wizard of Oz"* that is most like a Regulator. Why?

| | | |
|---|---|---|
| Dorothy | The Scarecrow | The Good Witch |
| The Tin Man | The Lion | The Wizard |

## MAIN POINT SUMMARY

Regulators are leaders. You may find that you either love them or hate them, depending on how you work with strong personalities.

Regulators want to move right into action. They also need to feel like they are in control of any situation. Although they can come off as cool and confrontational, the Regulator's ability to strive for the best can make them the most rewarding people to work with. If you are a Regulator salon professional, you may want to find some way to temper your impatience when people hesitate or have trouble making decisions.

## SELF-TEST/REVIEW

1. Place an "X" in the blank before each answer that accurately completes the following sentence. There should be four X's for the answer.

   Regulators tend to be:

   ____ Independent

   ____ Decisive

   ____ Always laughing

   ____ Take-charge types

   ____ Goal-oriented

   ____ Concerned about approval

2. As a Regulator, you generally are good at getting things done.
   Circle One:

   True or False

3. What are Regulators generally most concerned with?

   ______________________________________________

   ______________________________________________

4. When Regulator clients ask for something, it is best to:

   A. Give it to them right away

   B. Stay focused on what they want

   C. Give advice that is logical

   D. All of the above

5. What are main characteristics of a Regulator client?

______________________________

______________________________

______________________________

6. What opportunities do Regulator clients present to salon professionals?

______________________________

______________________________

______________________________

7. What challenges do Regulator clients present to salon professionals?

______________________________

______________________________

______________________________

8. How should you approach styling Regulator clients?

______________________________

______________________________

______________________________

Lesson 2.5

# Meeting the Energizer

Energizers are often creative and full of ideas. They can be enthusiastic and inspiring—they are natural in sales and salon work. They can have a tendency to shake up rules and not adhere to deadlines.

## OBJECTIVES

At the completion of this lesson, you will be able to:

- List what Energizers most likely care about
- Describe how Energizer salon professionals act
- Explain how Energizer clients generally act
- Identify what you need to do in order to maintain rapport with Energizer clients

## WHAT YOU NEED TO KNOW

Enthusiasm is the greatest strength of the Energizer personality style. They inspire and lead by believing deeply in what they say and do.

### Energizer Characteristics . . .

Energizers are oriented toward feelings when dealing with people and respond assertively when dealing with problems.

Energizers are not as concerned with:

- *Deadlines*
- *Rules*
- *Goals*

They tend to care more about:

- *Appreciation*
- *Change*
- *Approval*
- *Activity*
- *Excitement*

Energizers often exhibit the following characteristics:

- *Talkative*
- *Creative*
- *Energetic*
- *Outgoing*

## *Energizer Professionals . . .*

Energizers are likely the most expressive and creative salon professionals in the salon—they love to create while serving people. Energizers can be counted on to make clients feel good about their appearance. However, sometimes they can lose interest in things and not take deadlines and rules seriously.

**Energizer**

Energizers will usually:

*Smile*
*Crack jokes*
*Chat non-stop*
*Want your approval*

Their clients feel:

- *Positive*
- *Excited*
- *Inspired*

At the same time, Energizer salon professionals may not take appointment times seriously, which angers some clients. In addition, Energizers may feel hurt, and can become angry when they aren't getting approval from their clients.

**Energizers are the clients that let you experiment and take risks. At the same time, you need to get their agreement up front. If they don't like what you did, they're the clients who are most likely to let you know — in front of others.**

## *Energizer Clients . . .*

Energizer clients give you the most opportunity to express yourself as a salon professional. They are always ready to try something new and they will usually let you know in no uncertain terms if they don't like what you have done.

Energizers will usually:

- *Smile*
- *Crack jokes*
- *Chat non-stop*
- *Want your approval*

Energizers can be:

- *Active*
- *High risk-takers*
- *Charming*
- *Attention-getters*

Energizers are fun to work on because they are most often interested in cutting-edge styles and something unique.

As a salon professional, you may feel challenged because it's difficult:

- For Energizers to settle on a direction when they have so many good ideas.
- To get Energizers to put their desires into concrete terms you can act upon.

**In terms of the areas of behavior, Energizers are feeling-oriented and assertive.**

### *When Serving Energizer Clients. . .*

- Ask about their profession, likes and dislikes, to show your interest.
- Determine their ability to style their own hair and how much time they want to spend in the morning, to make sure they will like the style after they have left the salon.
- Agree on a plan of action before you begin cutting and styling to avoid their direct and public feedback if they don't like the result.
- Satisfy their need to feel important and appreciated by telling them you approve of them.

## In the Salon. . .

Sandy notices her client Rita rushing into the reception area, talking excitedly to the receptionist. "Let me see," Rita says to herself. "What have I seen lately that's new for long hair? What have I been wanting to try?"

Sure enough, Rita bounces over to Sandy and says, "Sorry I'm late. I just stopped at the mall, and will you look at this!" She pulls out her avant-garde purchase. "I want an up-do that is really chic and will match this cocktail dress!"

"Oh, Rita, it's beautiful," Sandy says. "I know just what I'll do. Let's do a french twist, but leave areas that can be crimped to create a contrast of textures. It'll look fabulous with that dress. Want to try it?"

"You bet."

Sandy and Rita talk non-stop through the service, sometimes talking right on top of one another. Neither seems to mind.

"Sandy, you did it again," Rita says when the style is finished. "I'll be the hit of the party tonight!"

"Thanks. But with so much to work with, how could I miss? Can I schedule your next cut on the way out?"

"Sure Sandy. Just make it in four weeks," Rita says, as she hurries out happily.

### REMEMBER

**Energizers are not consistent, so you have to work hard to retain them. Make sure they re-book before leaving the salon and confirm their appointment by phone or mail.**

| Energizers Are | Energizers Need |
|---|---|
| • Feeling and assertive | • To be admired and appreciated |
| • The life of the party | • Excitement |
| • Outgoing | • Change |
| • Creative | • Lots of activity |
| • Inspirational | |
| • Not time-structured | |
| • Not goal-oriented | |

Next in Lesson 3.1, *Defining Style Strengths, Weaknesses and Perceptions*, we'll deepen our understanding of the personality styles by comparing and contrasting them to see how they work, or don't work, when they mix.

## EXERCISES

1. Write the names of television or movie characters (past or present) whose primary personality patterns can best be described as an Energizer. Write your reason in the space provided.

| Character | Reason |
|---|---|
| ____________ | ________________________ |
| | ________________________ |
| | ________________________ |
| | ________________________ |
| ____________ | ________________________ |
| | ________________________ |
| | ________________________ |
| | ________________________ |
| ____________ | ________________________ |
| | ________________________ |
| | ________________________ |
| | ________________________ |
| ____________ | ________________________ |
| | ________________________ |
| | ________________________ |
| | ________________________ |

2. Circle the character in the *"Wizard of Oz"* that is most like an Energizer. Why?

| | | |
|---|---|---|
| Dorothy | The Scarecrow | The Good Witch |
| The Tin Man | The Lion | The Wizard |

________________________________________

________________________________________

3. Write a short essay that compares and contrasts the characteristics of the four personality styles. Look back at the person whose name you wrote down in the exercise in Lesson 2.1 (page 54) and keep that person in mind. Think about how that person is in relation to the four personality styles as you compare and contrast the styles.

## MAIN POINT SUMMARY

Energizers are clients who allow you to express your full creativity. They can also be frustrating because they don't care about time and don't understand if you can't fit them in when they're late.

You'll need to make sure your Energizer clients and colleagues feel important and appreciated.

If you're an Energizer salon professional, you may need to find some way to make sure you stay on track. Energizers flow with ideas—but sometimes fall short on delivery.

Depending on your client, you may need to temper your creativity, enthusiasm, and talkative nature.

## SELF-TEST/REVIEW

1. Place an "X" in the blank before each answer that accurately completes the following sentence. There should be four X's for the answer.

   Energizers tend to be:

   ____ Talkative

   ____ Outgoing

   ____ Creative

   ____ Time-structured

   ____ Approval seekers

   ____ Low risk-takers

2. Energizers are the most likely to be more expressive than other styles. Circle One:

   True or False

3. What are Energizers generally most concerned with?

   ______________________________________________

   ______________________________________________

4. If your client is an Energizer, he or she will most likely:

   A. Change hairstyles often

   B. Make more conversation than others

   C. Be prone to be late for appointments

   D. All of the above

5. What are main characteristics of an Energizer client?

______________________________________________

______________________________________________

______________________________________________

6. What challenges do Energizer clients present to salon professionals?

______________________________________________

______________________________________________

______________________________________________

7. How should you approach styling Energizer clients?

______________________________________________

______________________________________________

______________________________________________

## Unit 3:
# Relating: Analysis

## THE VISION

In Unit 1, you explored the transitions of a salon career over time through the stages of Novice, Professional, and Master. We hope you use these opportunities to develop a rich personal vision of the many opportunities the salon industry has to offer. Remember that in Unit 2 you learned the personality styles—observing the major types of behaviors that characterize each style. We'll now take a look at how salon professionals in each stage begin to apply their understanding of personality styles by looking at strengths, weaknesses, differences, and similarities. This will help you further to learn and envision what to expect for yourself, and the clients you serve.

### Novice

Novices tend to judge people quickly. Novices have not usually grasped how the strengths, weaknesses, similarities and differences of the personality styles can enhance relationships. Instead, they may use the style preference concept to pigeonhole clients into neat boxes as an easy way to label differences. The Novices are still firming up their technical basics and can feel more easily frustrated by more challenging personalities. They often need the guidance of a Professional or Master salon professional to learn to analyze, rather than judge clients. Being challenged by and focused on the technical side of the business, the adventure of interpersonal interactions awaits.

### Professional

Professionals are able to step back and look at people-problems objectively. They are able to analyze style preferences and the interactions of the personal styles. Salon professionals at the Professional level understand the strengths and weaknesses of each personality style, as well as similarities and differences, and use that knowledge to improve relationships when confronted with problems. However, they are still likely to wait until a problem presents itself and then accurately assess and fix the situation. They are beginning to use these skills as a matter of course and have a great deal of room for growth.

### Master

Masters are quick to analyze personalities encountered. They use their knowledge as a matter of course, without thinking about it. To Masters, every new interaction is appreciated because it provides an opportunity to improve their level of service delivery. Masters enter any given situation prepared and flexible enough to interact readily with all the variances in personality styles.

Master salon professionals understand the strengths and weaknesses of each personality style. They also understand the similarities and differences, know how to anticipate potential challenges, and build relationships. Master salon professionals can be role models for Professionals and Novices.

## What's Ahead. . .

The previous Unit, Observation, was designed to help you see how each of the personality styles is expressed with different behaviors and feelings. In this Unit, Analysis, you will learn to analyze what happens when the styles interact with each other.

As a result, you will begin to find opportunities to adjust your own behavior in order to have better relationships with others whose styles may be different from your own.

After completing this unit of *Relating with CARE*, you will:

- Be able to say how the personality styles relate to one another—what's compatible and what's incompatible.
- Be able to identify the strengths and weaknesses of your personality style so that you can begin enhancing your strengths in relationships with others and learning to adapt your behavior skills to compensate for your weaknesses.
- Begin to shift your actions and manner of speaking more fluidly in order to create better rapport with people of all personality styles.

### Unit 3: Relating: Analysis, consists of three lessons:

### Lesson 3.1: Defining Style Strengths, Weaknesses and Perceptions

### Lesson 3.2: Understanding Style Similarities and Differences

### Lesson 3.3: Building Rapport with Style Polarities

Lesson 3.1

# Defining Style Strengths, Weaknesses, and Perceptions

Now we're going to look at the strengths and challenges of each personality style. We'll also see how the style preferences are viewed by one another.
Then, you'll have a chance to apply the information you learn to your own situation.

## OBJECTIVES

At the completion of this lesson, you will be able to:

- Summarize each style's strengths and weaknesses
- Explain how each style perceives the other styles

## WHAT YOU NEED TO KNOW

By stepping back and noticing strengths, weaknesses, and perceptions, you are practicing the key skill of **analysis**. You are learning to make distinctions among the personality styles. That means you notice the differences among the styles, which helps you define them more precisely.

### Understanding Style Strengths and Weaknesses

Understanding both the strengths and the challenges you may encounter as a result of your personality style is important because awareness of your:

- Strengths—allows you to use them to your advantage
- Weaknesses—allows you to strengthen and work around them

Knowing how others perceive your personality style is a key step to increasing rapport.

Your knowledge of the style strengths, weaknesses and perceptions will increase your effectiveness in relating to clients. You learn to use your strengths to enhance rapport and manage your weaknesses.

Knowing the character traits of each personality style can help you to understand your clients and achieve even more fruitful professional relations. The richness of others will be emphasized rather than seeing people as good or bad, right or wrong.

The following tables outline the strengths and weaknesses of each of the four personality styles.

Keep in mind that strengths and weaknesses often complement one another, like the two sides of a coin. For example, one side may be represented as "I like to make people feel good," and the other side represented as "I have difficulty saying 'No.'"

By learning to see strengths and weaknesses in these "complementary pairs," you will deepen your understanding of others.

### Knowing the Cooperator's Strengths and Weaknesses

| Strengths | Weaknesses |
|---|---|
| • Enjoys working with people | • Difficulty saying no |
| • In tune and responsive to the needs of others | • More interested in relating to others than getting the job done |
| • Loyal | • May tend to seek security in relationships and deny own needs |
| • Creative and expressive | • Often lacks sense of internal direction; needs to be directed by others |
| • Good team player | • Does not place importance on time and deadlines |
| • Good at fostering group communication and understanding | • Quality of work suffers when they feel they do not have the affection and approval of supervisors, co-workers, clients |
| • Good counselor and advisor | • May spend more time on giving advice |
| • Keeps commitments | • May make decisions based on emotions |

### Knowing the Analyzer's Strengths and Weaknesses

| Strengths | Weaknesses |
|---|---|
| • Figures things out | • Can spend too much time gathering facts before making a decision and proceeding |
| • Understands how things work | • Not very in touch with own feelings or the feelings of others |
| • Precise and correct | • Hesitant |
| • Understands and need for and follows rules | • Shy |
| • Plans and sets goals | • May not be able to project confidence |
| • Diligent worker | • Can get too caught up in a task |

## Knowing the Regulator's Strengths and Weaknesses

| Strengths | Weaknesses |
|---|---|
| • Goal-oriented | • May not focus on the human side of the issue |
| • Decisive | • Can appear bossy and cold |
| • Good supervisor and leader | • Can be rigid and inflexible |
| • Projects confidence | • Has difficulty turning over control to others |
| • Gets a lot done | • Often forgets feelings and relationship |
| • Competent and effective | • Can act superior to others |

## Knowing the Energizer's Strengths and Weaknesses

| Strengths | Weaknesses |
|---|---|
| • Inspiring and charming | • Needs to be the center of attention, which may result in ignoring the needs of others |
| • Lots of energy and enthusiasm | • Lacks self-discipline |
| • Good at motivating others | • Not good at follow-through |
| • Creative and expressive | • May forget commitments or promises |
| • Confident | • Can be sarcastic and unkind when backed into a corner or feeling unappreciated |
| • Good social skills | • Makes excuses for work being late or incomplete |

## Exercise

List three of your strengths and their paired weaknesses.

| Strengths | Weaknesses |
|---|---|
| 1. ______________________ | ______________________ |
| 2. ______________________ | ______________________ |
| 3. ______________________ | ______________________ |

## Understanding Style Perceptions

This section outlines how each style perceives each of the other styles. Each style perceives the others from their own point of view. Because none of us is purely one style, but a unique mixture of styles, we can understand all of these combinations.

Try to see yourself and the people in your life in these pairs. In the line in the margin, write the name of someone you know who sees the world from the point of view outlined. See Exercise 1 on page 94 for an example.

## Perceptions of the Cooperator

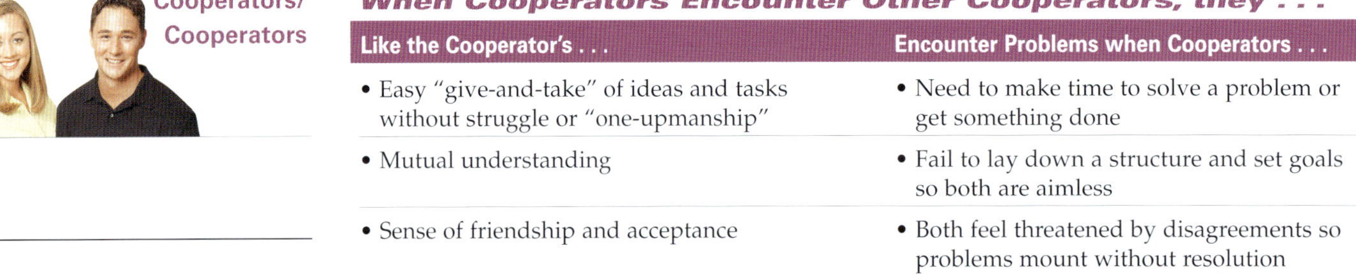

Cooperators/
Cooperators

### When Cooperators Encounter Other Cooperators, they . . .

| Like the Cooperator's . . . | Encounter Problems when Cooperators . . . |
|---|---|
| • Easy "give-and-take" of ideas and tasks without struggle or "one-upmanship" | • Need to make time to solve a problem or get something done |
| • Mutual understanding | • Fail to lay down a structure and set goals so both are aimless |
| • Sense of friendship and acceptance | • Both feel threatened by disagreements so problems mount without resolution |

Cooperators/
Analyzers

### When Cooperators Encounter Analyzers, they . . .

| Like the Analyzer's . . . | Encounter Problems when Analyzers . . . |
|---|---|
| • Concern for getting a job done without rushing | • Withdraw and talk little |
| • Ability to think things through | • Fail to express their feelings and desires |
| • Sense of order | • Insist on a structure or rules that Cooperators do not see a need for |

Cooperators/
Regulators

### When Cooperators Encounter Regulators, they . . .

| Like the Regulator's . . . | Encounter Problems when Regulators . . . |
|---|---|
| • Ability to manage and handle things the Cooperators would rather not be bothered with | • Seem demanding and bossy |
| • Assertiveness and self-confidence | • Show little concern for or sensitivity to feelings |
| • Willingness to take the responsibility for a decision, because the low risk-taking Cooperator would rather not commit to a decision | • Rush the Cooperator |

Cooperators/
Energizers

### When Cooperators Encounter Energizers, they . . .

| Like the Energizer's . . . | Encounter Problems when Energizers . . . |
|---|---|
| • Charm, friendliness, outgoing nature | • Seem self-centered |
| • Interest in people | • Become restless and impatient |
| • Energy and enthusiasm | • Take risks or make snap decisions |

## Perceptions of the Analyzer

Analyzers/ Cooperators

### When Analyzers Encounter Cooperators, they . . .

| Like the Cooperator's . . . | Encounter Problems when Cooperators . . . |
|---|---|
| • Patience with which they approach things and decisions | • Relate rather than plan |
| • Time they take to listen | • Focus on relationship rather than task and detail |
| • Measured way of working on projects or making decisions | • Follow Energizers on risky courses of action |

Analyzers/ Analyzers

### When Analyzers Encounter Other Analyzers, they . . .

| Like the Analyzer's . . . | Encounter Problems when Analyzers . . . |
|---|---|
| • Concern for detail | • Can't stop analyzing a situation or problem and choose a solution |
| • Precision and correctness | • Take forever to get things done |
| • Quiet ways and lack of chit-chat | • Will not risk giving an answer or suggesting a solution that might not be correct |

Analyzers/ Regulators

### When Analyzers Encounter Regulators, they . . .

| Like the Regulator's . . . | Encounter Problems when Regulators . . . |
|---|---|
| • Self-control | • Appear impatient and rushed |
| • Ability to get down to business with a minimum of talk and chatter | • Act overbearing or aggressive |
| • Emphasis on getting the job done | • Choose a course of action with which the Analyzer is uncomfortable |

Analyzers/ Energizers

### When Analyzers Encounter Energizers, they . . .

| Like the Energizer's . . . | Encounter Problems when Energizers . . . |
|---|---|
| • Excitement about ideas | • Seem self-centered |
| • Ability to inspire others to achieve a goal | • Become restless and impatient |
| • Energy and enthusiasm | • Take risks or make snap decisions |

Cooperator

Analyzer

Regulator

Energizer

# Perceptions of the Regulator

Regulators/ Cooperators

## When Regulators Encounter Cooperators, they . . .

| Like the Cooperator's . . . | Encounter Problems when Cooperators . . . |
|---|---|
| • Loyalty toward teammates and leaders | • Talk instead of working |
| • Ability to listen | • Appear too friendly or get physically too close |
| • Support of team projects | • Emphasize feeling rather than fact |
| • Ability to see the big picture | • Ignore problems rather than facing them |

Regulators/ Analyzers

## When Regulators Encounter Analyzers, they . . .

| Like the Analyzer's . . . | Encounter Problems when Analyzers . . . |
|---|---|
| • Ability to follow rules and do as they are told | • Take to much time to complete a task |
| • Precision and attention to detail | • Seem indefinite or unable to make a decision |
| • Work ethic and persistence | • Appear unable to show confidence or assert his or her opinions |
| • Logic, reason and consistence | • Seem to be uncertain or rigid |

Regulators/ Regulators

## When Regulators Encounter Other Regulators, they . . .

| Like the Regulator's . . . | Encounter Problems when Regulators . . . |
|---|---|
| • Ability to get a lot of work done | • Compete for the same thing or try to accomplish the same task |
| • Drive and desire to be the best | • Try to control or direct without agreement |
| • Directness and assertiveness | • Perceive his own purpose and goals as different from the others |
| • Self-confidence | • Get into a power struggle over whose way is best |

Regulators/ Energizers

## When Regulators Encounter Energizers, they . . .

| Like the Energizer's . . . | Encounter Problems when Energizers . . . |
|---|---|
| • Confidence | • Want to play or talk rather than work |
| • Assertiveness | • Fail to achieve a goal or meet a deadline |
| • Leadership | • Make excuses rather than take responsibility |
| • Creative abilities | • Demand more appreciation or approval than the Regulator feels is necessary |

# Perceptions of the Energizer

Energizers/ Cooperators

## When Energizers Encounter Cooperators they . . .

| Like the Cooperator's . . . | Encounter Problems when Cooperators . . . |
|---|---|
| • Interest in people | • Move too slowly |
| • Willingness to listen to and appreciate the Energizer | • Seem to lack energy |
| • Ability to express feelings and be understanding | • Remind the Energizer of the importance of loyalty and keeping his commitments |
| • Willingness to be inspired and motivated by the Energizer | • Seem to be boring or limited |

Energizers/ Analyzers

## When Energizers Encounter Analyzers, they . . .

| Like the Analyzer's . . . | Encounter Problems when Analyzers . . . |
|---|---|
| • Ability to focus on tasks | • Require the Energizer to focus on details, facts, and figures when the Energizer would rather be talking and creating |
| • Ability to take the Energizer's ideas and see them through to completion | • Take a of lot time to complete a project |
| • Willingness to handle little details that bore the Energizer | • Do not laugh at the Energizer's jokes or seem to be won over by the Energizer's charming ways |
| • Logic, reason and consistency | • Speak slowly or deliberately when explaining something |

Energizers/ Regulators

## When Energizers Encounter Regulators, they . . .

| Like the Regulator's . . . | Encounter Problems when Regulators . . . |
|---|---|
| • Leadership qualities | • Criticize the Energizer |
| • Assertiveness and self-confidence | • Try to dominate or control the Energizer |
| • Ability to get a lot of work done | • Do not respond to the Energizer's charm and enthusiasm |
| • Ability to take risks and make decisions | • Remind the Energizer of deadlines, goals, and work to be done |
| • Success ratio | • Do not show warmth, caring, love and approval to the Energizer |

Energizers/ Energizers

## When Energizers Encounter Other Energizers, they . . .

| Like the Energizer's . . . | Encounter Problems when Energizers . . . |
|---|---|
| • Energy and enthusiasm | • Are both vying for the limelight and attention of others |
| • Vision and ability to generate ideas | • Cannot seem to complete a project or stick to their own plans |
| • Willingness to forgive each other's faults (or not see them to begin with) | • Are competing for the same prize, and only one Energizer can win |
| • Willingness to give each other time to complete a project | • Do not follow through on agreements |
| • Lack of concern for deadlines and projects | • Do not expect enough from each other |

In Lesson 3.2, *Understanding Style Similarities and Differences*, you will learn how your personality style is similar to and different from the other styles.

## EXERCISES

1. Go back to pages 90-93 and look at each pair of perceptions. In the space under the pair designations in the margin, write the name of someone you know who predominately sees each style from the point of view outlined in the example below:

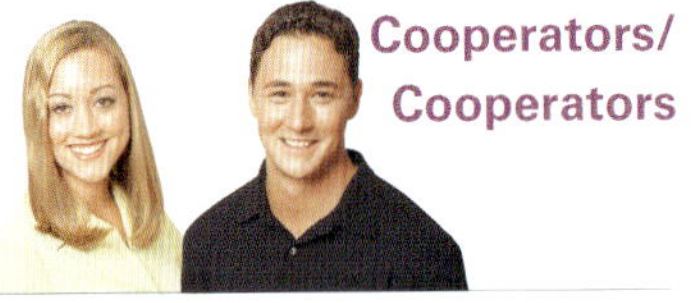


My Mom

**When Cooperators Encounter Other Cooperators, they . . .**

| Like the Cooperator's . . . | Encounter Problems when Cooperators . . . |
|---|---|
| • Easy "give-and-take" of ideas and tasks without struggle or "one-upmanship" | • Need to make time to solve a problem or get something done |
| • Mutual understanding | • Fail to lay down a structure and set goals so both are aimless |
| • Sense of friendship and acceptance | • Feel threatened by disagreements so problems mount without resolution |

2. Write your own primary personality style here:

________________________________________

Name at least two things about each of the four styles you:

**A. Like**

**B. Don't like**

*Cooperator* **A.**________________________________________

**B.**________________________________________

*Analyzer* **A.**________________________________________

**B.**________________________________________

*Regulator* **A.**________________________________________

**B.**________________________________________

*Energizer* **A.**________________________________________

**B.** ________________________________________

3. Give an example of one time you worked well with a personality style different from yours. For example, if you are an Energizer, explain how you worked well with a Regulator, a Cooperator, or an Analyzer.

______________________________________________

______________________________________________

______________________________________________

______________________________________________

______________________________________________

______________________________________________

What did you learn from the above experience?

______________________________________________

______________________________________________

______________________________________________

______________________________________________

4. Write a short essay on how you see your primary personality pattern. Use examples of how you think and feel, what kinds of problems you have with other people, and how you get along with others.

______________________________________________

______________________________________________

______________________________________________

______________________________________________

______________________________________________

______________________________________________

______________________________________________

______________________________________________

______________________________________________

## MAIN POINT SUMMARY

After this lesson, you should have a better appreciation of the styles and how they operate. For example, you may see that the feeling-oriented Cooperators and Energizers may have difficulty relating to thinking-oriented people like the Analyzers and Regulators.

Once we understand that each style has strengths and challenges, and each is neither right nor wrong, it's easy to work with others who are not like us—who have a different style preference.

In fact, we can begin to appreciate the other styles for what they can contribute, and not take their weaknesses so personally.

Ultimately, we want to find ourselves in the role of the Master salon professional—automatically using this knowledge and incorporating it into their daily life.

## SELF-TEST/REVIEW

1. Think of at least two strengths and two weaknesses of each personality style:

**Cooperator**

*Strengths* ______________________________

______________________________

*Weaknesses* ______________________________

______________________________

**Analyzer**

*Strengths* ______________________________

______________________________

*Weaknesses* ______________________________

______________________________

**Regulator**

*Strengths* ______________________________

______________________________

*Weaknesses* ______________________________

______________________________

**Energizer**

*Strengths* ________________________________________________

________________________________________________

*Weaknesses* ________________________________________________

________________________________________________

2. Identify at least one trait that a person with each pattern will like, and one that a person with each pattern will not like.

**Cooperator**

Other Cooperators will like:

________________________________________________

________________________________________________

Other Cooperators will not like:

________________________________________________

________________________________________________

Analyzers will like:

________________________________________________

________________________________________________

Analyzers will not like:

________________________________________________

________________________________________________

Regulators will like:

________________________________________________

________________________________________________

Regulators will not like:

________________________________________________

________________________________________________

Energizers will like:

______________________________________________

______________________________________________

Energizers will not like:

______________________________________________

______________________________________________

**Analyzer**

Cooperators will like:

______________________________________________

______________________________________________

Cooperators will not like:

______________________________________________

______________________________________________

Other Analyzers will like:

______________________________________________

______________________________________________

Other Analyzers will not like:

______________________________________________

______________________________________________

Regulators will like:

______________________________________________

______________________________________________

Regulators will not like:

______________________________________________

______________________________________________

Energizers will like:

______________________________________________

______________________________________________

Energizers will not like:

________________________________________

________________________________________

**Regulator**

Cooperators will like:

________________________________________

________________________________________

Cooperators will not like:

________________________________________

________________________________________

Analyzers will like:

________________________________________

________________________________________

Analyzers will not like:

________________________________________

________________________________________

Other Regulators will like:

________________________________________

________________________________________

Other Regulators will not like:

________________________________________

________________________________________

Energizers will like:

________________________________________

________________________________________

Energizers will not like:

________________________________________

________________________________________

**Energizer**

Cooperators will like:

Cooperators will not like:

Analyzers will like:

Analyzers will not like:

Regulators will like:

Regulators will not like:

Other Energizers will like:

Other Energizers will not like:

Lesson 3.2

# Understanding Style Similarities and Differences

**Now we're going to look at how your personality style is similar to, and different from, the other styles. If you know the traits you share with others, you can use your mutual concerns to focus and get the job done. And if you understand the differences, you are more likely to bridge any gaps.**

## OBJECTIVES

At the completion of this lesson, you will be able to:

- List the concerns and traits the personality styles have in common
- Identify on the traits you share with other personality styles so that you can build better rapport
- Recognize the differences between the personality styles in daily interaction
- Explain how to bridge gaps or avoid differences in values and traits

## WHAT YOU NEED TO KNOW

One of the easiest ways to create rapport is to emphasize your similarities with others. You and your close friends probably share many of the same interests. The more things you have in common with another person, the more likely you are to enjoy that person's company. Even when you have no common interests, you can still find things you share in your general personality concerns that can help you to build rapport.

### Focusing on Similarities

The CARE system allows you to emphasize **shared traits**, as well as similar qualities in attitudes and beliefs. It also helps you recognize and deal effectively with differences.

Understanding the four personality styles' shared traits can help you:

- Relate better to the personality styles with which you share traits
- Understand personality styles you don't share traits with, allowing you to build better rapport with those whom you share the fewest traits

## REMEMBER

**In Lesson 3.1, you learned that people tend to be either thinking-oriented or feeling-oriented. You also learned that people tend to be either passive or assertive. Finally, you learned that personality styles have similar degrees of thinking-feeling and passive-assertive traits. Shared personality style traits spring from those fundamental similarities.**

This section outlines the shared traits for each of the four pairs of personality styles: Cooperator-Energizer, Analyzer-Regulator, Regulator-Energizer, and Cooperator-Analyzer.

**Cooperators/ Energizers share the Feeling traits.**

**Cooperators and Energizers share . . .**

- Concern for people
- Concern for feelings
- Concern for team spirit
- Concern for relationships
- Creativity
- Willingness to talk and touch

**Regulators/ Energizers share the Assertive traits.**

**Regulators and Energizers share . . .**

- Vision
- Concern for direction
- Desire to win
- Desire for respect from others
- Concern for change and challenge
- Concern for position
- Ability to make decisions

**Analyzers/ Regulators share the Thinking traits.**

**Analyzers and Regulators share . . .**

- Concern for task
- Concern for time
- Concern for organization
- Concern for accuracy
- Concern for goals
- Concern for rules and policies

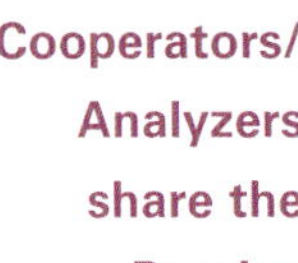

**Cooperators/ Analyzers share the Passive traits.**

**Cooperators and Analyzers share . . .**

- Concern for status quo
- Concern for security
- Desire to support visionaries
- Hesitancy to make decisions
- Low assertiveness

**Styles that seem to be opposites share concerns. Cooperators and Analyzers are both feelers and thinkers and share the Passive traits. Similarly, Regulators and Energizers share Assertive traits.**

## Visualizing Shared Traits

When you think about how personality styles are either feeling-oriented or thinking-oriented, passive or assertive, you may not initially see how the styles share **traits**. For instance, Cooperators are feeling-oriented while Analyzers are thinking-oriented. Both, however, are passive, so Cooperators and Analyzers share the passive traits.

### Shared Traits

In this diagram, the circle is shaded with the colors of the trait labels. Notice that the Feeling color, yellow, spans both the Cooperator and Energizer areas of the circle, while the Passive color, green, spans both the Cooperator and Analyzer areas of the circle. The color shadings show how those styles share traits.

To review Thinking-Feeling and Passive-Assertive traits, see pages 52-53.

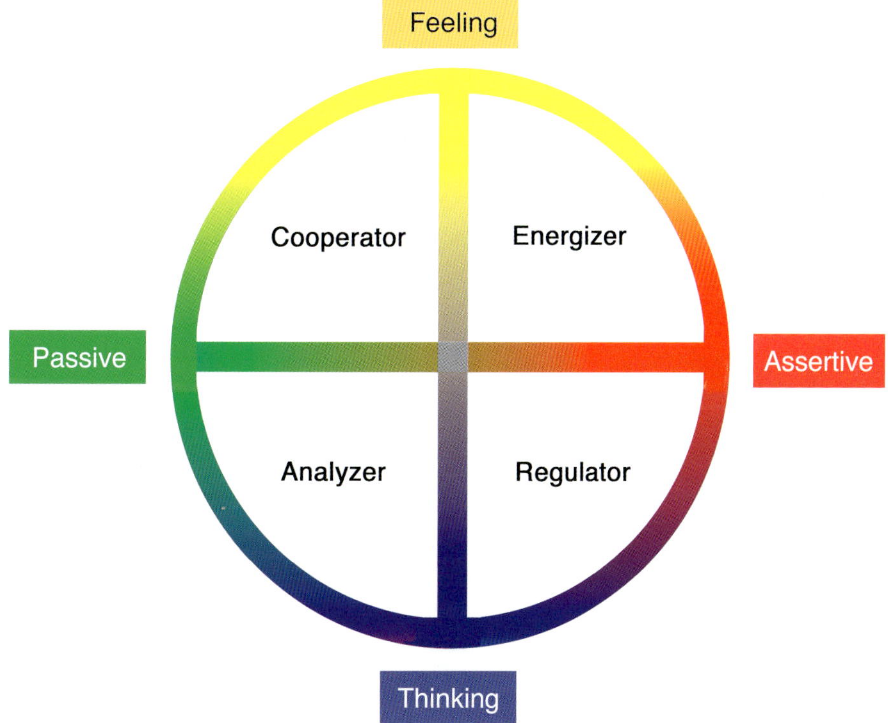

Now let's look at the differences. Differences are not opposites, but differing concerns and orientations. Here we look at differences between styles that have shared traits.

## *Understanding Differences*

Unrecognized differences can easily lead to dis-rapport. When you are aware that there are differences—and know how the style differences may play out in the salon—you can choose an alternative interaction rather than fight the difference. One good strategy is to build on similarities. Sometimes you can even have the differences enhance each other.

Each style views life differently due to emphasis on either feeling or thinking and either passive or assertive behaviors. Disagreements about life views are never resolved since they are neither right nor wrong.

Rather than facing immovable roadblocks to rapport, you can find a "detour" of similarities around differences. You then build "bridges" based on shared traits.

The following charts summarize the differences between the styles that share traits:

**Cooperator/ Energizer share a concern for feelings and for people.**

**Cooperators/Energizers differ because . . .**

- Cooperators are slower to move
- Cooperators care more about loyalty
- Cooperators care more about status quo
- Energizers show more enthusiasm
- Energizers move more quickly
- Energizers need more attention

**Regulator/ Energizer share a concern for change, action, and competition.**

**Regulators/Energizers differ because . . .**

- Regulators are less fluid and changeable
- Regulators focus more on tasks
- Regulators are more goal-oriented
- Regulators care less about people and feelings
- Energizers tend to have less follow-through
- Energizers care less about responsibility
- Energizers care more about people, outcomes, relationships and feelings

**Analyzer/ Regulator share a concern for task, time and structure needs.**

**Analyzers/Regulators differ because . . .**

- Analyzers care more about safety and security
- Analyzers are more concerned with precision and detail
- Analyzers are slow to change
- Analyzers have better listening skills
- Regulators take control
- Regulators are visionaries
- Regulators value challenge
- Regulators value change

**Cooperator/ Analyzer share a concern for security, patience, and listening.**

**Cooperators/Analyzers differ because . . .**

- Analyzers rely more on facts and figures
- Analyzers are more concerned with time and deadlines
- Analyzers are more concerned with tasks
- Cooperators focus more on feelings
- Cooperators focus more on relationships
- Cooperators are more likely to enjoy wandering, unfocused conversations

## In the Salon. . .

Understanding and appreciating differences can lead to smoother salon relationships, which leads to a welcoming atmosphere for clients. Top salon professionals, for instance, often display the Energizer personality style. Salon managers, in contrast, are often Regulators.

The Energizer brings creativity and enthusiasm to client relationships. The Regulator, on the other hand, keeps the Energizer on track and makes sure the salon runs effectively as a business.

The differences between the two styles complement one another, except when the Energizer's enthusiasm and "looseness" about time clashes with the Regulator's focus on discipline.

At that point, it's useful to remember an assertive trait the Energizer and Regulator share: a concern for being the best. By focusing on shared traits, the Energizer and Regulator can temper their conflict with the understanding that they both want the same outcome.

In Lesson 3.3, *Building Rapport with Style Polarities*, you will learn about how these similarities and differences between the personality styles combine to form an individual person.

**Understanding the similarities and differences can balance the styles. It allows you to maximize the strengths and minimize the weaknesses.**

## EXERCISES

### Comparing Style Similarities and Differences

This exercise helps you draw a picture of all you've learned about personality style similarities and differences.

#### Part 1

Read the list of different concerns for the personality styles for Style 1 and Style 2. Write the names of the styles described by the concerns in the circle. Do the same thing for Style 3 and Style 4.

| *Style 1* | | *Style 2* |
|---|---|---|
| *Hesitation* | *vs.* | *Action* |
| *Slow* | *vs.* | *Fast* |
| *Cooperative* | *vs.* | *Competitive* |

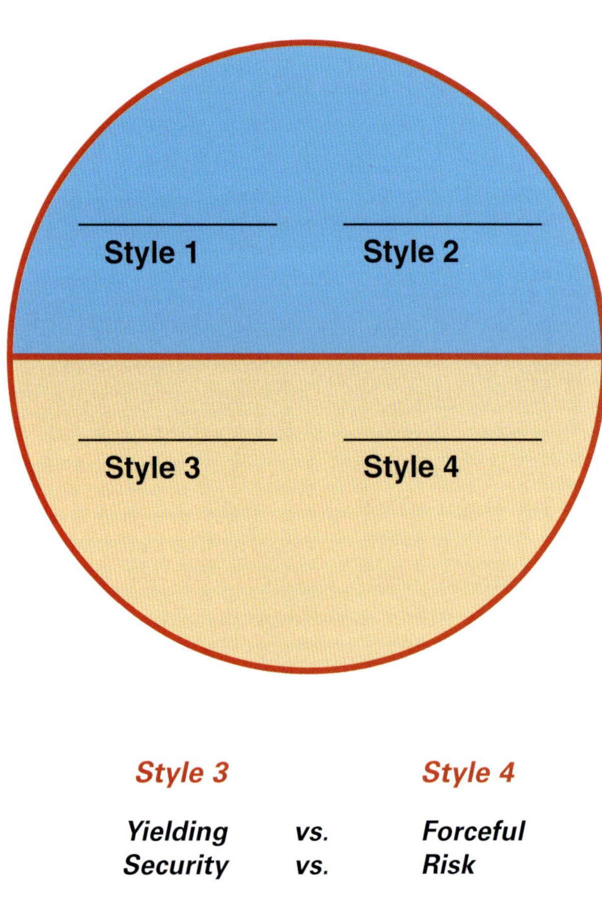


| *Style 3* | | *Style 4* |
|---|---|---|
| *Yielding* | *vs.* | *Forceful* |
| *Security* | *vs.* | *Risk* |

## Part 2

Read the list of traits on the top of the circle and write the names of the personality style they represent in the circle. Do the same thing on the bottom.

| *Style 1* | | *Style 3* |
|---|---|---|
| *Care* | *vs.* | *Fact* |
| *Process* | *vs.* | *Data* |
| *Express* | *vs.* | *Things* |

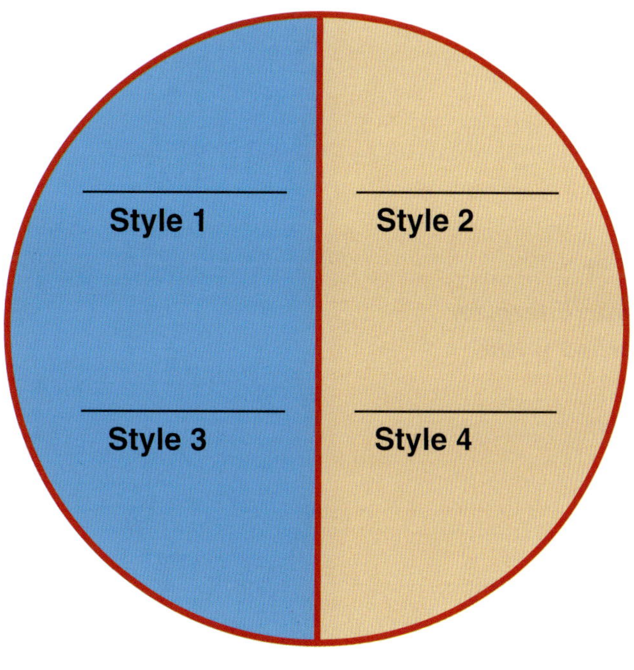


| *Style 2* | | *Style 4* |
|---|---|---|
| *Feeling* | *vs.* | *Respect* |
| *Trust* | *vs.* | *Results* |
| *People* | *vs.* | *Precise* |

## *Part 3*

Now look at the shape below. The names of the four styles are inside. For each pair of personality styles, identify three differences. Write your answers in the blanks provided.

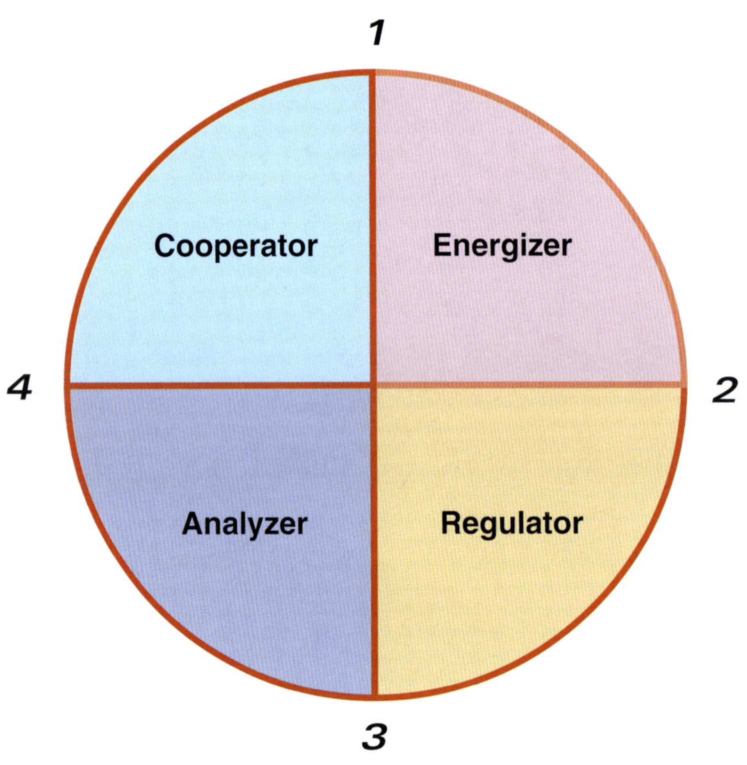


**1**
***Cooperator/Energizer***
***Concerned with:***

______________ vs. ______________

______________ vs. ______________

______________ vs. ______________

**3**
***Regulator/Analyzer***
***Concerned with:***

______________ vs. ______________

______________ vs. ______________

______________ vs. ______________

**2**
**Energizer/*Regulator***
***Concerned with:***

______________ vs. ______________

______________ vs. ______________

______________ vs. ______________

**4**
***Analyzer/Cooperator***
***Concerned with:***

______________ vs. ______________

______________ vs. ______________

______________ vs. ______________

## Journaling

Practice your people skills by identifying traits and concerns you have in common with each person you meet. You should be learning that more conflicts happen than you noticed before you learned the CARE Profile. You didn't notice them because you accept such lack of rapport as the normal course of events.

The next time you sense a conflict arising between you and someone else—be it with a manager, another salon professional, or a client—stop. Take a deep breath, a mental step back, and think about concerns you share with that person. Ask yourself, "What do we both want?" Once you have identified that shared concern, you can find ways to deal with the problem at hand more easily. It sometimes helps to keep a journal and jot down a few notes to help you see the conflict and resolution in writing.

1. Write about a conflict you have experienced.

______________________________________________

______________________________________________

2. What did you both want?

______________________________________________

______________________________________________

3. How could identifying your shared concerns have helped resolve the problem in a better manner?

______________________________________________

______________________________________________

## MAIN POINT SUMMARY

Understanding personality style similarities and differences allows you to build rapport with people whose styles differ from yours. Cooperators, for instance, may have trouble with Analyzers because of their concern for facts. Cooperators and Analyzers, however, value security and low-risk situations. They tend not to make decisions very quickly. That gives them a place to meet. Regulators may have trouble with Energizers because they are not as concerned with time and tend not to be as focused on task. At the same time, however, they share a desire to compete and win and a concern for change and challenge.

The differences can also give you a sense of how personality styles that share traits will react differently in particular situations. For instance, the "thinkers" (Analyzers and Regulators) share a concern for time and task, but a Regulator will take charge and may be more aggressive.

## SELF-TEST/REVIEW

1. When something is different, it is said to be opposite.
   Circle One:

   True or False

2. Differences between two individuals always lead to disagreement and discomfort. Circle One:

   True or False

3. Which two styles take risks? ________________, ________________

   Which two styles avoid risks? ________________, ________________

4. Which two styles emphasize relationships?

   ____________________, ____________________

5. Which two styles emphasize a concern for accuracy?

   ____________________, ____________________

6. The ____________________, values challenge and change,

   while the ____________________, likes to relate with others,

   while the ____________________, does not as much.

7. The ____________________, and ____________________, are

   both passive, but the ____________________, likes to relate to others,

   while the ____________________, does not as much.

8. The ____________________, and ____________________, are both

   assertive and want to win, but the ____________________, is not as

   disciplined or goal-oriented as the ____________________.

Lesson 3.3

# Building Rapport with Style Polarities

**Now we're going to look at the polar opposite personality styles. Understanding polar opposites can allow you to harness the power of differences to build great relationships.**

## OBJECTIVES

At the completion of this lesson, you will be able to:

- Identify the two pairs of polar opposite personality styles
- Discuss the differences between your primary personality style and your polar opposite personality style
- Determine how style polarities can provide a balancing force that support one another in their differences
- List ways to tap into the power of polar opposites

## WHAT YOU NEED TO KNOW

You may have noticed that two personality style combinations have no traits in common. They shared neither thinking-feeling traits nor passive-assertive traits.

### Managing Personality Style Polarities

Those relationships are polar opposite. They are as far from one another in basic personality traits and attitudes as the North Pole is from the South Pole.

Understanding polar opposites is important because polar opposites are more likely to conflict than the other styles. In truth, it is easiest for you to identify those who are least like you. And, it's your job to manage your judgments and maintain high-quality rapport.

Managing your style polarities means you can develop strategies that anticipate areas of potential conflict before they become interpersonal problems. This is something Master salon professionals do as a matter of course, and you can do it as you build your skills of observation and analysis.

Look at the diagram on the following page. Notice that the personality styles next to one another share either a feeling or thinking orientation. The preferences placed one on top of the other share either a passive or an assertive orientation.

## REMEMBER

**Similarities and differences in personality styles are based on the two fundamental personality orientations: thinking or feeling-oriented, and passive or assertive.**

The styles on a diagonal do not share an orientation. They are polar opposites, or polarities.

Based on what you already know about the style traits of each orientation, you can imagine the kind of conflicts these styles might experience.

As you can see, the two pairs of polar opposites are:

- Cooperator and Regulator
- Analyzer and Energizer

As you gain experience observing people, you will see that most personality style differences are a matter of degree with polarities. There may be a difference in "kind." They share neither thinking/feeling nor passiveness/assertiveness. This distinction is particularly important when working with polarities.

**Cooperators and Regulators are polar opposites. So are Analyzers and Energizers.**

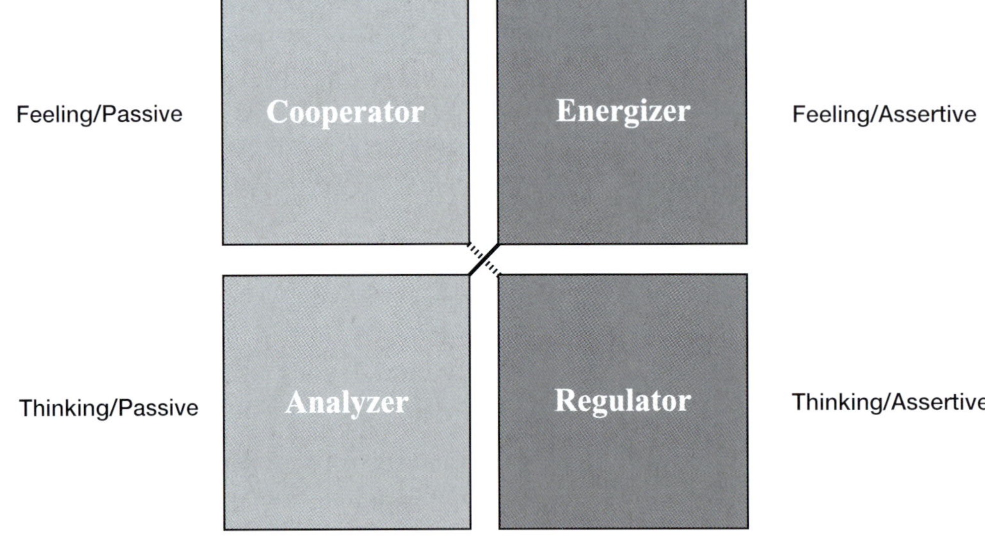


The greater the degree of polarity difference, the greater the potential for conflict. Managing the relationship between polarities is critical to your success—and the success of your salon. Well-managed, you can have a powerful team. Unmanaged, they can tear your salon apart.

**Interpersonal differences can be seen in terms of the degree to which we combine the characteristics of the CARE model. We are going to use the CARE Profile Graph to help us chart our differences. Then we can more easily anticipate areas of potential conflict with our polar opposites.**

When two polarities learn to appreciate and work with one another's differences, they begin to realize that their differences, when combined, provide increased strength. It is as if the two polarities, when joined together in rapport, make a whole and well-rounded style. In dis-rapport, all are diminished.

## Measuring the Degree of Your Polar Styles

The degree of personality style polarity depends on the score each person gets on his or her primary personality style.

For example, if you are high on "R" and low on "C," you are more likely to experience conflict with a Cooperator. If the difference between the polarity scores was smaller, you would have less opportunity for conflict. The same is true for any style that is particularly low in its polarity.

When you recognize that a person has a primary personality style that is opposite yours, you can take responsibility for how you act toward that person and capitalize on the strengths inherent in the polarities.

### Measure the Degree of Your Polar Personality Styles:

Refer back to your CARE Profile Graph on page 47. Look at your highest score, which is your Primary Style. Write down your Primary Style and Primary Score in the space below.

Primary Style ____________________ Primary Score ______

Look at your lowest score which is your Polar Style. Write down your Polar Style and your Polar Score in the space below.

Polar Style ______________________ Polar Score _________

Subtract your Polar Score from your Primary Score and write the result below.

Polarity Degree __________________

Here's how it works—if the difference between the two scores is 20 or greater, you are more likely to encounter conflict with people whose primary style is your polarity.

You can use your knowledge of personality styles to bridge differences. You will be better able to do this when you are able to quickly and accurately identify another's personality style.

## NOTE

**People who are high in polarities are often effective, but conflicted, team members and leaders. For example, high Regulators with high Cooperator scores must constantly sort out their conflicting concerns for relationship and goal accomplishment.**

## In the Salon. . .

People of polar opposite personality styles who work well together can be a potent force in a salon when they learn to bridge the differences. A Cooperator artistic director, for instance, may balance a Regulator manager. The Regulator can make sure the dollars and cents of the salon are in order, while the Cooperator provides a human balance by making sure that salon employees are courteous to clients.

Similarly, an Analyzer manager can pay attention to the details in order to provide an environment that fosters the Energizer salon professional's creative spark.

Because you can't give the CARE Profile Questionnaire to clients, the next lesson, 4.1, *Identifying Styles by Observing Behavior*, will help you identify a personality style just by meeting a person.

## EXERCISES

1. In the blanks below, list the names of people with whom you experience conflict. Your list may include a teacher, a co-worker, a client, a relative, or someone less central to your life like a neighbor who complains about your dog. What do you think that person's primary personality style is? Write a style next to each name. How many are opposites to your primary style?

| Name | Primary Style |
|---|---|
| ________________ | ________________ |
| ________________ | ________________ |
| ________________ | ________________ |

2. The next time you attend a show or seminar with your class or co-workers, team up with someone you know is your polar opposite. Even if it is someone you do not have good rapport with, talk with him or her and exchange perceptions of what you saw and learned at the event. See if the other person can give you some new insights or ideas.

3. Write down what you learned from this experience.

________________________________

________________________________

________________________________

## MAIN POINT SUMMARY

Polar opposites are styles that have neither thinking-feeling nor passive-assertive traits in common.

When you are aware of the traits of your polar opposite, you may see that your opposite has traits that you can benefit from. If you keep that in mind, you are more likely to build an effective relationship rather than take the differences personally.

Your knowledge of personality styles can help you bridge the differences you feel with certain people.

## SELF-TEST/REVIEW

1. Polarities are styles that are ______________________________ from our own.

2. The polarity of Energizer is ______________________________.

3. The polarity of Cooperator is ______________________________.

4. Why do style polarities cause conflict?

______________________________________________________________

______________________________________________________________

______________________________________________________________

______________________________________________________________

5. Pick one of the two polarity relationships and discuss how these styles can avoid conflict and work in harmony.

______________________________________________________________

______________________________________________________________

______________________________________________________________

______________________________________________________________

6. When two polarities work in harmony, they ______________________________ each other.

## Unit 4:
# Relating: Application

## THE VISION

In this unit, Application, we'll look at how salon professionals apply their understanding of personality styles to stay in rapport with their clients, co-workers and bosses.

In Unit 1, you learned about yourself and your own personality style. This will help you see how *People Skills* concepts can be applied as you you grow in your career. In Unit 2, you worked on learning and observing the personality styles. In Unit 3, you moved from Observation to Analysis—analyzing strengths and weaknesses, differences and similarities of the personality styles. Now, in Unit 4, Application, you will apply your observations and analysis to on-the-job rapport-building opportunities.

### Novice

When it comes to Application, Novice salon professionals tend to focus more on applying their new technical salon skills. On the interpersonal level, they may begin to think about building rapport, but they often do not have enough experience to handle challenges. Novices can learn from watching masters and Professionals, and asking them for advice.

### Professional

Salon professionals at the Professional level experiment with shifting styles to build better rapport. They are aware of discord, and when they try to build rapport, they tend to apply new techniques with uncertainty about whether the new techniques will work. But they can often identify the personality styles of new clients accurately and treat clients skillfully.

Successful salon professionals generally reserve experimentation with new skills for relationships between co-workers and bosses or in their private lives—rather than with clients, where the risk is perceived as higher. Professionals add skills purposefully and after careful consideration and analysis. The most effective Professionals knowingly face people skills challenges in all areas of their lives.

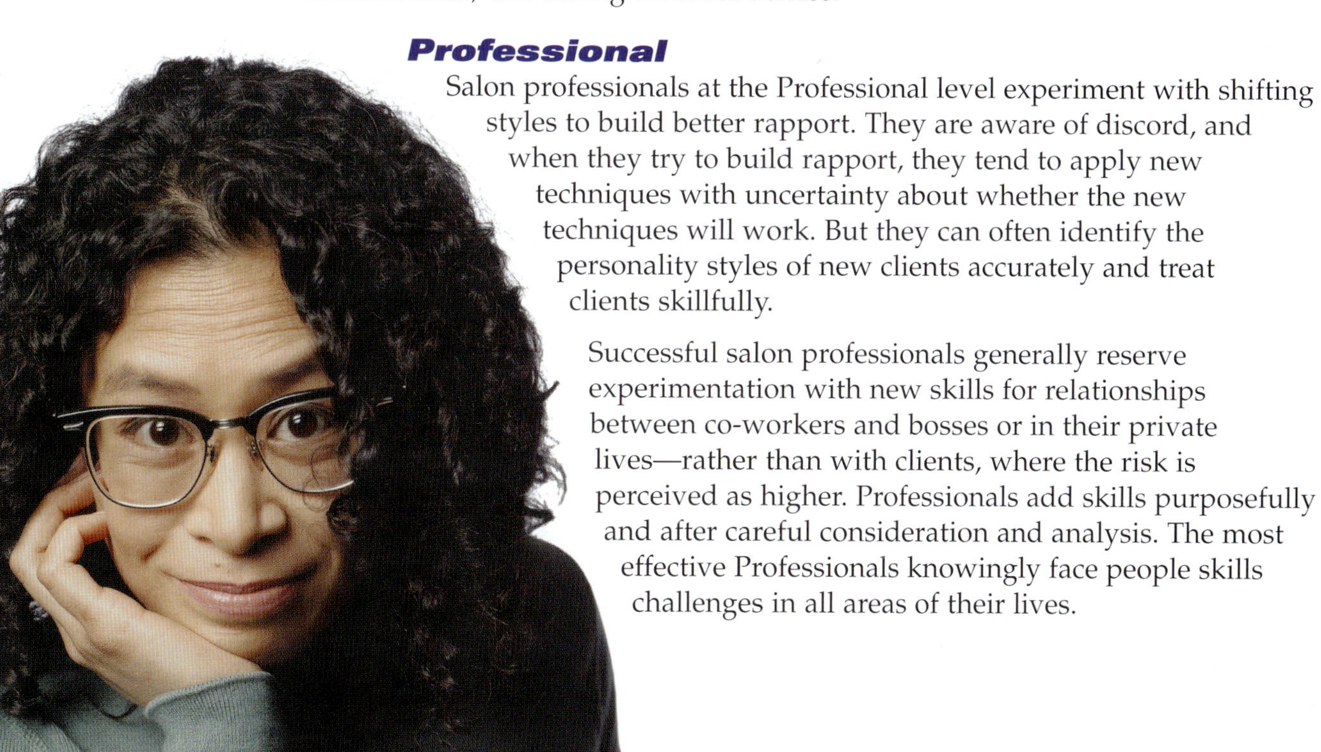

### Master

Master salon professionals enjoy being challenged by new clients and employees. Each new person represents an opportunity to demonstrate expert communication skills to win in the game of business and life.

Master salon professionals use their knowledge of personality styles to consistently identify the styles of others and shift their own actions to gain greater rapport. They focus on improving their own weaknesses, learning to expand their ability to shift styles for greater effectiveness and fulfillment. As a result, they find pleasure in seeing the results of enhanced rapport.

Masters are learning in all areas of life. Life is no longer two separate worlds for Masters. Work and personal life are united. Masters see fresh, new, and challenging opportunities where others may see only problems.

## What's Ahead. . .

In this unit of *Relating with CARE*, you will work on Application. Here, you will begin to apply the personality style preference concepts and start to use them to improve your relationships in the salon—and in your daily life.

At first, you will find that you use your own style as a basis of comparison in identifying the personality styles of others. Gradually, you will be able to shift your actions to relate better with people of different personality styles. As you gain skill, you will be able to create solid rapport with people of opposite personality styles.

After completing this unit of *Relating with CARE*, you will be able to:

- Identify the primary and secondary personality styles of others through observation.
- Use your own primary and secondary personality styles as a basis for adapting your style to improve relationships with an ever-widening range of clients.
- Appreciate the full range of differences in personality styles and shift your manner of speaking and acting in order to create rapport with people, no matter what their personality style.

### Unit 4: Application, consists of five lessons:

**Lesson 4.1: Identifying Styles by Observing Behaviors**

**Lesson 4.2: Identifying Styles by Listening to Speech**

**Lesson 4.3: Shifting to Build Rapport**

**Lesson 4.4: Responding to Styles to Build Rapport**

**Lesson 4.5: Creating Personal and Client Action Plans**

Lesson 4.1

# Identifying Styles by Observing Behaviors

You can't give your clients the CARE Profile Questionnaire, so you need to learn how to read their personality styles.

## OBJECTIVES

At the completion of this lesson, you will be able to:

- Recognize behavioral cues that provide clues to a person's personality style preference
- Match behavioral cues with the four personality styles
- Identify Cooperators, Analyzers, Regulators and Energizers by:
  - — the way they greet you
  - — their manner of speaking
  - — the clothes they wear
  - — the jobs they hold

## WHAT YOU NEED TO KNOW

In order to establish rapport with a wide range of clients, you need to sharpen your observation skills and pay attention to people you meet. Listen to them, watch their eyes and gestures. Observe how they dress. Use the information you learn about their primary and secondary personality styles to choose how to build lasting rapport.

### Behavioral Cues

To successfully identify another's personality style through observation, you need to learn what clues and signals to look for. You need to observe behavioral cues, ways people act and things people say that provide hints to their personality styles.

Use the tables on the next page to review cues under each category.

Note that the behavioral cues in the tables are only guides. People who are thinking-oriented, for instance, tend to be self-contained but some can be quite expressive.

By knowing the main focus of a client's personality style, you will better know how to interact with that client.

## Feeling or Thinking Behavioral Cues

| Feeling-Oriented Behaviors | Thinking-Oriented Behaviors |
|---|---|
| • Friendly smile | • Self-contained |
| • Looks you in the eye | • Waits until you introduce yourself before telling you his or her name |
| • Laughs a lot | • Maintains space between himself/herself and others |
| • Introduces self | • Waits for you to talk first |
| • Speaks before being spoken to | • Discusses activities, not people |
| • Warm | • Controlled voice, not many highs and lows |
| • Offers hand to shake | • Arms folded across chest |
| • Touches, hugs | |
| • Gestures with hands while talking | |

Now, we'll see how each style chooses to engage in particular behaviors.

## Assertive or Passive Behavioral Cues

| Assertive Behaviors | Passive Behaviors |
|---|---|
| • Looks at you when talking | • Says things like "I don't know, what do you think?" |
| • Says what he or she thinks | • Has difficulty making a decision |
| • Gives opinions | • Does not volunteer to answer a question |
| • Makes a decision quickly | • Takes time, moves slowly |
| • Has firm handshake | • Does not offer an opinion |
| • Speaks confidently | • Follows others |
| • Organizes | • Tentative, "shades of gray" statements |
| • Leads | • Soft handshake |
| • Acts confident | |

## REMEMBER

**Personality is the outward, observable action and attitude that reflect the self below the surface. Each of the four personality styles can be gauged in terms of whether they are:**

- **Feeling or thinking-oriented**
- **Passive or assertive**

## Overall Key Traits

Now you have some behavioral cues for identifying another person's primary personality style. The following table lists how those cues may show up in real life. Again, the table provides general tendencies, not absolute characteristics.

| | The Cooperator<br>Feeling and Passive, Tends to: | The Analyzer<br>Thinking and Passive, Tends to: |
|---|---|---|
| **Greeting** | • Smile | • Have a controlled, brief smile |
| | • Meet your eyes | • Look down and away |
| | • Shake your hand with loose grasp | • Wait for you to move first |
| | • Be warm and approachable | • Shake your hand with loose grasp |
| | • Hug you hello by second visit | • Withdraw hand quickly |
| **Dress** | • Choose warm, neutral shades (beige, rich brown) | • Choose functional, efficient clothes |
| | • Avoid "startling" fashions | • Place no importance on fashion or designer labels |
| | • Wear stylish but low-key fashions | • Look neutral or bland |
| **Talk** | • Speak with emphasis | • Be precise |
| | • Look to you to confirm | • Sound controlled |
| | • Speak slowly | • Speak slowly |
| | • Use words like "friends," "feeling," or "caring" | • Use facts and figures |
| **Job** | • Work in helping professions | • Work in analytical fields |
| | - Nurse | - Science |
| | - Social worker | - Engineering |
| | - Teacher | - Accounting |
| | - Therapist | - Computer programming |
| **Hair** | • Wear a basic but stylish cut | • Wear a functional cut |
| | • Want and take your advice | • Want same style each time |

| | The Regulator | The Energizer |
|---|---|---|
| | **Thinking and Assertive, Tends to:** | **Feeling and Assertive, Tends to:** |
| **Greeting** | • Have a reserved smile | • Have a broad, high-energy, expressive smile |
| | • Look you in the eye | • Look you in the eye |
| | • Wait for you to make the first move | • Have a firm handshake |
| | • Has firm handshake | • Introduce self first |
| | • Stiffen and withdraw if you get too close | |
| **Dress** | • Choose quality, expensive clothes | • Choose expressive, colorful, dynamic styles |
| | • Wear conservative, classic designs | • Wear fashionable, designer labels |
| | • Select separates that do double and triple duty | • Select expensive styles |
| **Talk** | • Be loud to make a point | • Be loud and excited |
| | • Sound monotone | • Sound expressive |
| | • Use a definite, reverberating tone | • Speak fast |
| | • Use commands and issue directions | • Use hands and arms |
| **Job** | • Work as leaders, achievers | • Work in "people" professions |
| | - Supervisors | - Salespeople |
| | - Lawyers | - Consultants |
| | - Doctors | - Speakers |
| | - Executives | - Politicians |
| | | - Political organizers |
| **Hair** | • Wear an attractive style | • Wear a creative style |
| | • Require easy care | • Be willing to try a new style |

To see other people more as they really are, remember to look for their secondary style as well as their primary style. It takes more mastery to start identifying more than one trait and using them all to create rapport.
If that seems too difficult, don't worry—over time you will be able to.
Your journey has just begun.

## Secondary Style Influence

Remember that a personality is multi-faceted. People are not purely one style. Everyone has traits of a Cooperator, an Analyzer, a Regulator and an Energizer to some extent. Usually, you operate from one of the styles most of the time, and your actions and attitudes reflect that style.

When you analyze your scores from the CARE Profile, you probably scored higher on one style. You identified your primary style and your secondary style. Keep in mind that your clients are just the same, and you need to take their secondary style into account in order to establish and maintain rapport.

### In the Salon. . .

Jean owns her own fashion boutique. She dresses like a Gypsy: bright colors, flowing scarves, dramatic hem lines, and glittery costume jewelry. She is usually friendly and outgoing, a ball of fire. She's definitely an Energizer.

But when it comes to her boutique, she's all business. She mentions the five-year business plan she is writing. That's goal-setting—the trait of a more self-controlled and goal-oriented individual.

She always makes her facial appointments on Tuesday morning, when her shop is less busy. In fact, she has made the next three ahead of time, the first Monday of the month for the next three months. When it comes to business, Jean is definitely a Regulator.

So if you make the mistake of assuming you can always be a little loose and breezy with Jean, and that running late won't bother her, you'll have to contend with a raging Regulator!

In Lesson 4.2, *Identifying Styles by Listening to Speech*, you will learn how listening to the way a person speaks helps to identify their personality style.

## EXERCISES

1. Identify personality styles in your family and friends.

   Use the behavioral cues to identify the personality styles of four people in your daily life, such as your mom, dad, any siblings, best friend, boyfriend or girlfriend, and co-workers. How does knowing the styles help you understand them more and relate to them better?

   **Person 1** **Primary Style**

   ______________________________________________

Knowing ________________'s personality style helps me understand and relate to them better because:

________________________________________________

________________________________________________

**Person 2** **Primary Style**

________________________________________________

Knowing ________________'s personality style helps me understand and relate to them better because:

________________________________________________

________________________________________________

**Person 3** **Primary Style**

________________________________________________

Knowing ________________'s personality style helps me understand and relate to them better because:

________________________________________________

________________________________________________

**Person 4** **Primary Style**

________________________________________________

Knowing ________________'s personality style helps me understand and relate to them better because:

________________________________________________

________________________________________________

2. Identify the Primary personality styles of the salon professional and client in Scenarios 1-4 on the following pages. Spaces are provided at the end of each scenario.

## Scenario 1

**Client: John**

**Salon Professional: Rebecca**

**John** saunters in wearing worn tan cords and a brown tweed jacket that looks very lived-in. His hands are in his pockets. He stops at the desk to chat with the receptionist a minute, then turns with a warm smile to Rebecca, showing rows of dimples and twinkling eyes.

**Rebecca** is standing at the styling station, cape in one hand and razor comb in the other, like a soldier at attention.

**John**, casually: "Hi, Rebecca, how are you? It's been so long. Hey, I'm really sorry I'm late, but I had to spend some extra time with my last patient. Someone going through a difficult time in their life and needed to talk a little more. I'm sure you understand."

**Rebecca**: (firmly) "Well, I certainly understand about clients making me late."

**John**: "Hey, I don't mind. That's why I'm in a people profession. I like talking to people, helping them with their problems."

**Rebecca**: "And I like helping clients with their styling needs—all my clients. It's a little hard to fit everyone in when some throw my schedule off and make me late."

**John**: "Rebecca, whoa, I feel a little anger here. Talk to me, kiddo, what's wrong? Problems at home?"

**Rebecca**: "No problems at home, John. And I'd rather not talk. I'd rather get to work. Shall we?"

**John's** primary personality style is:

______________________________

**Rebecca's** primary personality style is:

______________________________

## Scenario 2

**Client: Michael**

**Salon Professional: Albert**

**Michael** sits straight and stiff in the waiting area. His arms are folded across his chest. He is tapping his toe, glancing at his watch from time to time.

**Albert** walks up and says haltingly, "Um, hi Mike, oh, I mean Mr. Davis."

**Michael**: (in a deep, resonant voice) "Albert. Hello. You are fifteen minutes off schedule. I must be out of here in no more than forty minutes. I have an extremely important appointment with my firm's board of directors." He stares directly into Albert's eyes, and Albert looks away.

**Albert**: "Fine, fine. No problem. Let's go right to the shampoo bowl."

**Michael**: (with finality) "Skip the shampoo. Cut it dry this time. I showered after my tennis game this morning, so it's clean."

**Albert** (barely whispers) "Okay."

**Michael** strides to Albert's station. Albert practically has to run to catch up. He takes a neatly folded cape from the drawer and places it carefully around Michael. Michael glares impatiently.

**Albert** grows flustered. He fumbles for his tools and hesitates when putting the cape over Michael.

**Michael**, by now extremely upset, says from behind clenched teeth. "Albert, I told you I was in a hurry. Why are you taking so much time?"

**Albert** is becoming more withdrawn and silent. He appears to shrink in embarrassment as he sees others in the salon observing the scene.

**Michael's** primary personality style is:

______________________________

**Albert's** primary personality style is:

______________________________

## Scenario 3

**Client: Jane**

**Salon Professional: Cathy**

**Jane**: "Hi Cathy! How are you today? Great weather! Wow, let me tell you about last weekend!" Jane is wearing a tropical print shirt over bright aqua pants, and carrying a big canvas tote bag decorated with pins and buttons. As she enters the salon she takes off oversized sunglasses and carelessly tosses them onto the shelf at Cathy's styling station.

**Cathy**: (speaking slowly, warmly and with emphasis) says, "Hi Jane, I'm feeling good. I can tell you're feeling good, too. I love your shirt. It must have been some weekend. Tell me about it. I want to hear everything." Cathy is wearing khaki-colored slacks and a cream-colored Angora sweater under her salon lab coat. The two talk on for awhile. Then Jane glances at her multicolored wristwatch.

**Jane**: "Oh, dear! I'm going to be late! Hurry. Let's get going! I have to go to six stores and then get home and clean the house for a party I'm having tonight. I need my nails done—fast."

**Cathy**: "But you haven't picked out the polish yet, Jane. We need to talk about that a little before I just do something. What color will make you feel good?"

**Jane's** primary personality style is:

______________________________

**Cathy's** primary personality style is:

______________________________

## Scenario 4

**Client: Lisa**

**Salon Professional: Ethan**

**Lisa** is an older woman, whose brown hair is beginning to turn gray. She comes in after work, wearing a simple gray suit, white blouse, low-heeled black pumps, and no jewelry. This is her first visit to the salon. Ethan greets her in the waiting area, with a wide smile, taking her hand in his.

**Ethan**: "Hi, Ms. Jones, my name is Ethan. May I call you Lisa? Lisa, welcome to our salon. I'll be your salon professional today. I see you have made an appointment for a haircut. Come this way and sit down in my chair, while I have a look at your hair and we talk a bit about your style preferences." Lisa follows Ethan to his station silently. After she seats herself and smoothes her skirt, she speaks.

**Lisa**: "Hi, Ethan. Good to meet you. There is not very much to discuss about my hairstyle. Just trim it, following the same cut that's there already. I don't want anything else done with it."

**Ethan**: "Your hair appears dry, probably because it is beginning to gray, and the gray hair is more coarse than your other hair. A one-process color application in a warm chestnut brown would really brighten your image. We could do that next time, after we cut and condition it today. But for now I'd like to layer it a little on top, to give it the style some lift and softness—is that okay?"

**Lisa** has been listening the whole time, looking down and clutching her pocketbook in her lap. She speaks haltingly. "Maybe I made a mistake coming here. I've been going for years to a lady in my neighborhood who has a beauty parlor in her basement. But she had back surgery and can't work for a while. One of the car salesmen at the dealer where I work—I'm a bookkeeper—recommended this place. I'm not sure I'm ready for such a big change."

**Ethan**: "Whoa, Lisa, don't worry. Hey, it's okay, really! We're not talking a drastic change here, just a little image improvement. How about this—lets take it one step at a time. See how you like this cut, and think about the color for a while. We can do that whenever you're ready. I think you'd love it!"

**Lisa's** primary personality style is:

______________________________

**Ethan's** primary personality style is:

______________________________

## MAIN POINT SUMMARY

You don't have to give someone the CARE Profile Questionnaire to tell what his or her personality style is. What you do is listen to how someone speaks, look at his or her clothes—ask a lot of questions—and you will usually discover both primary and secondary personality styles.

## SELF-TEST/REVIEW

For each of the four clients below, look at the list of characteristics and behaviors. Label each client's primary and secondary styles in the space provided with either a Cooperator, Analyzer, Regulator, or Energizer.

### Client X Example

attention to feelings

low-risk

dramatic

listener

easy-going

wants to be liked

patient

Primary Style: Cooperator

Secondary Style: Energizer

In the example above, all traits were that of a Cooperator except for "dramatic," which is more the trait of an Energizer.

### Client 1

accurate

precise

competitive

thorough

analytical

self-controlled

Primary Style: ____________________

Secondary Style: ____________________

## Client 2

| | |
|---|---|
| expressive | persuasive |
| optimistic | people-oriented |
| flexible on time | cooperative |

Primary Style: ____________________

Secondary Style: ____________________

## Client 3

| | |
|---|---|
| self-confident | power-seeker |
| competitive | self-controlled |
| bossy | not punctual |

Primary Style: ____________________

Secondary Style: ____________________

## Client 4

| | |
|---|---|
| steady | caring |
| loyal | committed |
| cooperative | precise |

Primary Style: ____________________

Secondary Style: ____________________

Lesson 4.2

# Identifying Styles by Listening to Speech

**A person's speech provides accurate clues to their personality style preference. Listen to their volume, rate of speech, and tone—the way they speak as well as what they say is important.**

## OBJECTIVES

At the completion of this lesson, you will be able to:

- Recognize speech patterns that provide clues to a person's personality style
- Match speech patterns with the four personality styles
- Identify Cooperators, Analyzers, Regulators, and Energizers by their:
  - Content
  - Rate of speech
  - Tone
  - Word emphasis

## WHAT YOU NEED TO KNOW

A person's speech provides another way to identify a personality style. To identify personality styles by listening to speech you need to be able to listen to people as they speak and notice the volume, speed and tone of their voices. Once you've identified a style, you can begin to shift verbally to build rapport.

### Speech Characteristics

Usually, the way a person speaks reflects his or her primary personality style. Two people of different personality styles can use the same words, but the message behind the way they deliver the words will be very different. Speech consists of content and feeling.

**Content** refers to word choices.

**Feeling** includes volume, speed, emphasis, and tone of voice.

Speech patterns offer another set of clues to a person's personality style preference, in addition to the behavioral clues you learned to observe in the last lesson.

**Two things make up a person's speech: content and feeling. Content is the choice of words. Feeling is the volume, speed, word emphasis and tone.**

## *Identifying Language Styles*

Use the following table as a guide to speech characteristics in the areas of content and feeling.

However, you need to know that there are many people whose personality style will not match the speech characteristics listed in the table. For example, some Cooperators will speak rapidly instead of slowly, and some Regulators will speak softly instead of loudly.

So use the following characteristics only as a guide in "reading" people, not to fit them into a box. Identifying personality styles is simply a tool to establish rapport, and it is good rapport that wins a client's goodwill.

| | | ***The Cooperator*** | ***The Analyzer*** |
|---|---|---|---|
| | | **Feeling and Passive Tends To** | **Thinking and Passive Tends To** |
| | **Content** | • Emphasize words like "feel" and "love" | • Emphasize words like "think" and "like" |
| **Feeling** | Volume | • Use low volume | • Use low volume |
| | Speed | • Speak slowly | • Speak slowly |
| | Tone | • Sound warm and caring | • Sound flat and monotone |

| | | ***The Regulator*** | ***The Energizer*** |
|---|---|---|---|
| | | **Thinking and Assertive Tends To** | **Feeling and Assertive Tends To** |
| | **Content** | • Emphasize phrases like "I want," "I need," "I think," and "You" | • Emphasize words with exaggerated meanings, like "greatest," "best," "fantastic," and "outstanding" |
| **Feeling** | Volume | • Use high volume | • Use high volume |
| | Speed | • Speak fast | • Speak fast |
| | Tone | • Sound firm and commanding | • Sound excited |

## REMEMBER

**Just as there are no "pure" personality types, there are many people who will not fit the following speech patterns. Some Cooperators will speak rapidly instead of slowly, while some Regulators will speak softly instead of loudly.**

In Lesson 4.3, *Shifting to Build Rapport*, you will learn how altering your behavior and words to match the person you are communicating with can help build rapport.

## EXERCISES

1. What did you notice about the similarities in speech between the Cooperator and the Analyzer and Regulator/Energizer? Write your answers below.

*Cooperator/ Analyzer* ______________________________

______________________________

______________________________

______________________________

______________________________

*Regulator/ Energizer* ______________________________

______________________________

______________________________

______________________________

______________________________

## Identifying Styles by Listening to Speech

2. Read each sentence below, along with the clues on volume, speed and tone. In the blank preceding each number, write the first initial—C, A, R, or E—of the personality style you identify. The first one has been completed as an example.

| | Volume | Speed | Tone | Sentence |
|---|---|---|---|---|
| R | High | Fast | Firm | "Be sure to schedule your next appointment now. I'm getting very busy." |
| ________ 1. | High | Fast | Warm | Salon professional to client: "That is really a fantastic style on you. It looks really fabulous." |
| ________ 2. | Low | Slow | Flat | Salon professional to client, upon receiving a compliment: "Do you really think so?" |
| ________ 3. | High | Fast | Sharp | Client to salon professional: "I'm very busy. The style must be smart, yet easy to manage." |
| ________ 4. | Low | Slow | Probing | Client to salon professional: "Now, exactly why do you place the rollers at that angle?" |
| ________ 5. | High | Fast | Lively | Client to salon professional: "Oh, you just must go see that movie, it's simply the best movie that's come out this year." |
| ________ 6. | Low | Slow | Kindly | Client to salon professional: "You are good at this. How did you learn so much?" (Then listens to response.) |
| ________ 7. | High | Fast | Lecture | Salon professional to client: "Now do exactly as I told you, and you won't have any trouble. Tell me what I just said so I can be sure you understand." |
| ________ 8. | High | Fast | Assertive | Salon professional to client: "Now, sit down and I will decide what kind of perm you need." |
| ________ 9. | Low | Slow | Friendly | Salon professional to client: "How is your mother feeling? I've been so worried about her." |
| ________ 10. | High | Fast | Irate | Client to salon professional: "That was some number he pulled. I've never been so humiliated. It was just ghastly. The worst night of my life!" |
| ________ 11. | Low | Slow | Hurt | Salon professional to client: "I feel so badly that you don't just love this color. I was sure you would feel differently." |

## MAIN POINT SUMMARY

A person's volume, rate of speech, and tone can provide more clues to their personality style than the words they say, or content they use. These elements can also provide clues to the types of people you relate to best.

If you're an Analyzer, you probably like talking to a Cooperator because you speak slowly and softly. If you're a Regulator, Energizers can match your speed and volume.

Think about how a person emphasizes words when they talk. Use those words as your initial signal, and then put that together with the other clues, and you will probably be very close to identifying a style correctly.

## SELF-TEST/REVIEW

1. Speech consists of ______________________ and ______________________.

2. The "content" of communication is also called ______________________.

3. The four characteristics that make up the "feeling" of messages are:

   1. ______________________ 3. ______________________
   2. ______________________ 4. ______________________

4. Which two personality styles use high volume and fast speed?

   1. ______________________
   2. ______________________

5. Which two personality styles use low volume and slow speed?

   1. ______________________
   2. ______________________

6. How is Cooperator language the same as Energizer language?
   How is it different?

   ______________________________________________

   ______________________________________________

7. How is Regulator language the same as Analyzer language?
   How is it different?

   ______________________________________________

   ______________________________________________

Lesson 4.3

# Shifting to Build Rapport

**One effective way to establish rapport with people is to shift your behavior and words to match theirs. We call this style shifting. It requires that you take a risk and step outside of your own personality style.**

## OBJECTIVES

At the completion of this lesson, you will be able to:

- Demonstrate **language shifting** to build **rapport** with people of different personality styles
- Demonstrate how to shift your primary personality style to match another's style
- Explain why **style shifting** improves client communication and service

## WHAT YOU NEED TO KNOW

Now it's time to put together what you know about personality style interaction and identification and use that knowledge to change how you speak and act. You need to learn about: language shifting, in which you decide if you need to shift **volume**, **speed**, **tone** and/or choice of **words**. You also need to learn about style shifting, in which you shift your outlook to match that of another personality style.

Shifting your personality style and language makes it easier for you to establish rapport with clients of a style different from your own. This will broaden your base of potential clients because you are not limiting your potential clients to people who you naturally get along with.

### Shifting Your Language

Shifting your language to match another style is not as complicated as you may think. Each style shares several preferred forms of **communication**. If you are a Regulator, you may already be very much in rapport with an Energizer and vice versa. If you are a Cooperator, you and Analyzers may sound the same but use different words.

It is only when you are with someone whose style is your **polar opposite** that you may need to shift volume, speed, emphasis and tone. That will be easier once you practice shifting just words or tone.

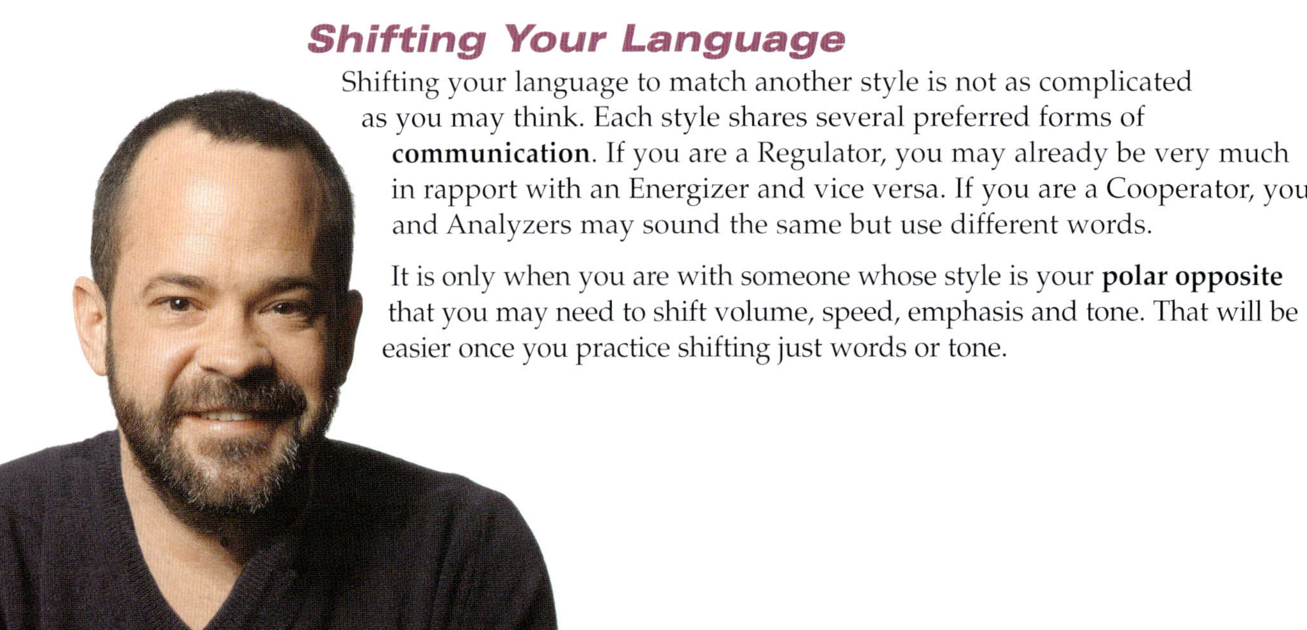

## Language Shifting Exercise

In this exercise, you will communicate based on your listener's primary personality style.

The following table outlines a style and a situation. Then, you will decide what to match—the words, the volume (high or low), and rate of speech (slow or fast). You will also provide a single word that describes the tone you will use.

### Example of a Language Shifting Situation:

After completing a service, adding up a ticket and collecting money from a client, you realize that you forgot to charge for a conditioning treatment. That can be an embarrassing and aggravating situation. How will you speak to each personality style to avoid conflict or discomfort? The main point is to match your client. That matching facilitates rapport encourages positive communication.

**Shifting your language is fairly easy. Take a look at the example and see how you can vary your speech to fit another style's patterns.**

| Style I am talking to: | Volume I use: | Speed I use: | Tone I take: | Words I say: |
|---|---|---|---|---|
| **Cooperator** | Lower | Slower | Concerned | "I'm so sorry, but I forgot to charge you for the conditioner." |
| **Analyzer** | Lower | Slower | Measured | "I just added your bill again and discovered I did not add in the conditioner, which brings the total to an additional ____." |
| **Regulator** | Higher | Faster | Straight-forward | "I made an error. I apologize for the inconvenience. I still have to charge you for the conditioner I applied." |
| **Energizer** | Higher | Faster | Upbeat | "I was enjoying talking with you so much that I completely forgot to add in the conditioner!" |

### *Language Shifting Situation #1:*

You are running 20 minutes late. You have to tell a waiting client in a way that helps him accept the delay without becoming upset.

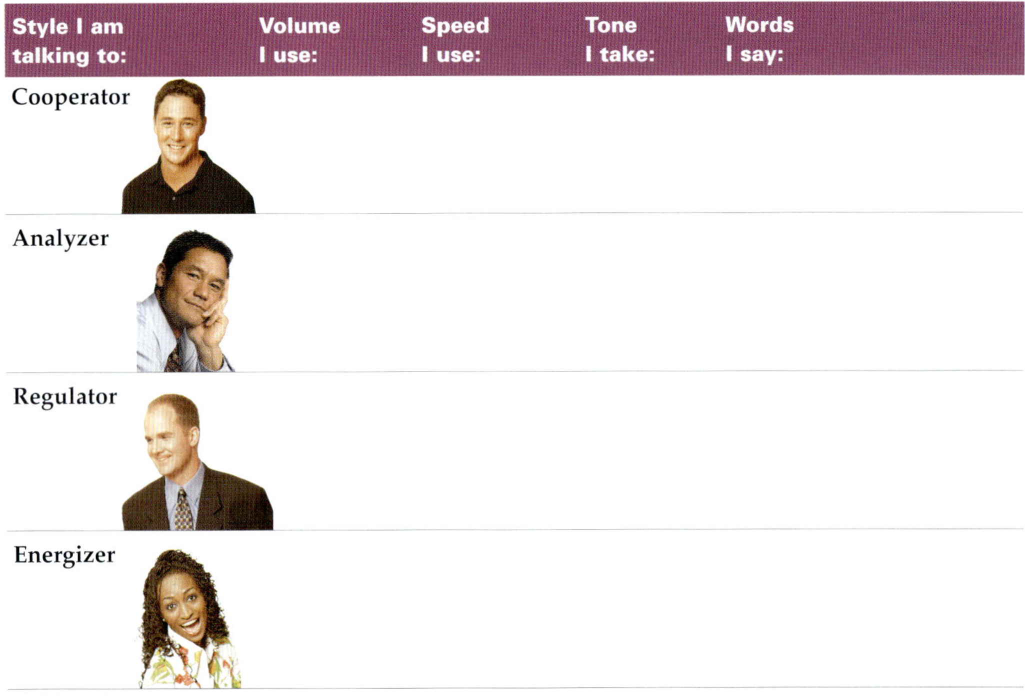

| Style I am talking to: | Volume I use: | Speed I use: | Tone I take: | Words I say: |
|---|---|---|---|---|
| Cooperator | | | | |
| Analyzer | | | | |
| Regulator | | | | |
| Energizer | | | | |

### *Language Shifting Situation #2:*

You have cut the hair of a client twice and both times noticed that the home hair color she is using is not a flattering shade. You want to have her accept your expertise—and your salon services—to change her hair color.

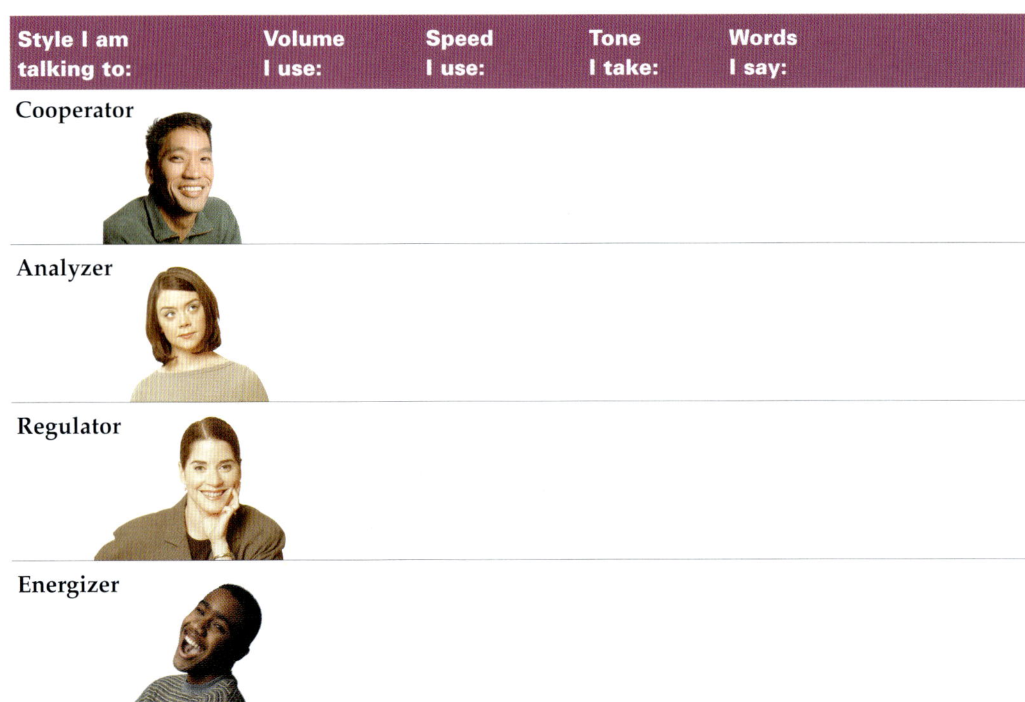

| Style I am talking to: | Volume I use: | Speed I use: | Tone I take: | Words I say: |
|---|---|---|---|---|
| Cooperator | | | | |
| Analyzer | | | | |
| Regulator | | | | |
| Energizer | | | | |

### Language Shifting Situation #3:

Your direct honesty about her dry, damaged hair has insulted your client. You can tell he or she is upset. What do you say?

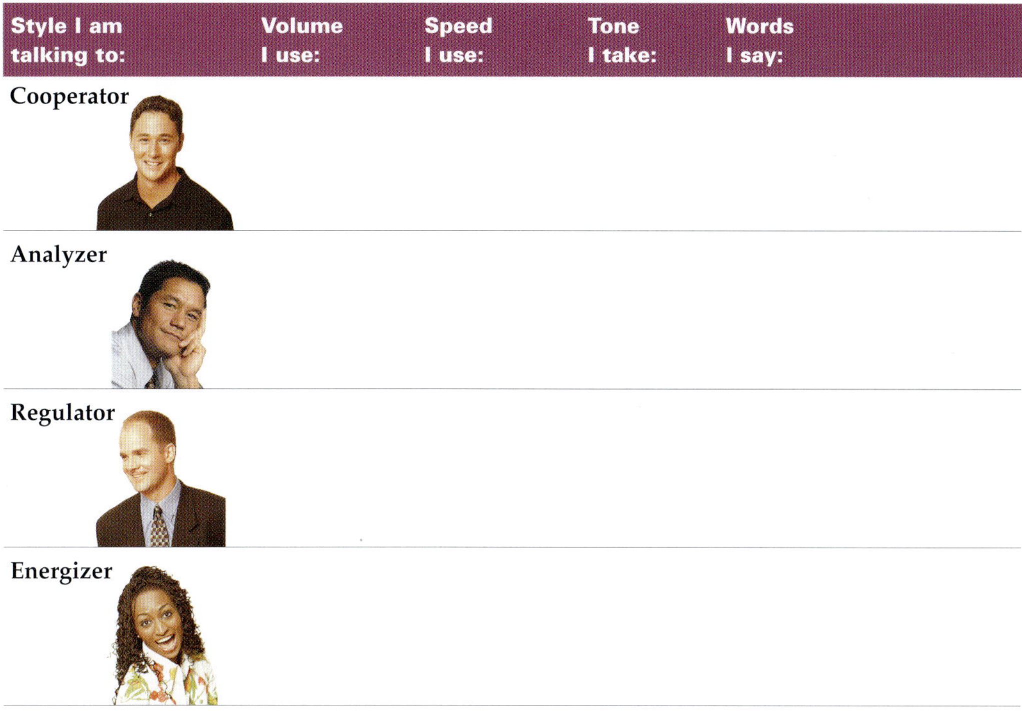

| Style I am talking to: | Volume I use: | Speed I use: | Tone I take: | Words I say: |
|---|---|---|---|---|
| Cooperator | | | | |
| Analyzer | | | | |
| Regulator | | | | |
| Energizer | | | | |

### Language Shifting Situation #4:

You are applying for a salon professional position that you really want and the manager asks you to sum up in one sentence why you think she should hire you. What do you say?

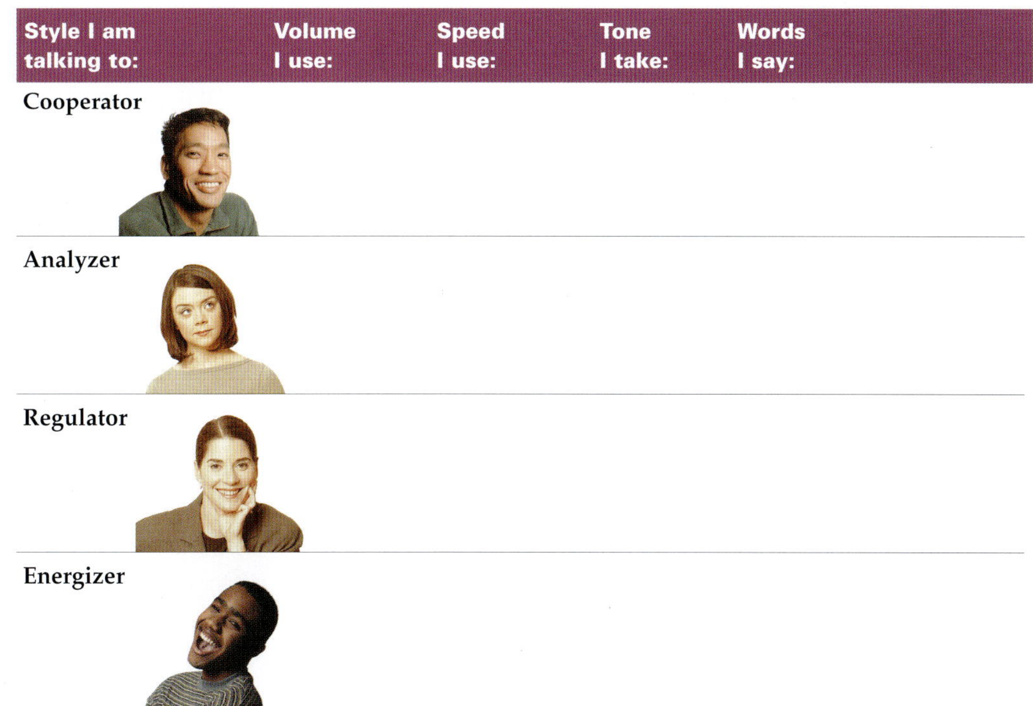

| Style I am talking to: | Volume I use: | Speed I use: | Tone I take: | Words I say: |
|---|---|---|---|---|
| Cooperator | | | | |
| Analyzer | | | | |
| Regulator | | | | |
| Energizer | | | | |

**Learn to match personality styles by style shifting. Shifting personality styles requires that you change the perspective from which you typically view people, the words you use, and the tone of your voice.**

## Shifting Your Personality Style

**Style shifting** is a *People Skills* technique that requires you to "step outside" of your **primary personality style** and into another style. When you shift styles, you learn to view people and situations from the perspective of a different personality style.

With style shifting, you are adding to the skills you just learned with language shifting. In addition to shifting the content and feeling of your speech, you are changing:

- The actions you take
- The perspective from which you view people and situations

When you take a few extra moments to see how a person of another personality style views a situation, you can create an atmosphere where your clients can be comfortable, relaxed, and have fun. In working toward rapport, you begin to see things from their point of view.

The extra effort you make to "come out" of your own personality style and meet clients on their own terms should pay off in:

- Client retention
- Client referrals
- Reputation growth

### *You Know Style Shifting*

Style shifting is not something new. If you think about it, you'll see that you have probably been shifting styles all of your life.

Think about when you were in school. You may have wanted to laugh out loud to a joke whispered to you in class. Instead, you stifled your giggle. Another example might be when you were angry at a teacher but didn't show your anger or talk about your disagreement so that you wouldn't be considered a "discipline problem."

In both of those cases, you shifted your behavior to meet the requirements of the situation and create a desirable outcome. You shifted your personality style.

## How You Do Style Shifting

Style shifting is like acting. You literally step out of your primary personality style and act like another.

You do not have to give up our own style. You may simply add the mannerisms and characteristics of your client's personality style to your own. Or you may tone down some of your characteristics that could grate against your client's style.

You need to experiment, of course—and experimenting involves risk. So, if you are a low-risk Analyzer or Cooperator this may be difficult for you, for example,

- If you are a passive Cooperator confronting an assertive Energizer, you have to stand firm or you may be overwhelmed by the force of the Energizer's personality.

Of course, it isn't necessarily any easier on the other side:

- If you are an assertive Regulator trying to establish rapport with a passive Analyzer, for instance, you would try to "ease up" and push less so you don't scare the Analyzer into his shell.

The following table summarizes the five main techniques of style shifting:

### Five Techniques of Style Shifting

| Five Techniques of Style Shifting |
|---|
| 1. Changing the way you communicate |
| 2. Changing your mannerisms |
| 3. Thinking differently |
| 4. Experimenting with new behaviors |
| 5. Taking risks |

Using these techniques effectively requires personality–style versatility, which is the subject of Lesson, 4.4, *Responding to Build Rapport*.

## EXERCISES

1. Practice style shifting with fellow students. Pick a style other than your own and stay in character for a whole class period.
   - How does it feel to you?
   - Who did best?
   - Why and how did they do it?
2. Practice style shifting with people in your everyday life. Think about how you would normally act in a situation with your boyfriend, girlfriend, spouse, or coworker, then act in a different way.
   - What effect did your different behavior have on the situation?
   - Did it improve the situation?
   - If so, how?

## MAIN POINT SUMMARY

Language and style shifting widens your range of behaviors. Both require that you take risks, especially for Cooperators and Analyzers.

With language shifting, you shift volume and speed. You can also shift your tone and the words you use.

Analyzers, for instance, like to hear facts, and Regulators want words that are straightforward. Cooperators go for "feeling" words more often, and Energizers really like to exaggerate everything.

When you shift styles, you also change the way you behave. That may require examining your attitudes toward other styles and act in different ways. It helps if you plan your risks.

## SELF-TEST/REVIEW

1. Language shifting is:

______________________________

______________________________

2. List the main variables in language shifting.

______________________________

______________________________

______________________________

3. What are the main differences in language between:

*Cooperators and Analyzers*

______________________________

*Cooperators and Regulators*

______________________________

*Cooperators and Energizers*

______________________________

*Analyzers and Regulators*

______________________________

*Analyzers and Energizers*

______________________________

*Regulators and Energizers*

______________________________

4. Style shifting is:

______________________________

______________________________

______________________________

5. What are the five elements of style shifting?

1. ______________________________
2. ______________________________
3. ______________________________
4. ______________________________
5. ______________________________

6. Listed below are four salon professional/client pairs. Try to imagine it is the client's first visit to the salon. For each pair, give a description of what the salon professional should do to style shift and make the client comfortable.

| Salon Professional | Client | Shifting Techniques |
|---|---|---|
| Energizer | Cooperator | |
| Regulator | Analyzer | |
| Cooperator | Regulator | |
| Analyzer | Energizer | |

Lesson 4.4

# Responding to Styles to Build Rapport

The Law of Requisite Variety gives you more control over a situation. By exhibiting a wide range of behavior, which language and style shifting allows you to do, you are more likely to build rapport with clients.

## OBJECTIVES

At the completion of this lesson, you will be able to:

- Use the **Law of Requisite Variety** to increase rapport
- Combine requisite variety and style shifting to respond to people of personality styles other than your own
- Practice responding to different personality styles in salon and personal situations

## WHAT YOU NEED TO KNOW

Responding to personality styles effectively builds rapport, and the effective way to respond to personality styles is to follow the Law of Requisite Variety. It goes like this:

***The element of any system with the widest range of behavior available to it will control that system.***

That law provides the greatest reason to practice **style shifting** by understanding and practicing requisite variety, you will have more behaviors to draw upon and have more control available to you in a given situation.

### Requisite Variety

Requisite variety is all about versatility. When you are versatile, you are willing and able to do a variety of things or exhibit a variety of behaviors.

The more things you can do and the more types of people you can relate to effectively, the more likely you are to have a sense of control and mastery in your work. And the more versatile you are, the more marketable you are.

So how can you be more versatile?

By style shifting. Style shifting is the way you increase your requisite variety.



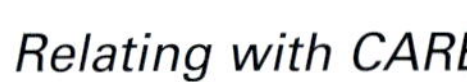

**Requisite variety requires versatility, the ability to do a variety of things or exhibit a variety of behaviors. Style shifting increases your versatility, which allows you greater control over your own destiny.**

Here are results you will see when you have requisite variety and have a better chance to control the outcome of a situation:

- Higher degree of work mastery
- More clients that you can serve and satisfy
- Ability to easily turn a negative situation into a positive one
- Greater work satisfaction
- More tools and opportunity for success
- Greater rapport with more people, which leads to more income for you and your salon

## Requisite Variety Risks

Practicing requisite variety—increasing control through style shifting—means trying new things and acting in new ways in order to find out what works in any given situation. That requires taking risks.

To shift styles and increase requisite variety, you risk your comfort zone by acting in a way different from your normal behavior. To put it another way, you risk feeling comfortable or confident by acting in a way that is not your first choice.

Your first choice generally corresponds to your primary personality style. Keep that in mind as you practice responding to different personality styles in the following exercises. Also keep in mind that the polarities will have the greatest difficulty shifting to each other's styles, as the following table shows.

### Requisite Variety Risks for Polar Opposites

| Style | Polar Opposite | Risk |
|---|---|---|
| **Cooperator** | Regulator | Feeling like they are hurting another person's feelings when being more directive like a Regulator |
| **Analyzer** | Energizer | Feeling out of control as they express more and stand out "in the spotlight" to act like an Energizer |
| **Regulator** | Cooperator | Feeling like they are being too soft as they act like the more feeling-oriented Cooperator |
| **Energizer** | Analyzer | Feeling impatient as they slow down and consider options more carefully in acting like the fact-oriented Analyzer |

If your actions seem like you are making fun of other styles, you may need to develop empathy in order to understand and see the validity in other styles. Regardless, a richer life awaits those who shift styles and increase their requisite variety.

## In the Salon. . .

Clarissa, an Energizer designer, has finally convinced Elyse, an Analyzer, to perm her long, straight hair. Unfortunately, the perm turned out too curly. Rather than looking ravishing, with increased body in her raven-colored hair, Elyse looks like she stuck her finger in a light socket.

Fortunately, Clarissa increased her requisite variety by practicing style shifting. She feels excited and wants to blurt out the problem and what can be done, but, knowing she is talking to an Analyzer, Clarissa restrains herself.

"Elyse, I respect your intelligence too much to give you anything but the facts," Clarissa says. "As you can see, your perm is curlier than you requested. I'm sorry that it happened, but there is a logical solution."

By sticking to the facts, a stretch for an Energizer, Clarissa speaks in a way Elyse can hear—and salvages an otherwise difficult situation.

In Lesson 4.5, *Creating Personal and Client Action Plans*, you will learn how to put people skills into action by writing plans down to make them real.

## EXERCISES

1. Think of someone in your life that you did not like or get along with when you first met, but later came to like. Write answers to the following questions in the spaces provided.
   - Who was the person?

     ______________________________

   - What happened?

     ______________________________

     ______________________________

   - Who took the risk to make an effort, change an attitude, and understand the other person?

     ______________________________

   - What risk did that person take?

     ______________________________

     ______________________________

- How does requisite variety and style shifting help you understand the situation better?

2. Create and present a role-play like the "In the Salon" story on p. 146. In that situation, an Energizer salon professional shifted her style to correspond to an Analyzer client. Base your role play on these considerations:
   - A problem experienced by a client in your specialty area. If you are a nail technician, for instance, base your role play on a problem with artificial sculptured nails.
   - A client with a personality style that is your polar opposite. If you are a Cooperator, then make the client in your play a Regulator.

   Present your skit in class. Write a short essay on what you learned.

3. Create a role-play based on this situation. A boyfriend and girlfriend (or spouses) are going to see a movie. She wants to see a "chick flick." He wants to see an action movie. Act out the situation as it would normally occur with someone. Then act it out with one partner increasing requisite variety through style shifting.

4. Talk a friend into changing her hairstyle, hair color, nail color, or using a skin-care service that she has never used. Use your knowledge of requisite variety and style shifting in talking to your friend. What happened? How did style shifting help?

## MAIN POINT SUMMARY

The Law of Requisite Variety provides an effective way of responding to different personality styles. The law states that the element of any system with the widest range of behavior available to it will control that system.

Requisite variety means being versatile, and the way you can increase your versatility is through style shifting. Practicing requisite variety through style shifting requires taking the risk to act in a way that is not your first choice, especially when shifting your personality style to its polar opposite.

## SELF-TEST/REVIEW

1. In everyday language, the Law of Requisite Variety states:

______________________________

______________________________

2. List the benefits of requisite variety.

______________________________

______________________________

3. What does it mean to be "versatile" and how do you increase your versatility?

______________________________

______________________________

4. In most situations, what is your first choice of action likely to be based on?

______________________________

5. List the main risks in increasing requisite variety for the four styles:

Cooperator ______________________________

Analyzer ______________________________

Regulator ______________________________

Energizer ______________________________

Lesson 4.5

# Creating Personal and Client Action Plans

**In this lesson, you will develop plans and set goals for how you will relate to clients. It is an opportunity to turn rapport-building into a reality.**

## OBJECTIVES

At the completion of this lesson, you will be able to:

- Create a Personal Action Plan and a Client Interaction Plan
- Discuss your plans with others to receive feedback
- Make commitments for your growth in relationships

## WHAT YOU NEED TO KNOW

To put your people skills into action, it is important to plan. It isn't enough to talk about plans. You need to write them down to make them real.

### Planning and Goal Setting

Planning helps you to accomplish goals, both tangible and intangible.

A study of graduates from one school found that 20 percent had financial goals. After 20 years, those with financial goals were earning or worth 80 percent of the total earnings of the class. Furthermore, those who wrote their goals down and reviewed them regularly were earning 80 percent of the 80 percent.

The lesson is clear. Goal setting and planning are critical to success.

By planning and setting goals, you will:

- Work with a sense of direction
- Take decisive action
- Improve your rapport with clients, friends, co-workers and associates
- Measure your personal and professional success in relationships.

In forming a **Personal Action Plan**, you learn to face your personal limitations and work on them. In forming a **Client Interaction Plan,** you decide what your communication strategy will be with each individual client.

Before we look at the plans, let's review the four CARE personalities.

## Personality Style Review

Use the following table to review the traits of each personality style. Read down the chart to compare style preferences. Read across to get a picture of the style preferences for one personality style.

| | Traits | Primary Question | Statement | Fear |
|---|---|---|---|---|
| C | • Is concerned about feelings<br>• Cares less about facts<br>• Is flexible<br>• Prefers low-risk situations<br>• Avoids threatening situations<br>• Is people-oriented<br>• Is cooperative<br>• Verbalizes less than others | • How? | • Tell me how you feel | • Loss of security<br>• Change |
| A | • Is a low risk-taker<br>• Uses time precisely<br>• Works with facts and figures | • Why? | • Give me the facts | • Criticism of work |
| R | • Appears cool and distant<br>• Precise about use of time<br>• Will take interpersonal risks<br>• Prefers telling others what to do<br>• Is competitive<br>• Exerts self-control<br>• Is task-oriented | • What? | • I know I do<br>• Do this | • Being used<br>• Losing<br>• Being taken advantage of |
| E | • Is verbal and fast-acting<br>• Shows feelings and concerns<br>• Is extroverted and a high risk-taker<br>• Is persuasive<br>• Is optimistic<br>• Is competitive<br>• Is people-oriented | • Who? | • Let me tell you | • Loss of social approval |

## Creating Personal and Client Action Plans

| | Strengths | Responds To | Barriers | Develop for Effectiveness |
|---|---|---|---|---|
| **C** | • Commitment<br>• Steadiness<br>• Caring<br>• Loyalty<br>• Cooperation | • Sincerity<br>• Loyalty<br>• Assurance<br>• Cooperation | • Lack of direction<br>• Uncertainty<br>• Slow to move | • Emotional control<br>• Action-oriented tendency<br>• Risk-taking ability<br>• Objectivity<br>• Critical thinking |
| **A** | • Accurate<br>• Detail-oriented<br>• Thorough<br>• Analytical | • Facts<br>• Cooperation<br>• Reasons | • Slow to move<br>• Rigidity<br>• Fear of risk | • Flexibility<br>• Appreciation of others<br>• Verbalization skills<br>• Participation<br>• Sensitivity to feelings |
| **R** | • Power<br>• Risk-taking<br>• Regulation<br>• Self-confidence<br>• Delegation | • Confrontation<br>• Challenge<br>• Competition<br>• Interpersonal risks | • Can be insensitive<br>• Control | • Rigidity decreased<br>• Human relations skills<br>• Team cooperation<br>• Ability to compromise |
| **E** | • Enthusiasm<br>• Sales ability<br>• Creativity<br>• Energy | • Challenge<br>• Big picture<br>• Competition<br>• People<br>• Excitement | • Flightiness<br>• Doesn't follow through<br>• Lack of commitment | • Attention to detail<br>• Long-range planning<br>• Practical approaches<br>• Realistic deadlines<br>• Task-orientation |

> **The Personal Action Plan shows what you are going to do in order to create rapport with personality styles that are difficult for you. You'll know what actions you need to take and what goals you'll need to set in order to succeed.**

## *The Personal Action Plan*

The **Personal Action Plan** is your opportunity to:

- Review yourself.
- Re-examine your primary and secondary personality styles.
- Decide what traits you need to work on to become a more effective salon professional.

It's called an action plan because "action" is the act of doing something. You take control of the situation by setting a plan, which you can think of as a roadmap to guide your actions. As you know, this section of *People Skills* is about application.

The actions in your plan may consist of goals. Goals may be tangible or intangible.

Tangible goals are things you can see, feel, touch, or measure. Wanting to make $60,000 a year is a tangible goal.

Intangible goals, on the other hand, are difficult to sense. Wanting your clients to feel at ease in your chair is an intangible goal.

Building a plan and setting goals is important because it leads to accomplishment. There's an old saying, "When you fail to plan, you plan to fail." So to accomplish something, you must have a goal and a plan for getting to that goal. You can think of it as a formula:

**Accomplishment = Plan + Goals**

The Personal Action Plan and Client Interaction Plan function as a roadmap to success.

Here's an example of a Personal Action Plan to help you create your own:

Relating: Application
Creating Personal and Client Action Plans

### Sample Personal Action Plan

Name: *Dale Christensen*

Date: 12/15/01

My primary personality style is: *Analyzer*

My secondary personality style is: *Cooperator*

**I need to do the following to improve my relationships with others:**

***Primary Style:***

1. Overcome my shyness and risk speaking more in new situations. Speak first to others. Learn to introduce myself. Smile.
2. Focus more on relationship than accuracy.
3. Don't analyze things to death. Take more risks and make decisions more quickly.

***Action Step(s) I will take are:***

Choose a low-risk decision and make it within 10 minutes.

I will take these steps by ______________________.
(date)

***Secondary Style:***

1. Set more goals and get more done.
2. Stop letting others take advantage of me in the name of friendship.
3. Learn to take risks.

***Action Step(s) I will take are:***

Practice risk-taking by talking to one person I don't know, each day for one week, starting ______________________.
(date)

**The personality style in others that gives me the most problem is:**

*Energizer* because I perceive them as: *Impatient, loud, rowdy and bossy,* and because I do not perceive them as: *Loyal, committed and trustworthy.*

Relating with CARE

154

*Before you begin the Personal Action Plan, remember to photocopy the form so you have extras.*

## Personal Action Plan

Name______________________________________

Date______________

My primary personality style is_____________________

My secondary personality style is____________________

**I want to do the following to improve my relationships with others:**

***Primary Style:***

1. __________________________________________________
2. __________________________________________________
3. __________________________________________________

***Action Steps I will take are:***

____________________________________________________

I will take these steps by ____________________________________
(date)

***Secondary Style:***

1. __________________________________________________
2. __________________________________________________
3. __________________________________________________

***Action Steps I will take are:***

____________________________________________________

I will take these steps by ____________________________________
(date)

**The personality style that gives me the most problem is:**

____________________________________________________

because I perceive them as:

____________________________________________________

and because I do not perceive them as:

____________________________________________________

Now you'll make a plan for how you'll improve your rapport with clients. You will focus on building relationships with those who are least like you—with whom you are the least comfortable.

## The Client Interaction Plan

You will now begin to use planning and goal-setting skills to improve problem relationships. The **Client Interaction Plan** is just that: a plan of action for managing your clients more effectively and successfully.

The Client Interaction Plan takes the Personal Action Plan a step further. It helps you learn to set strategy for each individual client or other person in your life. The Client Interaction Plan is a roadmap for how you plan to relate to other people in the future.

Salon professionals who achieve the greatest success consistently apply the knowledge and techniques they have acquired to satisfy the client. They become Masters because they automatically develop action plans without thinking about it. They draw on both their **technical skills** and **people skills** in order to gain the rewards of serving their clients.

### Completing the Client Interaction Plan

Until your people skills become second nature like the Master, complete a written Client Interaction Plan for each client using the form provided. This will move you to the Professional level of career development.

Think of two people—a client, a fellow student, teacher, co-worker, or relative—with whom you would like to improve your relationship.

Are you having a problem thinking of two people? Look around the classroom or salon:

- Is there anyone there you try to avoid?
- Is there someone in your life whose traits you dislike, whom you do not enjoy spending time with?
- Are there people that give you an uneasy or uncomfortable feeling, or a queasiness in your stomach when you are around them?

Those are all signs that a relationship moves you out of your comfort zone and offers the opportunity to learn and grow.

The next page shows an example of how you can write a plan that will help you identify the action steps needed to improve relationships.

Relating: Application
Creating Personal and Client Action Plans

## Sample Client Interaction Plan

Client Name: *John Rogers*

Primary Personality Style: *Regulator*

Secondary Personality Style: *Energizer*

I want to do the following to improve my relationship:

**Acknowledge his/her strengths**: His leadership qualities, strong achievement needs, ability to set goals and meet those goals, make decisions, and take risks.

**I realize I have problems with**: His aggressiveness, his need to dominate me, and his lack of sensitivity.

**To succeed with less frustration, I will**: Be more assertive. Be sure of my opinions and decisions, and state them clearly with logical reasons why I believe in them. Stick to business and avoid being overly friendly or too chatty.

**I will style shift by:** Grasping his hand firmly when I shake it, speaking in a louder voice, and increasing my work speed.

**I will increase Requisite Variety by:** Acting with more assertiveness and authority in my general manner. Showing a greater sense of self-confidence in my technical skills.

**I will grow by:** Feeling more self-confident in the way I work with all of my clients as a result of acting with increased assertiveness and authority with John.

**I will take the following actions**: Tell at least one other person what I have decided before I see John. Limit my greeting to John to, Hi, John. Let s get started, shall we?

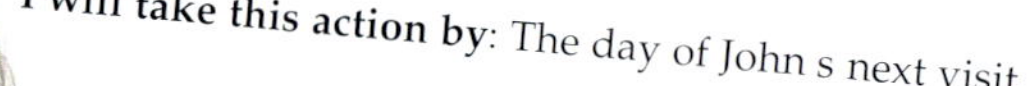

**I will take this action by**: The day of John s next visit.

157

Relating with CARE

*Before you begin the Client Interaction Plan, on the next page remember to photocopy the form so you have extras.*

## Client Interaction Plan

Client Name: ________________________________________

Primary Personality Style: ________________________________

Secondary Personality Style: ______________________________

**I plan to do the following to improve my relationship:**

Acknowledge his/her strengths: ____________________________

I realize I have problems with: ____________________________

To succeed with less frustration, I should: ____________________

I will style shift by practicing: ___________________________

I will increase requisite variety by: ________________________

I will grow by: _______________________________________

I will take the following actions: __________________________

I will take this action by: _______________________________
(date)

**The best way to ensure success is to use what you've learned on the job. Make notes about each personality style on your client cards, which give you a reminder of a whole set of relationship strategies.**

### *Recording Client Information*

Most salon professionals and salons are familiar with one kind of record keeping. It is otherwise known as a "client card" or "client file" and is completed for each client.

Client cards contain basic information such as the client's name, address, date of birth, color formulas, and last perm date. Savvy salon professionals also record more than just a mailing address and color formula. They use what they learn about personality styles, shared traits, differences, polarities, and language styles to identify each client and create a plan of action for building rapport and a good salon professional/client relationship. They can use their relationship skills to serve their clients better, which provides them with more personal satisfaction and success.

Realistically, you see too many clients over the course of time to remember the personality style of each client. Your client won't say to you, "I'm an Analyzer, so don't push or rush me. Speak slowly and give me facts."

So write down what you know, even if eventually it is only to put a "C" or an "A" in pencil at the top of the client card.

## EXERCISES

1. When you have completed your plans, share them with others to get feedback. Likewise, listen to the plans of classmates and co-workers. Then, contribute your insight into their Client Interaction Plans.

2. Review your Personal Action Plan from time to time and change it depending on how well you are doing.

## MAIN POINT SUMMARY

The key lesson in *People Skills* is that it is important to understand yourself as a way to understand others. Important steps toward that involve completing two types of plans.

The Personal Action Plan allows you to review yourself and find out what you need to work on to be a more effective worker and "people person."

The Client Interaction Plan allows you to define strategies that will improve your rapport with important people in your life

That's what managing your career with CARE is all about.

## SELF-TEST/REVIEW

1. The two things that equal accomplishment are:

   ______________________ + ________________________.

2. List the main advantages to planning.

   ______________________________________________

   ______________________________________________

   ______________________________________________

3. What happens when you fail to plan?

   ______________________________________________

   ______________________________________________

   ______________________________________________

4. How are the written Personal Action and Client Interaction Plans like road maps?

   ______________________________________________

   ______________________________________________

   ______________________________________________

5. What are some clues that a relationship is causing you problems?

   ______________________________________________

   ______________________________________________

   ______________________________________________

   ______________________________________________

# Congratulations!

You have completed *Relating with CARE*, Part 1 of *People Skills for the Salon Professional*. You've come a long way:

In Unit 1, *Relating: Fundamentals*, you learned about rapport and how it's the key skill to building and maintaining good relationships, not only with clients but also with friends, family members, and co-workers. You also discovered your personality style by completing the CARE Profile.

In Unit 2, *Relating: Observation*, you learned more about the thinking-feeling and passive-active behavioral characteristics of the four CARE personality styles. Then you met the Cooperator, Analyzer, Regulator, and Energizer and discovered those characteristics in your own personality.

In Unit 3, *Relating: Analysis*, you deepened your understanding of the personality styles by contrasting each of the four styles. You learned the strengths and weaknesses of each style, then looked at the similarities and differences. You also learned about the challenges of building relationships with polar opposites.

In Unit 4, *Relating: Application*, you learned how to take your knowledge of personality styles to work, both in the salon and at home. You leaned how to identify the personality styles of others by observing their behavior and listening to their speech. Then you learned how to shift your personality style to increase rapport with people whose styles are different than your own. You learned about the Law of Requisite Variety and how it allows you to increase your range of relationships. Finally, you filled out your own Personal Action Plan and Client Interaction Plan to put your newly learned people skills to use.

Now you're ready for *Serving with CARE*, Part 2 of *People Skills for the Salon Professional*, in which you'll learn how your people skills will help you provide excellent service.

In *Relating with CARE*, you learned three elements for building rapport:

- Understanding yourself
- Understanding your clients
- Managing your relationships

In *Serving with CARE*, we'll add two more:

- Understanding the phases of the Service Cycle
- Managing the phases of the Service Cycle

These 5 elements of *People Skills* are called the Building Blocks of Rapport. Master them and you will be able to accomplish your professional goals.

# Part Two:
# Serving with CARE

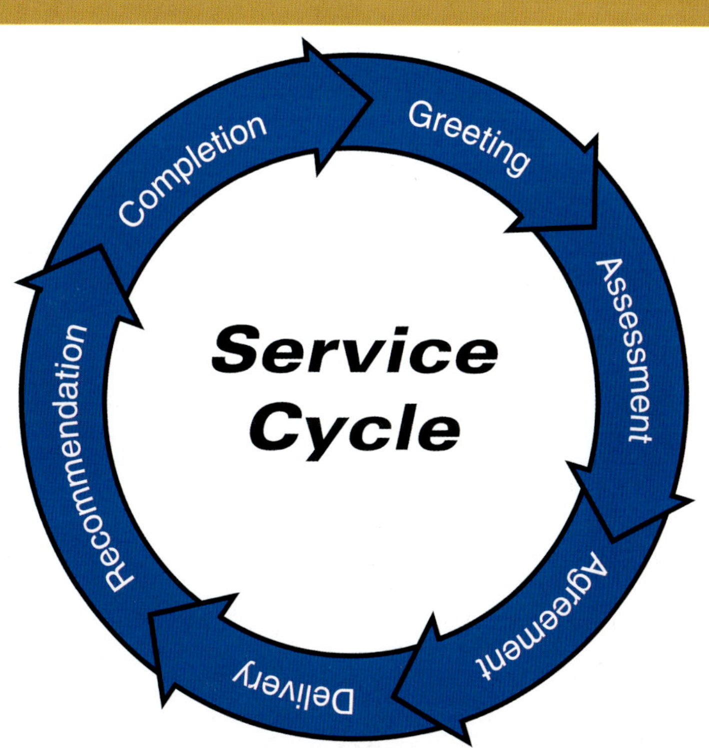

# Part Two: Serving with CARE

## Unit 5 Serving: Introduction

## Unit 6 Serving: Fundamentals

## Unit 7 The Service Cycle

## Unit 8 Service Development

## Unit 5
# Serving: Introduction

## THE VISION

Understanding service fundamentals is a solid bedrock upon which to build a service career. Fundamentals allow salon professionals to automatically deal with problems while seeing opportunities for advancement, development, and fulfillment. Understanding the fundamentals of service is also the first step on a mutual journey of personal and professional growth for both salon professionals and their clients.

Salon professionals *serve* and *are served* by their clients. As salon professionals help their clients achieve a desired image, they come to realize that their clients provide mirrors through which salon professionals gain feedback about themselves. As a result, salon professionals learn how to better serve *all* of their clients. While advancing from Novice to Master, salon professionals grow to know their clients better and help them reach their image goals. This allows salon professionals to reach their own goals and potential.

### Novice

Novices spend most of their time and energy honing their technical skills. They are less aware of their limitations in relating to people, serving people, and managing the service phases to full advantage. Novices are just learning the fundamental skills of service. They tend to be less concerned with rapport, only paying attention to it when problems arise. They also tend to accept a client's look, and duplicate it, directing most of their attention to delivering the cut or service. Over time, Novices learn how to understand their clients' lifestyles and assess how they currently wear their hair or do their nails. They are most likely to understand service in terms of their own experience as a customer and are learning how to serve by correcting the things they dislike about service they have received.

### Professional

Professionals have established technical skills to the point that they have become second nature. They fully understand the fundamental skills of service; they put greater emphasis on building personal relationships with their clients. They are more aware of their limitations in people skills. Professionals establish deeper rapport and actively engage in the challenge of developing people skills. Professionals discuss how their clients feel about their look and appearance, identify lifestyle issues, and suggest ways to refine a client's appearance. Professionals are also constantly learning about service from the way they are treated as customers.

### Master

Masters are highly proficient in both the creative and technical skills as well as in people skills. They are so adept that they are most often unaware of their skills. They easily establish rapport with a wide range of people. They know that people are not all the same, and they enjoy learning and appreciating the differences between individual clients, co-workers, bosses, and vendors. Master salon professionals experiment freely with relationships, learning and growing through all they do. Masters also tend be role models and to coach others in the behaviors of excellent service in the salon.

## What's Ahead . . .

The lessons in this unit are designed to introduce you to the fundamentals of service. You will learn what service is and how to practice excellent service. This unit also introduces the Service Cycle, the main service tool in the *People Skills* program.

This unit introduces the Service CARE Profile, which helps you understand your personality style both as a consumer of service and as a giver of service. You may also see how your personality style differs when looked at from a service perspective.

In addition, you will review the key concepts introduced in *Relating with CARE*:

- Rapport and how to build it.
- The characteristics of the four personality styles.

Finally, this unit introduces the service characteristics of the four personality styles and provides an overview of how you best serve each style.

### Unit 5: Serving: Introduction, consists of three lessons:

### Lesson 5.1: Expanding Your Relationship Skills

### Lesson 5.2: Your Service CARE Profile

### Lesson 5.3: CAREing for Clients: Review

Lesson 5.1

# Expanding Your Relationship Skills

As a salon professional, you can choose how much you enjoy your job. By learning how to care for your clients, you will establish strong relationships, increase your income and create a fulfilling lifestyle.

## OBJECTIVES

At the completion of this lesson, you will be able to:

- Define "service"
- Distinguish "service" from "servitude"
- Explain how service is a skill you can learn and improve throughout your career
- List the six phases of service

## WHAT YOU NEED TO KNOW

In *Relating with CARE*, you learned about rapport. You learned about the differences between people through understanding four basic personality styles. And you learned how to style shift in order to create greater rapport with your clients.

In *Serving with CARE*, you will learn ways to use people skills to serve your clients better, build satisfying relationships, and increase your income. You'll explore a proven method of providing top-flight service to clients through the Service Cycle—and we'll use our understanding of the four personality styles every step of the way to ensure that client visits create productive, lasting relationships.

A major contribution that you can make to your clients is simply understanding their feelings, learning about their circumstances, and having strong rapport. That, along with good technical results, gains their trust and very possibly gives you the opportunity to help them move to a greater sense of self-confidence and self-worth. That is service at its finest!

Before we start on our journey into service, let's review rapport, the key concept from *Relating with CARE*.

### Review of Rapport

Establishing effective rapport is the focus and goal of *People Skills for the Salon Professional*. The tools and skills you learned in *Relating with CARE* are designed

**Rapport refers to a relationship of harmony and agreement. When rapport is established, the people you are *in rapport* with feel understood by and drawn to you. You have put yourself in someone else's shoes.**

to help you establish and maintain rapport with a client so that you can:

- Relate to your clients better during service
- Forge stronger relationships with clients

When in rapport with the Analyzer, for instance, a Cooperator can appreciate the Analyzer's more deliberate approach. When not in rapport, the Cooperator is likely to feel hurt and rejected by the Analyzer's indifference to emotion and relationship.

Rapport is an abstraction, like a feeling or thought. You can't touch or measure it. You know that it is there and can sense when it is not. It varies on different days and with different people.

The receptionist establishes rapport as she greets the client.

Keep in mind that establishing rapport is a skill that can be learned. The rapport itself may often seem intangible, but the skills used to attain it certainly are not.

High-quality rapport is our highest aim in *People Skills*. With rapport, your fulfillment and satisfaction will increase throughout your career beyond your imagination.

## REMEMBER

**Establishing rapport is a skill you can learn. It's a two-step process:**

1. **Understanding the differences or barriers that exist between you and others.**
2. **Learning how to overcome barriers by drawing on the strengths of your *own* personality style.**

**For a more complete review, see Lesson 1.1, "Building Rapport," in *Relating with CARE*.**

Now let's take a closer look at what "service" means, and does not mean.

## Understanding Service

- Have you ever gone into a salon and had to wait while the receptionist finished a conversation with a co-worker?
- Have you ever stood at a counter waiting for a clerk who was nowhere to be found?
- Have you ever been in a restaurant and felt ignored by the server?

Of course you have. About one-third of service businesses have this situation occurring daily.

**Service requires a personal touch that brings you in closer contact with your clients. As you see the difference you make in your clients' lives, you'll gain a deeper appreciation of the value of your work.**

Businesses that operate in this way are missing one of the most critical values required for success in business: an orientation toward service. In the *People Skills* program, providing excellent professional service is the core value for achieving business success, which leads to personal fulfillment.

Salon professionals who provide personal attention to their clients are more likely to retain them over time, build a rewarding base of business and, perhaps, gain friends along the way. Currently, client turnover at salons is at an all-time high. The quality and extent of personal service, in large part, determine whether clients return for more of the salon's technical services.

### *Service Defined*

But what is service? According to Webster's *New World Dictionary*, service is "work done, or duty performed, for another or others; friendly help; also professional help or attention." *Serving with CARE* is based on that definition of service, particularly emphasizing professional attention.

Salon professionals who have a negative view of service confuse service with "servitude." According to the same dictionary, "servitude" means "the condition of a slave, serf, or the like; slavery or bondage; labor imposed as punishment for a crime."

True salon professionals don't confuse providing service with something demeaning or beneath them, as with servitude. Rather, they give service willingly and well, seeing it as part of their entire package of skills and talents.

Have you ever gone into a salon and had to wait while the receptionist finished a conversation with a co-worker?

### *Service Practiced*

Some people are naturally service-oriented, but everyone can learn how to provide excellent service. Service is a set of skills you build with clients over time.

In learning and developing any skill, it is helpful to identify your place along the continuum. That way you, your co-workers, and your boss know what to expect regarding your service ability.

For salon professionals, the two basic elements of service are technical skills (technique) and people skills (relationship). When you begin your career, your main orientation is, naturally, technique. That's the Novice level.

As your technical skills become more natural to you, your focus broadens to include a greater understanding of your client as a person. That's the Professional level.

As you develop technical mastery, your orientation shifts to people and relationships. Your understanding of your client as a person comes first, and your technique can be a means of personal transformation. At the highest level of service mastery in the salon business, you become a "trusted advisor." You are intimately involved in helping clients achieve their dreams by developing their total image. That's the Master level.

The following table summarizes the three **levels of service** used throughout *Serving with CARE* to help you gauge your career development and direction.

#### *Service Levels of Skill*

| Level | Pays attention to . . . | Works with clients to . . . |
|---|---|---|
| Novice | • Technique | • Understand and duplicate their image |
| Professional | • Technique, then relationship | • Understand their lifestyle and modify their image |
| Master | • Relationship, then technique | • Understand their lifestyle and transform their image |

So why develop your service skills?

At its most basic, service makes you and the client look and feel good, and is what the client pays for. At its highest level, your work becomes a daily adventure in human relations: You approach each client as a person to meet, understand, and serve someone with whom you establish a caring relationship.

That feeling of caring adds meaning to your work. It is the spark that fires up your creativity.

## The Service Cycle

Service businesses are *people* businesses. That's why people skills are so important. They make it possible for you to put service into action.

Think of service as a journey. Just as a journey has a beginning, middle, and end, so does service. Service has a cycle of its own, beginning with a greeting and ending with a completion or goodbye. Service is a cycle of separate and distinct phases, as the following illustration shows.

### The Greeting Phase

The first step in service is the Greeting Phase, where you begin to establish rapport with your client. Most of us know how to greet people and know the difference between an effective greeting and an ineffective one. The challenge is to consistently do it well, as a poor greeting may mean lost business, especially from new clients.

There are as many valid styles of greeting as there are people. Even so, you can learn key skills that will increase your effectiveness. In this course, you will explore your own style of greeting, the best way to listen during the greeting, and how to greet the different personality styles most effectively.

### The Assessment Phase

The Assessment Phase represents the greatest possibility for your career growth. It calls upon all your communication and listening skills, patience, technical knowledge, and understanding to determine exactly what the client wants and needs. In the coming pages, you will learn about the wealth of opportunities available to you as you help your clients decide how to look their best.

### The Agreement Phase

It is not by accident that the Agreement Phase is the middle phase. It is a pivotal point in the Service Cycle. Without firm agreement, you risk losing client satisfaction, for reasons ranging from cutting hair too short to misunderstandings about the cost of additional services. If you secure agreement, the rest of the service can unfold with greater ease and rapport.

Agreement allows your skills as a salon professional to shine. You propose a plan of action, fine-tune the plan, and reach agreement with your client.

Once you have agreement, you and the client have firmed up your partnership. You understand each other better, rapport is secure, and you have both taken responsibility for the outcome. Now high-quality rapport is easier to maintain.

### The Delivery Phase

The actual technical work varies with each new client. Delivering technical services while remaining connected to your client through the entire delivery is the challenge. You will learn to use conversation and touch to maintain rapport and keep your client informed, but not bored.

### The Recommendation Phase

Full service is not complete without reviewing the products your client is currently using, then recommending the products your client will need to easily maintain his or her look at home.

### The Completion Phase

Now it is time to acknowledge and review what you have done. It is important that what was agreed upon was provided, and to be sure that the client is satisfied.

The six phases of the Service Cycle are covered in the following lessons. Learn them completely so you are able to recognize the particular needs of your clients in each phase.

In Lesson 5.2, *Your Service Care Profile*, you will identify your CARE personality styles as a service provider and a customer.

## EXERCISE

1. Visit a few restaurants and assess the service they provide. Write about one positive and one negative service experience.

Positive:________________________________________

Negative:________________________________________

## MAIN POINT SUMMARY

Professional service is a critical means of achieving business success and personal accomplishment.

Knowing your clients well allows you to appreciate the value of your work. When you have rapport with your clients, you are serving someone whom you care about, and adding meaning to your work.

## SELF-TEST/REVIEW

1. List four phrases found in Webster's definition of "service."

   1. ______________________________

   2. ______________________________

   3. ______________________________

   4. ______________________________

2. What does "servitude" mean, and why is it important for the salon professional to differentiate "service" from "servitude"?

   ______________________________

   ______________________________

   ______________________________

3. Name and describe the characteristics of the three levels of salon mastery.

   1. ______________________________

   2. ______________________________

   3. ______________________________

4. Name and describe the six phases of the Service Cycle.

   1. ______________________________

   2. ______________________________

   3. ______________________________

   4. ______________________________

   5. ______________________________

   6. ______________________________

Lesson 5.2

# Your Service CARE Profile

The Service CARE Profile helps you understand your personality style as it relates to providing and receiving service.

## OBJECTIVES

At the completion of this lesson, you will be able to:

- Complete the Service CARE Profile
- Identify your CARE personality styles as a service provider and as a customer
- Compare your Service CARE Profile with your general CARE Profile

## WHAT YOU NEED TO KNOW

In *Relating with CARE*, you completed the CARE Profile Questionnaire, scored it, and determined your primary and secondary personality styles. In *Serving with CARE*, you will complete the Service CARE Profile Questionnaire and determine your Service CARE personality styles.

The Service CARE Profile fine-tunes your understanding of the personality styles learned in *Relating with CARE* because it is designed to help you understand your personality in both delivering and receiving service.

All of the same personality style traits you learned in *Relating with CARE* apply to the personality profile you build here in *Serving with CARE*. Keep your Service CARE personality styles in mind as you give and receive service. This gives you a way to sort out your personal tastes, behaviors, and beliefs from those of others. This new level of understanding helps improve your service skills.

Some people find that they are more passive as a *consumer* and more assertive as a *giver* of service. Others find they are more passive when giving service than in other situations. You will gain a greater understanding of yourself and the way you interact with clients as a service provider.

- If you are highly assertive in your service style, you may want to tone it down, especially when you are serving Cooperators and Analyzers.
- If you are more passive when giving service than in other situations, you may want to step it up so your clients feel more confident in your abilities.

**Remember that the Service CARE Profile Questionnaire is not a test. Answer as honestly as you can, and you'll get a good picture of your service style.**

In short, the Service CARE Profile, like the CARE Profile itself, shows you where you may need to shift your style for your own as well as your clients' satisfaction.

## Completing the Service CARE Profile Questionnaire

The Service CARE Profile Questionnaire contains 12 questions in two parts. The six questions in Part 1 are designed to show your CARE Profile as a service provider. The six questions in Part 2 are designed to show your CARE Profile as a client, or customer.

Like the CARE Profile in *Relating with CARE*, the Service CARE Profile is not a test. Unlike the CARE Profile, the questions require that you rank order each choice, rather than select a single answer.

First, read each question. Then look at the four statements under it. Rank each choice from highest (4) to lowest (1), according to the degree that it reflects your actions or beliefs. Mark 4 for the choice you agree with most, and mark 1 for the choice you agree with least.

Answer all of the questions in this manner.

The following two pages show you a completed Service CARE Profile Questionnaire to show you how to mark your answers.

## Sample Service CARE Profile Questionnaire

Serving: Introduction
Your Service CARE Profile

### The Service CARE Profile Questionnaire

Rank order choices A-D for each question. Mark 4 for the choice you agree with most strongly and 1 for the choice you agree with least, and so on until you have marked each statement 1, 2, 3 and 4. Use each number only once per statement.

#### 1. With Clients/Customers

1. My greatest pet peeve with customers is when they . . .
   - A. __4__ Don't work with me
   - B. __3__ Misstate what they want
   - C. __1__ Think I have all the time in the world
   - D. __2__ Complain about details

2. I like customers who care about . . .
   - A. __1__ Precision
   - B. __2__ Getting the job done, no matter what
   - C. __3__ Team spirit
   - D. __4__ Relationships

3. I have the most trouble when a client is . . .
   - A. __2__ Indecisive
   - B. __3__ Pushy
   - C. __1__ Dull
   - D. __4__ Erratic or irrational.

4. In focusing on my business, I most care about . . .
   - A. __4__ Establishing solid relationships
   - B. __2__ Getting projects done on time
   - C. __1__ Having a thorough and detailed plan for operating
   - D. __3__ Generating excitement in the venture for staff and clientele

5. I pride myself on my . . .
   - A. __4__ Enthusiasm
   - B. __3__ Friendliness
   - C. __2__ Logical reasoning
   - D. __1__ Drive to get things done

6. My biggest weak point is my . . .
   - A. __4__ Impatience
   - B. __2__ Lack of attention to detail
   - C. __3__ Follow-through
   - D. __1__ Getting upset over change

*Serving with CARE* 177

Serving: Introduction
Your Service CARE Profile

## 2. As a Client/Customer

7. The biggest problem I see with service providers and their service is their . . .
   - A. 4 Inaccuracy
   - B. 3 Lack of motivation and excitement
   - C. 1 Lateness
   - D. 2 Failure to include others.

8. The most important aspect of a service team is . . .
   - A. 1 That everyone is excited about working with me
   - B. 4 Good relationships among team members
   - C. 3 Having each member be thorough with their own tasks
   - D. 2 Seeing that everyone is moving forward quickly and productively

9. My greatest pet peeve with service providers is . . .
   - A. 3 Their failure to complete a task.
   - B. 4 When they don't communicate and work with me
   - C. 2 Inattention to detail
   - D. 1 When they aren't self-motivated

10. When I'm being served, I most want the person serving me to . . .
    - A. 4 Deliver thorough, competent service
    - B. 2 Be sensitive to my needs
    - C. 3 Give me accurate information and responses
    - D. 1 Be interesting and engaging

11. When it comes to travel, I . . .
    - A. 3 Hate waiting in lines
    - B. 2 Don't like imprecision in planning
    - C. 4 Prefer to have an unplanned adventure
    - D. 1 Prefer to travel with a group

12. When I have a problem at a restaurant, I hate it most when the server . . .
    - A. 2 Is slow to respond
    - B. 4 Treats me rudely
    - C. 1 Makes careless mistakes
    - D. 3 Ignores me

## The Service CARE Profile Questionnaire

Rank order choices A-D for each question. Mark 4 for the choice you agree with most strongly and 1 for the choice you agree with least, and so on until you have marked each statement 1, 2, 3 and 4. Use each number only once per statement.

### 1. With Clients/Customers

1. My greatest pet peeve with customers is when they . . .
   A. ____ Don't work with me
   B. ____ Mis-state what they want
   C. ____ Think I have all the time in the world
   D. ____ Complain about details

2. I like customers who care about . . .
   A. ____ Precision
   B. ____ Getting the job done, no matter what
   C. ____ Team spirit
   D. ____ Relationships

3. I have the most trouble when a client is . . .
   A. ____ Indecisive
   B. ____ Pushy
   C. ____ Dull
   D. ____ Erratic or irrational

4. In focusing on my business, I most care about . . .
   A. ____ Establishing solid relationships
   B. ____ Getting projects done on time
   C. ____ Having a thorough and detailed plan for operating
   D. ____ Generating excitement in the venture for staff and clientele

5. I pride myself on my . . .
   A. ____ Enthusiasm
   B. ____ Friendliness
   C. ____ Logical reasoning
   D. ____ Drive to get things done

6. My biggest weak point is my . . .
   A. ____ Impatience
   B. ____ Lack of attention to detail
   C. ____ Follow-through
   D. ____ Getting upset over change

## 2. As a Client/Customer

7. The biggest problem I see with service providers and their service is their . . .
   - A. ____ Inaccuracy
   - B. ____ Lack of motivation and excitement
   - C. ____ Lateness
   - D. ____ Failure to include others

8. The most important aspect of a service team is . . .
   - A. ____ That everyone is excited about working with me
   - B. ____ Good relationships among team members
   - C. ____ Having each member be thorough with their own tasks
   - D. ____ Seeing that everyone is moving forward quickly and productively

9. My greatest pet peeve with service providers is . . .
   - A. ____ Their failure to complete a task
   - B. ____ When they don't communicate and work with me
   - C. ____ Inattention to detail
   - D. ____ When they aren't self-motivated

10. When I'm being served, I most want the person serving me to . . .
    - A. ____ Deliver thorough, competent service
    - B. ____ Be sensitive to my needs
    - C. ____ Give me accurate information and responses
    - D. ____ Be interesting and engaging

11. When it comes to travel, I . . .
    - A. ____ Hate waiting in lines
    - B. ____ Don't like imprecision in planning
    - C. ____ Prefer to have an unplanned adventure
    - D. ____ Prefer to travel with a group

12. When I have a problem at a restaurant, I hate it most when the server . . .
    - A. ____ Is slow to respond
    - B. ____ Treats me rudely
    - C. ____ Makes careless mistakes
    - D. ____ Ignores me

## Building Your Service CARE Profile

Building your Service CARE Profile is a three-step process:

1. Transfer your answers from the questionnaire to the Service CARE Answer Sheet (see p. 180 for an example).
2. Score your Service CARE Profiles.
3. Graph the results to see your Service CARE Profiles.

### 1. Transferring Your Service CARE Answers

When you have completed the questionnaire, transfer your numbers to the Service CARE Answer Sheet. For each of the 12 questions, transfer your rankings for choices A-D to the white square across from the choice.

*See the sample Service CARE Answer Sheet on the next page.*

### 2. Scoring Your Service CARE Profile

Once you have transferred all your numbers to the Service CARE Answer Sheet, add up the numbers in each of the four columns C, A, R, and E. Note that you will have two totals, one for the columns for questions 1 through 6 and the other for the columns for questions 7 through 12.

*See the sample scored Service CARE Answer Sheet on the next page.*

### 3. Graph Your Service CARE Profile

Finally, you graph your Service CARE Profiles. You have two profile graphs, one for the total of questions 1 through 6 and the other for the total of questions 7 through 12. The first graph represents your Service CARE Profile for yourself as a service provider. The second graph represents your Service CARE Profile for yourself as a client.

Graphing your Service CARE Profile is a five-step process:

1. Find your total C, A, R, and E scores for questions 1 through 6.
2. On the first, or C column of the graph, enter the total of the C column on the Answer Sheet. Plot that number by darkening the circle on the Service CARE with Clients/Customers Graph, which appears on p. 184.
3. Plot your scores from columns A, R, and E of the Answer Sheet on A, R, and E of the CARE Graph.
4. Connect the dots to create your graph.
5. Repeat those steps for questions 7 through 12, except use the the Service CARE as a Client/Customer Graph on p. 185.

*See the sample Service CARE graphs on pp. 182-183.*

## Sample Service CARE Answer Sheet

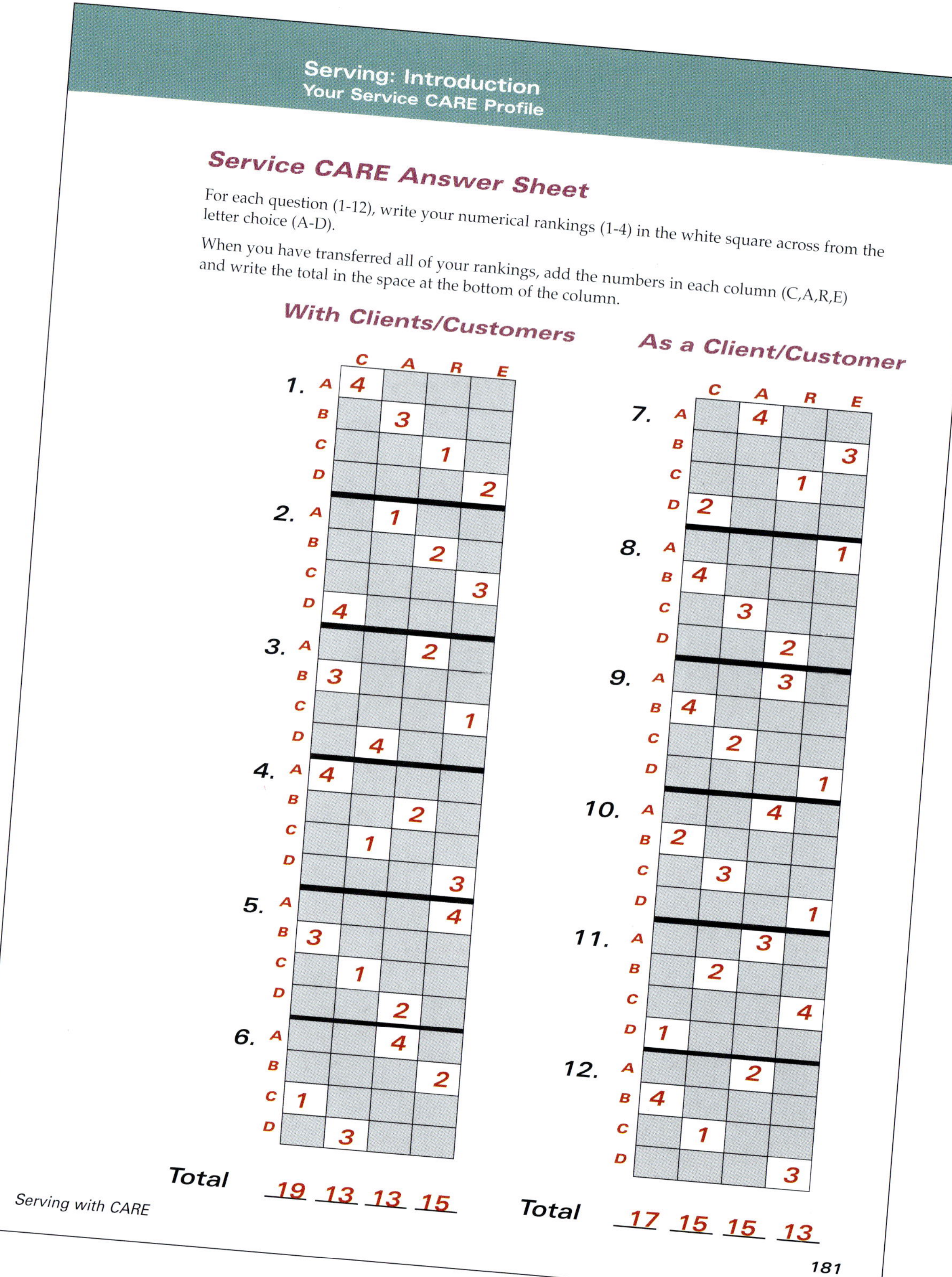


### Service CARE Answer Sheet

For each question (1-12), write your numerical rankings (1-4) in the white square across from the letter choice (A-D).

When you have transferred all of your rankings, add the numbers in each column (C,A,R,E) and write the total in the space at the bottom of the column.

**With Clients/Customers**

| | | C | A | R | E |
|---|---|---|---|---|---|
| 1. | A | 4 | | | |
| | B | | 3 | | |
| | C | | | 1 | |
| | D | | | | 2 |
| 2. | A | | 1 | | |
| | B | | | 2 | |
| | C | | | | 3 |
| | D | 4 | | | |
| 3. | A | | | 2 | |
| | B | 3 | | | |
| | C | | | | 1 |
| | D | | 4 | | |
| 4. | A | 4 | | | |
| | B | | | 2 | |
| | C | | 1 | | |
| | D | | | | 3 |
| 5. | A | | | | 4 |
| | B | 3 | | | |
| | C | | 1 | | |
| | D | | | 2 | |
| 6. | A | | | 4 | |
| | B | | | | 2 |
| | C | 1 | | | |
| | D | | 3 | | |
| Total | | 19 | 13 | 13 | 15 |

**As a Client/Customer**

| | | C | A | R | E |
|---|---|---|---|---|---|
| 7. | A | | 4 | | |
| | B | | | | 3 |
| | C | | | 1 | |
| | D | 2 | | | |
| 8. | A | | | | 1 |
| | B | 4 | | | |
| | C | | 3 | | |
| | D | | | 2 | |
| 9. | A | | | 3 | |
| | B | 4 | | | |
| | C | | 2 | | |
| | D | | | | 1 |
| 10. | A | | | 4 | |
| | B | 2 | | | |
| | C | | 3 | | |
| | D | | | | 1 |
| 11. | A | | | 3 | |
| | B | | 2 | | |
| | C | | | | 4 |
| | D | 1 | | | |
| 12. | A | | | 2 | |
| | B | 4 | | | |
| | C | | 1 | | |
| | D | | | | 3 |
| Total | | 17 | 15 | 15 | 13 |

## Service CARE Answer Sheet

For each question (1-12), write your numerical rankings (1-4) in the white square across from the letter choice (A-D).

When you have transferred all of your rankings, add the numbers in each column (C,A,R,E) and write the total in the space at the bottom of the column.

### With Clients/Customers

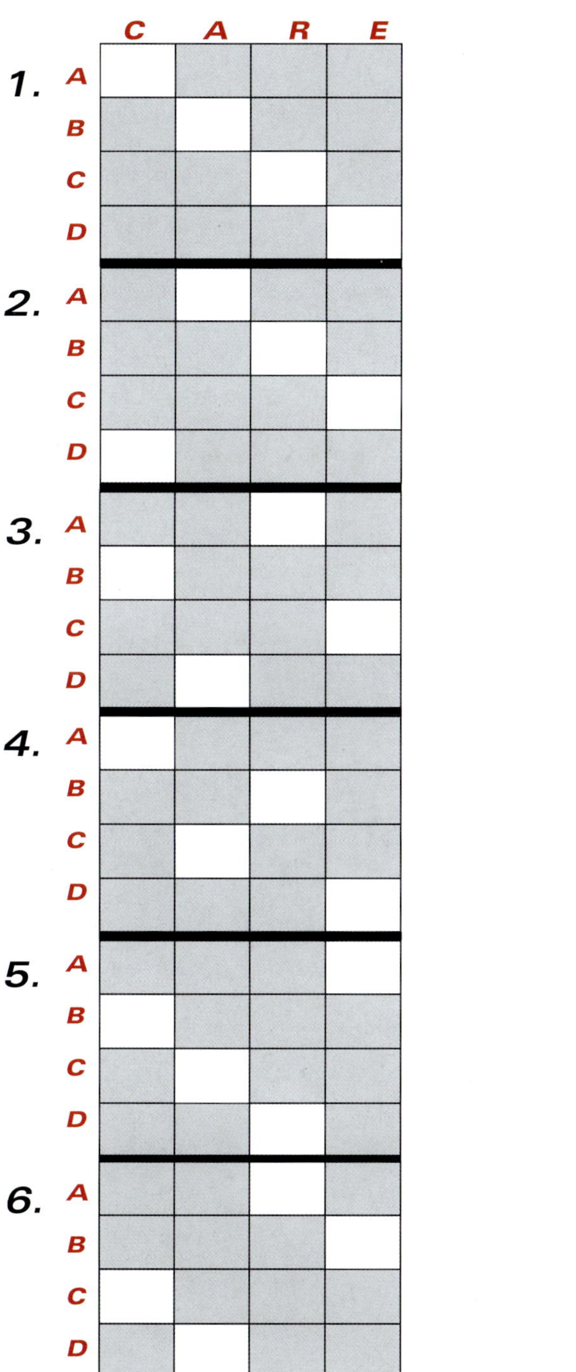

Total ___ ___ ___ ___

### As a Client/Customer

| | | C | A | R | E |
|---|---|---|---|---|---|
| 7. | A | | | | |
| | B | | | | |
| | C | | | | |
| | D | | | | |
| 8. | A | | | | |
| | B | | | | |
| | C | | | | |
| | D | | | | |
| 9. | A | | | | |
| | B | | | | |
| | C | | | | |
| | D | | | | |
| 10. | A | | | | |
| | B | | | | |
| | C | | | | |
| | D | | | | |
| 11. | A | | | | |
| | B | | | | |
| | C | | | | |
| | D | | | | |
| 12. | A | | | | |
| | B | | | | |
| | C | | | | |
| | D | | | | |

Total ___ ___ ___ ___

## Service CARE with Clients/Customers

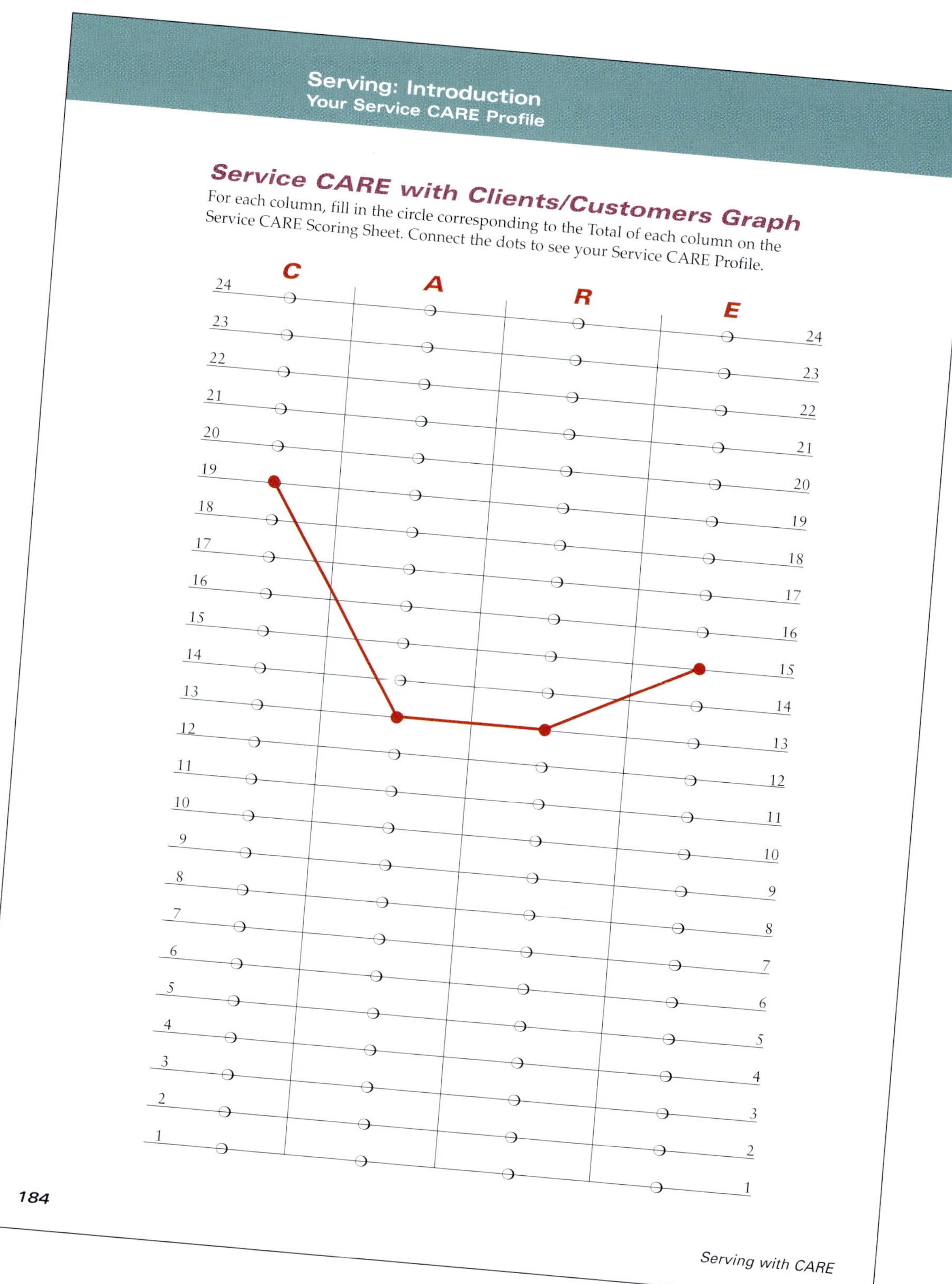

## Service CARE as a Client/Customer

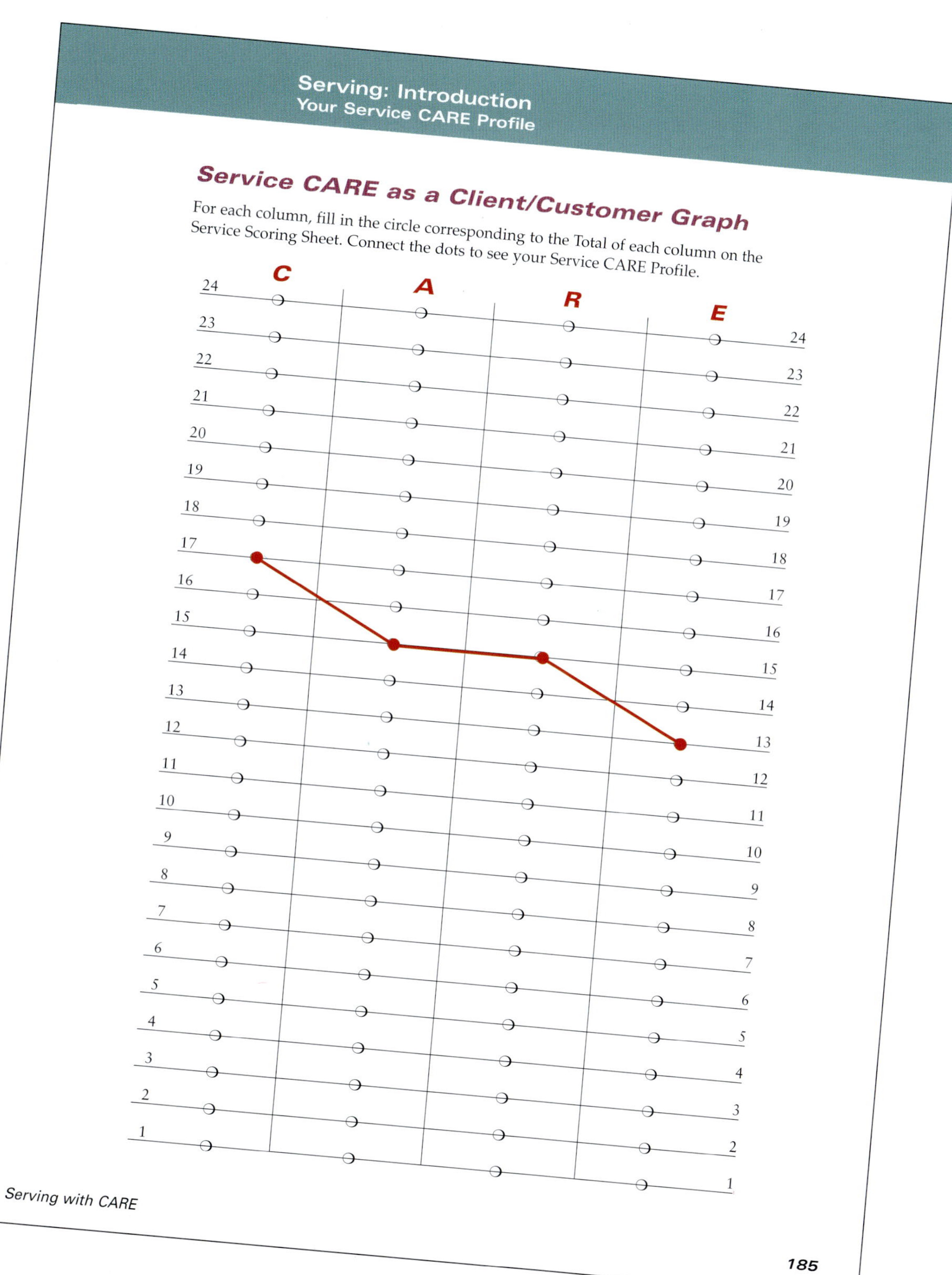

## Service CARE with Clients/Customers Graph

For each column, fill in the circle corresponding to the Total of each column on the Service CARE Scoring Sheet. Connect the dots to see your Service CARE Profile.

| | C | A | R | E | |
|---|---|---|---|---|---|
| 24 | ○ | ○ | ○ | ○ | 24 |
| 23 | ○ | ○ | ○ | ○ | 23 |
| 22 | ○ | ○ | ○ | ○ | 22 |
| 21 | ○ | ○ | ○ | ○ | 21 |
| 20 | ○ | ○ | ○ | ○ | 20 |
| 19 | ○ | ○ | ○ | ○ | 19 |
| 18 | ○ | ○ | ○ | ○ | 18 |
| 17 | ○ | ○ | ○ | ○ | 17 |
| 16 | ○ | ○ | ○ | ○ | 16 |
| 15 | ○ | ○ | ○ | ○ | 15 |
| 14 | ○ | ○ | ○ | ○ | 14 |
| 13 | ○ | ○ | ○ | ○ | 13 |
| 12 | ○ | ○ | ○ | ○ | 12 |
| 11 | ○ | ○ | ○ | ○ | 11 |
| 10 | ○ | ○ | ○ | ○ | 10 |
| 9 | ○ | ○ | ○ | ○ | 9 |
| 8 | ○ | ○ | ○ | ○ | 8 |
| 7 | ○ | ○ | ○ | ○ | 7 |
| 6 | ○ | ○ | ○ | ○ | 6 |
| 5 | ○ | ○ | ○ | ○ | 5 |
| 4 | ○ | ○ | ○ | ○ | 4 |
| 3 | ○ | ○ | ○ | ○ | 3 |
| 2 | ○ | ○ | ○ | ○ | 2 |
| 1 | ○ | ○ | ○ | ○ | 1 |

## Service CARE as a Client/Customer Graph

For each column, fill in the circle corresponding to the Total of each column on the Service Scoring Sheet. Connect the dots to see your Service CARE Profile.

| | C | A | R | E | |
|---|---|---|---|---|---|
| 24 | ○ | ○ | ○ | ○ | 24 |
| 23 | ○ | ○ | ○ | ○ | 23 |
| 22 | ○ | ○ | ○ | ○ | 22 |
| 21 | ○ | ○ | ○ | ○ | 21 |
| 20 | ○ | ○ | ○ | ○ | 20 |
| 19 | ○ | ○ | ○ | ○ | 19 |
| 18 | ○ | ○ | ○ | ○ | 18 |
| 17 | ○ | ○ | ○ | ○ | 17 |
| 16 | ○ | ○ | ○ | ○ | 16 |
| 15 | ○ | ○ | ○ | ○ | 15 |
| 14 | ○ | ○ | ○ | ○ | 14 |
| 13 | ○ | ○ | ○ | ○ | 13 |
| 12 | ○ | ○ | ○ | ○ | 12 |
| 11 | ○ | ○ | ○ | ○ | 11 |
| 10 | ○ | ○ | ○ | ○ | 10 |
| 9 | ○ | ○ | ○ | ○ | 9 |
| 8 | ○ | ○ | ○ | ○ | 8 |
| 7 | ○ | ○ | ○ | ○ | 7 |
| 6 | ○ | ○ | ○ | ○ | 6 |
| 5 | ○ | ○ | ○ | ○ | 5 |
| 4 | ○ | ○ | ○ | ○ | 4 |
| 3 | ○ | ○ | ○ | ○ | 3 |
| 2 | ○ | ○ | ○ | ○ | 2 |
| 1 | ○ | ○ | ○ | ○ | 1 |

## Interpreting Your Service CARE Profiles

Now that you've built your Service CARE Profiles, you can be more aware of how your personality works when providing service to clients and also when receiving service. Throughout this course, you will be asked to notice how you provide and receive service as a way to improve your service skills.

As you most likely know, each column in the CARE Profiles represents one of the four personality styles:

**C**ooperator

**A**nalyzer

**R**egulator

**E**nergizer

The highest peak on the graph represents your Primary personality style, while the second highest peak represents your Secondary personality style. You now have a picture showing the relative "weight" of each personality style within your individual personality as a service provider and as a consumer.

The relative weight is important because it's your mix of styles that helps to make you unique. Nobody has a pure single-note personality style. In fact, everybody is a mix of all four styles.

- My Customer Profile: Primary _______________ Secondary _______________
- My Provider Profile: Primary _______________ Secondary _______________

### Your Styles as a Service Provider and a Consumer

Many of you score the same. However, others will notice differences between your scores with clients and as clients. Those differences may indicate ways where you may need to adjust your style or grow in your behavior.

For instance, you may find that you are more assertive as a service provider than as a consumer—higher in Regulator than Cooperator. As a service provider, you may be well-suited to take charge of service delivery, but as a consumer, you may need to increase your self-esteem and demand more.

Or, you may have a high Regulator score as a consumer but a low Regulator score as a provider. You may need to work on feeling as entitled when you provide service as you do when you receive it.

Or you may find that you have a high Energizer score as a service provider and a low Analyzer score. You may have the enthusiasm required to help people change their image, but you may not be asking the questions to get the detailed information required to fully understand your client. You may want to work on bringing out the Analyzer side of your personality when you provide service.

Whatever your mix, remember that your goal is to build rapport with the greatest variety of people possible—both when you are providing service to clients and when you are receiving service as a customer.

## EXERCISES

1. Compare your Service CARE Profile as a service provider with your Service CARE Profile as a customer. List five similarities you notice. List five differences.

| Similarities | Differences |
|---|---|
| 1. ______ | 1. ______ |
| 2. ______ | 2. ______ |
| 3. ______ | 3. ______ |
| 4. ______ | 4. ______ |
| 5. ______ | 5. ______ |

2. Compare your Service CARE Profiles with your overall CARE Profile from *Relating with CARE*. List five similarities you notice. List five differences.

| Similarities | Differences |
|---|---|
| 1. ______ | 1. ______ |
| 2. ______ | 2. ______ |
| 3. ______ | 3. ______ |
| 4. ______ | 4. ______ |
| 5. ______ | 5. ______ |

3. How do you think those similarities and differences affect the way you provide service? What do you think you need to learn in order to provide better service?

______

______

______

______

4. How do you think those similarities and differences affect the way you are as a consumer? What do you think you need to learn in order to be more effective as a customer?

5. Describe one or two very positive service experiences you have enjoyed as a client or customer. Relate this to your Service CARE Profile as a client/customer.

6. Describe a negative service experience you have had as a client or customer. Relate this to your Service CARE Profile as a client/customer.

Lesson 5.3

# CAREing for Clients: Review

**Remember, creating rapport with clients is the goal of the *People Skills* program and the foundation of excellent service. Reviewing the four personality styles reminds you of the basics you will use in *Serving with CARE*.**

## OBJECTIVES

At the completion of this lesson, you will be able to:

- Describe the traits, strengths, and weaknesses of the four personality styles
- Discuss the service challenges for each of the four personality styles

## WHAT YOU NEED TO KNOW

Remember that knowing the CARE personality styles provides a way for you to create rapport with a wider variety of people. In this review, you'll deepen your understanding of the personality styles to maintain high-quality rapport throughout a client's visit to the salon.

### Personality Styles Recap

In *Relating with CARE*, you learned how to identify a person's personality style, and you learned how to shift your behavior and language to build rapport with each of the four personality styles.

Your CARE skills help you give excellent service because they provide clues to a person's likes, dislikes, behavior, and thinking. Before we look at how to serve each of the four styles, use this review to identify their main traits, strengths, and weaknesses.

# Cooperator

## Cooperator Trait Review

| Cooperators Tend to Be | Cooperators' Key Needs Include |
|---|---|
| • **Feeling** and **passive** | • To be accepted |
| • Concerned about people | • To be liked |
| • Concerned about feelings | • To get along |
| • Patient | • To belong |
| • Good listeners | |
| • Not time-oriented | |
| • Not risk-takers | |

## Cooperator Strengths and Weaknesses Review

| Strengths | Weaknesses |
|---|---|
| • Enjoys working with people | • Difficulty saying no |
| • In tune with and responsive to the needs of others | • More interested in relating to others than getting the job done |
| • Loyal | • May tend to seek security in relationships and deny own needs |
| • Creative and expressive | • Often lacks sense of internal direction; needs to be directed by others |
| • Good team player | • Does not place importance on time and deadlines |
| • Good at fostering group communication and understanding | • Quality of work suffers when they feel they do not have the affection and approval of supervisors, co-workers, clients |
| • Good counselor and advisor | • May spend more time on giving advice |
| • Keeps commitments | • May make decisions based on emotions |

## Analyzer

### Analyzer Trait Review

| Analyzers Tend to Be | Analyzers' Key Needs Include |
|---|---|
| • **Thinking** and **passive** | • Security |
| • Factual | • Time to think |
| • Methodical | • Facts to rely on |
| • Not risk-takers | |
| • Not fast-paced | |

### Analyzer Strengths and Weaknesses Review

| Strengths | Weaknesses |
|---|---|
| • Figures things out | • Can spend too much time gathering facts before making a decision and proceeding |
| • Understands how things work | • Not very in touch with own feelings or the feelings of others |
| • Precise and correct | • Hesitant |
| • Understands the need for and follows rules | • Shy |
| • Plans and sets goals | • May not be able to project confidence |
| • Diligent worker | • Can get too caught up in a task |

## Regulator

### Regulator Trait Review

| Regulators Tend to Be | Regulators' Key Needs Include |
|---|---|
| • **Thinking** and **assertive** | • To direct |
| • Independent | • To dominate |
| • Cool and in-control | • To win |
| • Take-charge types | • To compete |
| • Doers | |

### Regulator Strengths and Weaknesses Review

| Strengths | Weaknesses |
|---|---|
| • Goal-oriented | • May not focus on the human side of the issue |
| • Decisive | • Can appear bossy and cold |
| • Good supervisor and leader | • Can be rigid and inflexible |
| • Projects confidence | • Has difficulty turning over control to others |
| • Gets a lot done | • Often forgets feelings and relationships |
| • Competent and effective | • Can act superior to others |

## Energizer

### Energizer Trait Review

| Energizers Tend to Be | Energizers' Key Needs Include |
|---|---|
| • **Feeling** and **assertive** | • To be admired and appreciated |
| • The life of the party | • Excitement |
| • Outgoing | • Change |
| • Creative | • Lots of activity |
| • Inspirational | |
| • Not time-structured | |
| • Not goal-oriented | |

### Energizer Strengths and Weaknesses Review

| Strengths | Weaknesses |
|---|---|
| • Inspiring and charming | • Needs to be the center of attention, which may result in ignoring the needs of others |
| • Lots of energy and enthusiasm | • Lacks self-discipline |
| • Good at motivating others | • Not good at follow-through |
| • Creative and expressive | • May forget commitments or promises |
| • Confident | • Can be sarcastic and unkind when backed into a corner or feeling unappreciated |
| • Good social skills | • Makes excuses for being late |

## *Providing Service with CARE: Review*

Each client you meet presents a different service challenge. Some of those challenges are unique to that person's lifestyle and history, but others are related to their personality style.

As you gain mastery, you intuitively understand the service challenges a particular client presents. Until that point, however, you can use your knowledge of the personality styles to help you:

- Establish and maintain high-quality rapport by shifting styles so that you experience the greatest rapport with a wide range of people.
- Maintain this high-quality rapport throughout the client's entire visit to the salon.
- Ensure that your clients return again and again.
- Experience the fulfillment of long-term partnerships and personal growth with clients.

When you combine your CARE skills with an effective Service Cycle, you have a complete guide to client service and satisfaction. The following overviews illustrate how to serve each personality style.

**Establish and maintain high-quality rapport by shifting styles so you experience the greatest rapport with the widest range of people.**

### *Serving the Cooperator: Review*

The Cooperator is generally warm and friendly but can be slow-moving and unassertive. This client responds to caring and values relationship. Don't rush this client or expect them to deliver straightforward fact-oriented suggestions. Instead, your style recommendations should consider the Cooperator's high concern for relationships and harmony, their need to have friends, and be liked. Because this person may have a difficult time making decisions and setting goals, you may help by gently suggesting a salon program and schedule.

**Be friendly but firm with the Cooperator. Suggest styles that show warmth.**

## *Serving the Analyzer: Review*

This person needs facts upon which to base a decision and time to think them over. The Analyzer tends to be slower paced, logical, and fact-oriented. In demonstrations of affection or touching, be alert to your client's level of tolerance. Excessive contact may make this personality style withdraw and become even less communicative. In the meantime, just be your professional self, and the Analyzer will come to trust you.

**Give the Analyzer time when considering new moves. Don't rush decisions with the Analyzer. Offer facts. With certain Analyzers, be aware that they are more likely than others to be uncomfortable with touch.**

### *Serving the Regulator: Review*

The Regulator is generally assertive and logical. This client often wants to be in control, so provide your professional advice without pushing and be sure to let the Regulator make the final decision. You must act professionally and business-like at all times. As with the Analyzer, note the client's comfort level with affection. You may need to refrain from displays of emotion and affection. Appear decisive in your actions and speech.

**You may have better rapport if you are decisive, business-like, and professional with the in-control Regulator.**

### *Serving the Energizer: Review*

The Energizer generally hungers for attention and to be in the limelight. Like all of us, the Energizer wants to be acknowledged, approved of, and appreciated, but the Energizer is more likely to feel hurt or rejected without your approval. A high risk-taker, the Energizer may willingly change his or her appearance, but if problems occur, you may be blamed and criticized more by the Energizer than others. So make sure the Energizer understands exactly what you are suggesting and mention potential problems. The Energizer will be less concerned with time and more likely to cancel or not show than, say, the Analyzer. If tardiness and no-shows become a problem, explain the salon's policies with a smile. Better yet, have the receptionist telephone in advance or send a reminder postcard to help the Energizer arrive on time.

**Be even more appreciative and approving toward the Energizer. Approach undesired behavior in a non-critical way.**

You will learn more about how a person's values affect their behaviors in Lesson 6.1, *Valuing Service*.

## EXERCISES

1. List several service traits associated with each personality style that should be kept in mind when performing a service.

   Cooperator

   ______________________________

   ______________________________

   Analyzer

   ______________________________

   ______________________________

   Regulator

   ______________________________

   ______________________________

   Energizer

   ______________________________

   ______________________________

## MAIN POINT SUMMARY

Rapport leads to a sense of harmony that we experience when we feel we can understand others and be understood by them. Learning how to establish rapport is the focus of the *People Skills* program. To be successful, salon professionals must learn to establish rapport and maintain it.

An understanding of the four personality types will prepare you to build rapport with any client. The Cooperator, the Analyzer, the Regulator, and the Energizer all have unique traits that you must learn to honor for full success.

Applying your knowledge from the CARE personality styles provides clues to your clients' needs and desires, but clients are definitely more complex than the specific traits of the four personality styles.

In order to provide the highest levels of service, you also need to understand their basic values and how they are reflected in your client's total lifestyle and behavior.

## SELF-TEST/REVIEW

1. What is the goal of the *People Skills* program?

   1. ____________________

   2. ____________________

2. How can you establish rapport with a wide range of people?

   ____________________

   ____________________

   ____________________

   ____________________

3. Match each personality type to the correct set of attributes listed below:

   ____ Cooperator

   ____ Analyzer

   ____ Regulator

   ____ Energizer

   A. Thinking and passive; methodical; plans and sets goals; needs time to think; hesitant; shy

   B. Thinking and assertive; take-charge type; needs to dominate; projects confidence; can be rigid and inflexible

   C. Feeling and assertive; outgoing; creative; lacks self-discipline; good social skills; needs excitement

   D. Feeling and passive; not a risk-taker; needs to be accepted; enjoys working with people; has difficulty saying no

4. It is only necessary to maintain rapport at the beginning of the salon service. Circle One:

   True or False

Unit 6

# Serving: Fundamentals

## THE VISION

In Unit 5, you were introduced to the basics of serving each of the four personality styles. You also completed the Service CARE Profile and learned how your personality style influences your behavior as a service provider and as a customer. Now we'll take a look at the fundamentals of service: understanding values and effective listening. Interacting with clients is not simply a matter of doing a job or delivering services, but an intimate and nourishing opportunity to engage in meaningful relationships.

### Novice

Novices are just learning to identify their personal values and recognize the values of their salon. Novices assume that most people have the same values as they do and are just awakening to the richness of differences from client to client, and the differences between clients and themselves. They are beginning to learn how values are reflected in the behaviors of others and in the surroundings of the homes and businesses they visit. With regard to listening skills, Novices miss some of the facts and much of the more subtle context that a client may be communicating. Their focus is still on the techniques of the service rather than on building the relationship with clients.

### Professional

Salon professionals at this level are clear on their values and how these values are reflected in their actions and physical surroundings. They recognize the differences between their values, their clients' values and the differences in values from client to client. As listeners, Professionals rarely miss the facts that clients communicate and are beginning to establish deeper levels of communication with clients. They can use listening skills and techniques as a way to get clients talking, which allows them to obtain a deeper understanding of their clients' image preferences and desires. Listening is becoming a way to build rapport and results in their clients feeling valued and appreciated.

### Master

Masters know their own values and how they compare to the values of others. They are also less prone than Novices and Professionals to judge the values of others when they differ from their own. They are able to compare values instantly and can shift to match the values of others. As listeners, Masters rarely miss facts and use the skills and techniques of listening to facilitate communication with clients. They understand the subtleties clients communicate through their skill in listening to context as well as facts. Masters are also in a position to teach both Novices and Professionals about the subtleties in listening to clients.

## What's Ahead . . .

The two lessons in this unit are designed to teach you the fundamentals of service. By understanding values, you gain a greater appreciation of yourself and your clients, and how you are similar to and different from those clients. By learning how to listen, you can gain a better understanding of what your clients want.

After completing this unit of *Serving with CARE*, you will:

- Understand your values and how to portray them.
- Begin to recognize the values of your clients.
- Understand the different types of listening.
- Learn the three techniques of listening: responding, acceptance/understanding, and paying attention.
- Understand how to listen to the four personality styles.

**Unit 6: Serving: Fundamentals, consists of two lessons:**

**Lesson 6.1: Valuing Service**

**Lesson 6.2: Effective Listening**

Lesson 6.1

# Valuing Service

**Value: the quality of being desirable. When you are aware of your own values, and those of your clients, you are better able to provide professional service with rapport.**

## OBJECTIVES

At the completion of this lesson, you will be able to:

- Describe how a person's behavior reflects their values
- List your personal values
- Recognize how you communicate your personal values
- Explain how a salon's appearance reflects the values of its owners and salon professionals
- Identify value differences in both personality and lifestyle
- Practice cataloging the values reflected by a salon
- Discuss how understanding your values, and your client's values, allows you to provide better service

## WHAT YOU NEED TO KNOW

"Value" is the quality of being valuable or desirable, useful, important. Values are best known as social principles, goals, or standards held or accepted by an individual, class, or society. We pay more for what we value more. The word "value" refers to the things we hold more dear.

The qualities that you feel are desirable and the standards held by salon management directly reflect the quality of service you provide. To provide the best service, it helps to understand:

- What you and your salon value
- How you communicate those values

### Understanding Values

A person's values are all of those things that person esteems as a whole. You evaluate your clients and co-workers by looking at their personality style, their relationships, and their lifestyle. Your evaluation is based on your values. You learn to tailor your salon services according to what you and your clients value, just as you learned style flexibility to establish rapport.

When providing salon services, you respond to people according to what they value. A person's values are reflected in their personality styles, relationships, and lifestyle.

### *Importance of Values*

Understanding values is important because people base their choices on what they value, and they behave according to what they value. It's like journeying down a river in a canoe: The canoe of action floats on a current of values, and each person is traveling on a unique stream.

When you are aware of your values, and those of your clients, you are even better able to establish rapport and provide the kind of professional service that clients value and therefore want to patronize.

That does not mean you need to have the same values as your clients. In some cases you will, and in others you won't.

But it does mean working in a way that respects your clients' values and shows that you respect and appreciate them.

### *Categories of Values*

To understand what values are and how they influence behavior, it helps to break values into categories. People have values in every area of life. In a salon setting, values in these two areas are the most critical:

1. Personality/Relationship

2. Lifestyle

***Personality Values*** are the things that matter to a person and are reflected, at least in part, by a person's personality style. This includes ***Relationship Values***, which are the things a person considers important when relating to other people.

CARE personality styles reflect both personality and relationship values, as summarized in the following table.

#### *Personality Values and Relationship Values*

| Personality Style | Personality Values | Relationship Values |
|---|---|---|
| Cooperator | • Relationships | • Intimacy |
| Analyzer | • Accuracy | • Accountability, privacy |
| Regulator | • Completion | • Leadership, teamwork |
| Energizer | • Enthusiasm | • Expression |

By understanding personality, relationship, and lifestyle values, you gain a deeper appreciation of yourself and your clients, which leads to better service.

***Lifestyle Values***, on the other hand, are not dependent on the personality styles although they may be influenced by them. These values are reflected in the things a person considers important to the way they live. Examples include:

- Finances
- Activities
- Appearance
- Possessions
- Comfort
- Aesthetics
- Employment

Lifestyle values can be seen in things like cars: Jaguar (sexy), Volvo (safe), Mercedes (status), or Chevy (practical). Lifestyle values tend to be based on a person's upbringing, self-perception, and life circumstances, such as age, job, neighborhood, and friends. A "suburbanite" varies from a city-dweller just as a wealthy person likely has different lifestyle habits than a person of modest means.

Values are like personality styles. One person's values are not necessarily "better" than another person's, just as one personality style is not necessarily "better" than another.

What matters is that you recognize and respect another's values. This helps you develop rapport. You may develop rapport based on mirroring your client's values, or you may actually contrast with their values. It is the recognition and respect that matter. Of course, your success will be assured if your highest values are service and gratitude for the opportunity to work with your clients.

Are you expressing your highest values? Let's find out.

**Values are personal and are largely unspoken. But that doesn't mean your values aren't communicated. All behavior conveys values.**

## Communicating Values

Just as two people working in harmony to paddle a canoe forward, two people communicating in harmony experience high-quality rapport.

You communicate your values at all times: in your dress, your voice, and your actions. Your success as a salon professional (and human being) depends on your ability to understand those communications, and to make them as effective and positive as you can.

When you intentionally communicate to your clients that they are important to you, they will feel valued and be more likely to return.

Salon professional and client maintain harmony and rapport.

### Know Your Values

Remember that how you act reflects what you believe, and that what you believe flows from what you value. Imagine that you are on the phone when a client comes up to the reception area where you are standing. If you make someone wait until your phone call ends to even establish eye contact, what value are you communicating? You may say you value the client but your behavior communicates something different.

Your appearance and manner, as well as the environment of your salon, are critical because they all express the value you place on client service.

How you dress and speak also communicates your values. As the saying goes, "Beauty is in the eye of the beholder," which means that different clients will perceive things differently. Your appearance is the first impression your client has that reflects your values. You should be aware of how a particular client is likely to react to your dress, speech, and actions.

- If you dress sloppily, your clients *may* feel that you take them for granted.
- If you dress professionally, your clients are more likely to feel that you consider them worthy of special treatment.
- If you dress fashionably, your clients *may* feel confident about your concern for image. Remember that flamboyant dress may threaten more conservative clients. Be sure to let them know you recognize and respect their values.

The appearance of your workspace also reflects your values. You may show that you value personality and self-expression through personal photos or items at your station. You may keep an impeccable space, with every tool in its place, to show you value neatness and efficiency. Or you may show your knowledge of trends and what's "in" through celebrity or fashion photos. What value does hair on the floor, from five prior clients, communicate to your current client as they walk to your chair?

### Know Your Salon's Values

Now consider the salon itself. When you walk into a salon, you can immediately tell what its owners and staff value.

If it's a glitzy salon and nobody greets you, for instance, it's quite possible that the salon values appearance more than interpersonal contact. Here are some other values that a salon environment can reflect:

- Comfort
- Health/Cleanliness
- Community
- Entertainment
- Appearance/Image

A salon waiting area that is full of life communicates an enjoyable, atmosphere to clients.

**Throughout this book, you will see behaviors that guarantee an unsuccessful day. The choice is yours: Will you choose to make each interaction with the client an opportunity to serve?**

The values your salon management chooses will influence to a large extent the types of clients the salon will attract. Salon management and client values reflect one another, and a salon's environment and "culture" can come in many different flavors.

Some salons appeal to a neighborhood clientele, in which warm, casual, easy-going values define the salon's atmosphere. In this case, a casual manner fits with the salon's values.

Other salons specialize in media personalities and require a higher level of glitz. In that environment, a casual demeanor might be misinterpreted. Still other salons seek to create an oasis of warmth, acceptance, and ease amidst a demanding, high-pressure urban environment. In setting up your station and salon, make sure your highest values are fully reflected so you can attract and keep clients in-tune with you.

### *Know Your Clients' Values*

Just as it is important to understand *your* values and what *you* communicate as you provide salon services, it is also important to understand what your *clients* value and are communicating by their appearance, speech and mannerisms. Your clients' values provide the clues you need to provide excellent service.

Think about how you communicate you r values through your manner of speech and dress. Think about other ways that *your* personality style is manifested. Key in on the same types of clues to discover what your clients value. Revisit the personality style overviews in Lesson 5.3, *CAREing for Clients* for a review of some of the values for each personality styles. Remember, we are all a unique combination of personality styles and our values reflect that combination.

To be successful, avoid projecting your values onto others and try to understand what your clients value. For instance:

- You may value an exciting, expressive nail color, while your client values a convenient, easy-to-manage natural nail.
- You may value the savings from a large economy-size body lotion, while your clients prefers new experiences with smaller sizes of skin care products.
- You may wear an expressive hairstyle because you are single and value attracting a romantic partner, while your client may want a style that's easy to manage because she's married with children and on the run a great deal.

You will learn another fundamental of service in Lesson 6.2, *Effective Listening.*

## EXERCISES

1. Compare your values to those of two other people in the areas of:

**Personality**

My values:______________________________

______________________________

__________'s values:______________________________

______________________________

__________'s values:______________________________

______________________________

**Relationship**

My values:______________________________

______________________________

__________'s values:______________________________

______________________________

__________'s values:______________________________

______________________________

**Lifestyle**

My values:______________________________

______________________________

__________'s values:______________________________

______________________________

__________'s values:______________________________

______________________________

What differences in values do you see between yourself and your parents?

My values:______________________________________________

______________________________________________

_______________'s values:______________________________________________

______________________________________________

2. Visit three different salons. Salon values are reflected in many variables such as salon location, what is in the salon, and how things are arranged.

   From a list of items and their arrangement, list the values you saw reflected in each salon.

   **Salon 1**

   Location:______________________________________________

   ______________________________________________

   What is in the salon?______________________________________________

   ______________________________________________

   What does this salon value?______________________________________________

   ______________________________________________

   **Salon 2**

   Location:______________________________________________

   ______________________________________________

   What is in the salon?______________________________________________

   ______________________________________________

   What does this salon value?______________________________________________

   ______________________________________________

**Salon 3**

Location:________________________________________

_____________________________________________

What is in the salon?__________________________________

_____________________________________________

What does this salon value?______________________________

_____________________________________________

## MAIN POINT SUMMARY

A person's manner of relating to others, their personality type, and their lifestyle all reflect that person's values and beliefs. People tend to act according to their values and to base their choices on the deep-seated values that they hold.

When you are aware of your own values, and those of your clients, you are better able to provide professional service with rapport. A successful working relationship occurs when values, different or similar, intersect harmoniously in the context of productive rapport between client and salon professional.

As a salon professional, it is crucial that you understand how you communicate your own values to your clients, and that you are able to correctly interpret the values of your clients and to provide service according to their needs.

## SELF-TEST/REVIEW

1. List the two different kinds of values, and give some examples of each.

   1.________________________________________

   ________________________________________

   2.________________________________________

   ________________________________________

2. How can you demonstrate that you respect the values of your clients even if they are different from your own values?

   ________________________________________

   ________________________________________

   ________________________________________

3. What are some unspoken ways that you communicate your values?

   ________________________________________

   ________________________________________

   ________________________________________

4. List some ways that you can communicate your values through the appearance of your workspace.

   ________________________________________

   ________________________________________

5. What are three ways that a salon's values are reflected?

   1. ________________________________________

   2. ________________________________________

   3. ________________________________________

6. Why is it important to learn what your clients value?

______________________________________________

______________________________________________

______________________________________________

7. Match each personality style on the left to the personality value on the right.

| | |
|---|---|
| _____ Cooperators | A. Place a high value on accuracy. |
| _____ Analyzers | B. Find great value in getting things done. |
| _____ Regulators | C. Tend to value enthusiasm and excitement. |
| _____ Energizers | D. Value relationships highly. |

Lesson 6.2

# Effective Listening

**Without high-quality listening, you cannot provide quality service. You will miss important clues that tell you how to adjust service to match your client's desire.**

## OBJECTIVES

At the completion of this lesson, you will be able to:

- Explain the differences between factual (literal) listening and feeling (empathic) listening
- Demonstrate how to use the responding techniques of repeating and paraphrasing—to help keep clients talking
- Recognize the requirements for effective listening
- Tailor the way you listen to each personality style
- Identify listening requirements for the six phases of service

## WHAT YOU NEED TO KNOW

Listening is important during every phase of service. On average, people spend more of their time listening than talking. Effective listening allows us to learn the emotional state of our clients. If they are excited, we can join them in that excitement. If they are troubled, we can listen with understanding and empathy. Through this kind of awareness, and by providing a tailored and effective response, we increase our rapport. Stronger rapport leads to more rewarding relationships and better technical service. The skill of listening is important in every phase of your career.

Without the ability to listen well, you will:

- Have greater difficulty determining a person's needs.
- Struggle more often to be in rapport.
- Fail to adjust your own communications to meet those of the other.
- Face more problems when services do not go as planned.

Failure to learn listening skills can cost you financially and in personal fulfillment. When you listen effectively, your clients will become more real to you. You will recognize their needs, establish better rapport, and learn to serve more kinds of people—not to mention increase your income.

## Building Rapport Through Listening

Your ability to listen is important in retaining clients, since the quality of your service is in direct relation to your listening and interpreting skills.

In *Relating with CARE*, you learned how building rapport supports the foundations of client relationships. With the absence of rapport, strong and lasting relationships are difficult to establish.

Similarly, accurate, effective listening contributes to building powerful, lasting relationships. By listening effectively, you respond with greater impact and strengthen rapport. You create the positive client contact necessary for providing exceptional service.

Salon professional listens to Regulator client during the Assessment Phase, where listening skills are especially important.

Rapport is the common thread that connects *Relating with CARE* and *Serving with CARE*. As you become a better listener, your rapport skills deepen. Conversely, as your rapport skills deepen, you become a better listener and understand your clients more fully.

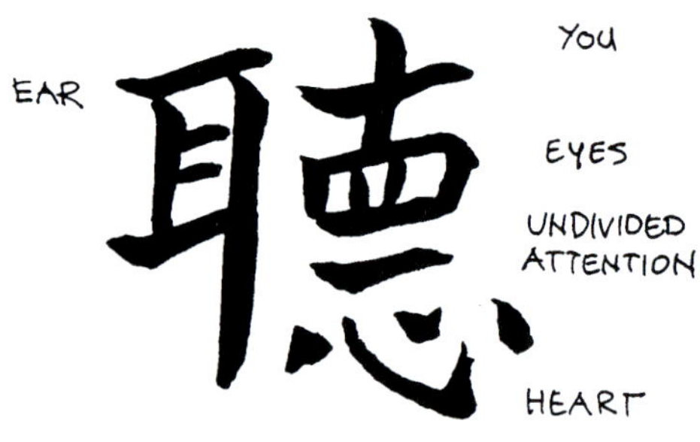


Chinese verb "to listen"

The act of understanding others is a gift. You have the unique opportunity to help them look better and feel better through both your technical and your people skills. With better listening skills, you also have an opportunity to honor them even more. The Chinese symbol for the verb 'to listen' identifies the critical elements of listening. Look at the symbol on the left and guess what the verb 'to hear' would be. Hearing is a biological response and does not require as much from you nor does it offer much in return.

Effective listening is a skill you can learn, just as carpentry, playing a musical instrument, knitting, and cutting hair are skills.

**Listening is a skill that you learn by studying its component parts. There are two types of listening: factual and feeling.**

## *Listening Defined*

When you listen to someone talk, you notice the words they say. But you also notice something more—a sense of what they are saying that is not in the words themselves but in the feeling behind the words. Indeed, all listening consists of recognizing and understanding facts and feelings. To become a good listener, you need to understand:

- Factual (literal) listening
- Feeling (empathic) listening

### *Factual Listening*

Factual listening, which is also called literal listening, serves to obtain facts, details, and information. Listening for the facts can give you answers to questions, but is also limited since just having the facts cannot tell you exactly what a person means. Factual listening often ignores context and misses feeling. Context is the specific situation and feeling is the emotion, tone and sensations.

Some experts say that factual listening accesses only 10 to 20 percent of the message. The missed 80 to 90 percent can make the difference between a satisfied customer and an unsatisfied one, and enjoyment or frustration for you.

So we see that factual listening is important and cannot be ignored. Just think how often we miss important information by not paying attention.

If you listen only to the literal meanings of words, however, they can be misleading. If you can "read between the lines" and hear them in context, the same words form a complete picture. That's where the second kind of listening comes in.

Empathic listening—where you listen for context and feelings—is especially important with Energizers.

### *Feeling Listening*

Unlike factual listening, feeling listening gets to the deeper or hidden meaning that's often unspoken. This is likely to be especially true with Energizers and Cooperators, who concern themselves less with factuality. With feeling or empathic listening, you can often build stronger rapport because the speaker senses that you heard their underlying truth. This generally causes them to talk more and give you even more high-quality information.

Unlike the skill of literal listening, listening for feeling does not focus on data or factual information. Instead, it focuses on awareness of nonverbal messages, body language, and tone of voice. It also focuses on the flow of expression.

In both factual and feeling listening, your goal is to encourage the flow of communication from the client. One way to achieve that goal is to "mirror" back to the clients what they are saying in a way that shows you value their communication. This "mirroring" can be repeating back or paraphrasing the client's part of the conversation.

Now let's look at the requirements for effective listening: responding, acceptance/understanding, and paying attention. Mastering these skills helps your client feel heard.

## Listening Skills

Being an effective listener, instead of someone who just hears what is said, requires skill and practice. Effective listening skills consist of:

- Responding
- Acceptance/understanding
- Paying attention

As a listener, your own personality style also comes into play and has its own strengths and weaknesses. The strengths and weaknesses are influenced by your values, as discussed in the previous lesson. We generally listen for the things that we value and are more likely to pay attention to people who share those values.

"Mirroring" the client by repeating or paraphrasing what they said helps build rapport through listening

Providing a relevant response shows your client that you understand. It may be as simple as a nod of the head, but should be a response that matches what the client says and shows that you are listening.

### Responding

How you respond shows your client whether or not you are listening to them—and that determines whether or not they continue talking. If clients see that you are listening, they are more likely to continue. Otherwise, they may stop talking altogether if they see you are not paying attention—then you will have broken rapport.

When you respond, you are "reinforcing" the client's self-expression, which increases the flow of their conversation. With increased flow, your rapport with and knowledge of the client increases. You improve your ability to deliver personalized services. It is like rolling a tire by pushing it with your hand. Once it is rolling, it only takes little nudges to keep it going.

To keep the conversation rolling, it helps to know how to respond in a way that encourages the conversation. These encouraging responses are called **relevant responses**.

The purpose of giving a relevant response is to allow clients to feel that your response is directly related to their concerns. You can give a relevant response by simply reflecting your clients' message back to them.

In addition to standard techniques such as questions and sharing information, the following two simple techniques are particularly effective types of relevant responses:

- Repetition
- Paraphrasing

### *Repetition*

Repetition is repeating back exactly what the client said. This allows the client to see whether or not you understand what was said and correct you if you are not accurate. Notice the factual information in the following example and how the salon professional repeats it to check for accuracy.

## In the Salon . . .

During the Assessment Phase, Marie, the salon professional, asks her first-time client Frieda about her experience in salons. She repeats Frieda's comments to encourage expression and build rapport.

**Marie:** Why did you leave your last salon?
**Frieda:** I was disappointed.
**Marie:** You were disappointed?
**Frieda:** Yes, they made me feel unimportant.
**Marie:** Really? How?
**Frieda:** I had an appointment for 1:00, but I waited until 1:30 and they never called me. They forgot about me completely.
**Marie:** Your appointment was at 1:00, and they let you sit there a half an hour and still never called you? What happened then?
**Frieda:** I walked to the nearest designer and told her why I was upset.
**Marie:** How did she handle it?
**Frieda:** She said she knew nothing about it since all the designers kept their own books, and she knew I wasn't on her book. Then she went back to cutting hair!
**Marie:** She just went back to cutting?
**Frieda:** Yes, can you beat that? I felt six inches tall. I walked out and I'll never go back there again.

### *Paraphrasing*

Paraphrasing is a similar technique of reflecting speakers back to themselves, except it isn't a literal reflection. Instead, you use different words to confirm to the speaker the essence of what he or she said.

Paraphrasing is used more with feeling listening. In paraphrasing, you read the emotion or reaction to the client's communication and mirror that back. This invites the client to respond with even more emotional, expressive sharing.

There are still other simple techniques of reflecting back to the speaker in order to show you are listening—they don't even need to be words. Any sign of encouragement may do, including:

- Head nods
- Short "Uh-huhs"
- A well-placed "Oh, really?"

Notice how the salon professional's responses to the "feeling" in the client's voice encourage expression. High-quality information helps us know, understand, or empathize with the client better, as shown below.

## In the Salon . . .

Alison, the designer, asks her first-time client Michelle about her salon experiences. She paraphrases Michelle's answers to build rapport.

**Alison:** What was your best salon experience?

**Michelle:** I'll never forget it. It happened when I was in Australia on assignment and I needed a manicure. I met a remarkable nail technician.

**Alison:** It sounds like they made quite an impression on you.

**Michelle:** She sure did. It wasn't just the excellent manicure. She made it warm and fun, and I felt great.

**Alison:** It sounds very pleasant.

**Michelle:** Yeah, I wish more people in your profession understood that. I'd spend more time in salons if they did.

**Alison:** Can you tell me more about what she did?

**Michelle:** I don't know. Maybe being friendly just comes naturally to Australians. She took extra time to talk to me, kind of like what you're doing here. She smiled warmly. She seemed really to care what it felt like to be working away from my home and my family. We were laughing at everything. I ended up staying for a facial and a cup of tea. I was there two hours and I didn't want to leave.

**Alison:** So, you see the salon visit as potentially more than just a haircut or a manicure—perhaps as coming to a place where you can relax and feel welcomed and understood?

**Michelle:** Exactly! And, by the way, that's how you're making me feel now.

**You build rapport and gain credibility by listening closely to your clients. Tailor your listening to the requirements of each personality style for the deepest rapport and understanding.**

## Listening to the Cooperator

| Listening Type | What to Listen or Watch for | How to Respond |
|---|---|---|
| Factual | • Information about their lives, such as names of family members, because Cooperators value relationship and will feel heard.<br><br>• Words that may indicate uncertainty so you can then help clarify the details. Cooperators sometimes speak ambiguously because they do not want to offend or assume you will not be interested. | • When you hear a name, repeat it back in conversation. For instance, you may hear a Cooperator say, "My daughter Eileen is very particular about her hair, too." You can say back, "Eileen must be a lot like you."<br><br>• If they use words and phrases such as "Maybe," "Is it okay if..." "I don't really care," then put form to the words. This encourages them to continue. Phrases like, "You are uncertain about..." show interest, invite expression, and provide comfort. |
| Feeling | • The feelings behind words in the face and body language Cooperators may smile to show excitement, but more likely they will fidget when they are not satisfied because they are hesitant to say anything negative. | • Ask what they are feeling and if there is anything more to be done to reassure them that they can tell you what is on their mind. |

## Listening to the Analyzer

| Listening Type | What to Listen or Watch for | How to Respond |
|---|---|---|
| Factual | • Pay attention! Analyzers give you facts, information, and details, but you may need to encourage more flow. | • Repeat information back to them as you hear it, which may require you to sharpen your literal listening skills if you are a Cooperator or an Energizer.<br><br>• Confirm what they want in detail, and they will be more likely to trust and respect you. |
| Feeling | • This can be the hardest style to read empathically. Analyzers are not all that comfortable with your ability to empathize with them. | • If Analyzers are not forthcoming with information or details, it may be an indication that they are not satisfied. Ask!<br><br>• If Analyzers are silent, do not think it means they are angry or upset. Analyzers like to be quiet. Let them have their space. They will appreciate less chit-chat and more technique. |

## Listening to the Regulator

| Listening Type | What to Listen or Watch for | How to Respond |
|---|---|---|
| Factual | • Listen for facts and be sure you have them straight. Regulators do have high energy, however, so you might find that they are challenging to keep up with once they start talking. | • Repeat information back to them as you hear it, which may require you to sharpen your literal listening skills if you are a Cooperator or an Energizer.<br>• Confirm what they want in detail, and they will more likely trust and respect you. |
| Feeling | • Regulators are less open to your empathy, like Analyzers. Don't give up! Remember that Regulators have feelings too—they just hide them more. | • Regulators have many feelings and usually aren't afraid to share them if they recognize them. They might resist having anyone interpret those feelings for them. They will more likely appreciate being heard and then moving on.<br>• Check in with them from time to time to make sure they aren't feeling left out of the decisions, or worse yet, not in charge. |

## Listening to the Energizer

| Listening Type | What to Listen or Watch for | How to Respond |
|---|---|---|
| Factual | • Listen carefully and closely, as you may have some difficulty listening to the literal parts of an Energizer's conversation. They often jump from topic to topic. | • You can put some structure into what they are saying, but you probably won't get a lot of details or definitive decisions from them. |
| Feeling | • Meet Energizers at the feeling level. This is where they live. | • Use the same words they do—exciting, fun, huge, big, great, and wonderful.<br>• Show them you understand how important something is to them, and they will give you more information about what they need. |

A Cooperator salon professional's head nod shows she understands what the Energizer client wants.

**Acceptance is at the root of feeling heard. You may not agree with your client and don't have to, but your client needs to feel accepted and understood.**

### *Acceptance/Understanding*

Regardless of their CARE personality style, all clients value listening and being heard. Feeling accepted is a universal need. Understanding this universal need is a key to building the rapport necessary to serve your clients.

It is important to realize that ***acceptance and agreement are not the same thing***. It is quite possible to *understand* what a person is saying and *accept* them, but not *agree* with what they are saying. Be aware that acceptance may be a difficult skill to master if you feel that you must always be "right," or if you believe in most situations that there is only one "right" answer.

When clients say, "I really just want the basics," and you know they need more than that, you may not agree and you may have difficulty *accepting* what they are saying.

That's where your factual listening can come in handy. By declaring, "I understand you want the basics," you show that you accept and understand what they are saying. This can cause them to say more so you can understand.

Once you have displayed acceptance and understanding, you can more readily offer your own opinion. If, on the other hand, you only offer your opinion and fail to show that you understand and accept their point of view, your client will most likely feel misunderstood or ignored, and you will have broken rapport.

Each of us is a unique mixture of the styles. One listening style alone will not work for any of us. Read the following charts, knowing that you are expanding your style shifting and that each type of response is a guide, not a rule.

Acceptance and understanding flow naturally from sensitive listening. The very act of listening communicates acceptance for many. It helps further to demonstrate acceptance with affirming statements such as "I see,"

"I understand," or even, "I feel the same way." Listening to understand others first before expecting them to understand you will be a valuable salon skill.

### Accepting/Understanding the Cooperator

| How You React | What You Say | How You Proceed |
|---|---|---|
| • Accept their need for the status quo. | • "I hear you. It's a nice style that still works well for you."<br>• "Having the basics would be simple to do. Not a problem!" | • Once you have shown Cooperators you understand and accept that they don't want to "rock the boat" or do anything too different, you can then proceed with more suggestions. |

### Accepting/Understanding the Analyzer

| How You React | What You Say | How You Proceed |
|---|---|---|
| • Accept what they are saying. | • Repeat what they say. Analyzers aren't interested in interpretation but want to know you understand the facts.<br>• "Yes, I understand that you want the basics." | • Once the Analyzer knows that what they have said is accepted, you can introduce new data and could even get a new decision from them. |

### Accepting/Understanding the Regulator

| How You React | What You Say | How You Proceed |
|---|---|---|
| • You may not agree and may have other ideas about how to do what they say they want. | • Don't make the mistake of being intimidated by Regulators' confidence. Usually, they are open to creative ideas even if they have strong ideas of their own. | • As long as you have shown that you have heard them, that you accept what they have offered, you are on much better ground to present other ideas or to simply move into whatever action they have in mind.<br>• Quickly repeat what they said and present your alternatives. |

## Accepting/Understanding the Energizer

| How You React | What You Say | How You Proceed |
|---|---|---|
| • Pay attention to them. You don't really need to accept what Energizers say. Acceptance is not as important to them. | • They will be engaged and want you to be, too, in whatever they are saying. | • Join them in whatever they are saying. Most of the time it will be a creative process.<br>• Energizers are usually flexible. You can show that you are able to accept the Energizer by "going with the flow." |

## In the Salon . . .

Art is a Cooperator stylist who has felt dominated and rejected by Stan, a Regulator client. After taking *People Skills*, Art was thrilled at his ability to get quiet clients like Stan talking. When he finally did get Stan talking using factual and feeling listening, he was shocked to learn about Stan's past.

To Art, Stan had appeared to be the typical spoiled, rich businessman. Art had assumed Stan was born with a silver spoon in his mouth. Nothing could have been further from the truth. As it turned out, Stan was the oldest of seven children. He'd quit school at 16 and gone to work to help support the family.

A good worker, Stan had moved from helper in construction work to supervisor and eventually president of a large construction firm. Behind his gruff exterior was a man who felt embarrassed at not having graduated from high school. As Art listened over a number of appointments, Stan continued to let his story unfold.

Stan did not change, but with increasing empathy, Art did. Art began looking forward to Stan's appointments. Stan began helping Art develop his retirement strategy, and Art's acceptance helped Stan boost his self-esteem. Art was on his way to Master with his first major victory in developing hard-won rapport.

Giving another person your full attention builds rapport.

**Attention is just that: attending to your client. Listen for both content and nonverbal feeling in order to increase rapport.**

## *Paying Attention*

Hand-in-hand with acceptance and understanding goes "attending to," or "paying attention to," your clients. This can mean attending to their mood, words, or posture.

Paying attention can be as simple as looking at them when they are talking or as complicated as minimizing distractions and ensuring that you are both comfortable. For example, you could ask if they'd like a cup of tea if they are a tea drinker. You could even change the music to match their mood or tastes.

Giving clients your full attention means remaining "present" with them. Even if you don't agree with them and even if you'd rather be doing something else, you should be engaged with your clients—at all times. Otherwise, you could miss important details or misinterpret nonverbal messages and jeopardize rapport. A client can feel when you are paying attention and when you are not.

The following tables show how to effectively pay attention to each of the four basic personality styles.

### *Paying Attention to the Cooperator*

| How You Pay Attention | What Matters to the Person | What You Do |
|---|---|---|
| • Show you are paying attention by telling the Cooperator how much you like what she is saying, or that she is contributing to you in some way. | • Cooperators like things to be comfortable. Asking if they are comfortable is always a good way to attend to them.<br>• Pay attention to the mood by being sure there isn't too much noise or distraction. A Cooperator could be putting up with irritating music or conversation just because she doesn't want to say anything or cause a problem. | • Let Cooperators know you enjoy giving them your attention. Relate stories that are similar to theirs, and they will definitely feel you are listening to them. |

## Paying Attention to the Analyzer

| How You Pay Attention | What Matters to the Person | What You Do |
|---|---|---|
| • Keep it straightforward and simple. | • Details matter to the Analyzer, and when you get the facts right, he knows you are listening to him.<br>• Neatness is important. Keep things neat and clean when Analyzers are around. | • Ask specific questions. Do they like their coffee black or with sugar? Two packets or only one? |

## Paying Attention to the Regulator

| How You Pay Attention | What Matters to the Person | What You Do |
|---|---|---|
| • Know that their attention needs are strong, but they don't want to be catered to. | • Regulators appreciate good performance and high standards, and they expect you to provide those. | • Regulators like to make decisions, so attend to them by asking just what they would to like. Then be sure you give it to them. |
| • Regulators will appreciate your attention and your desire to hear exactly what they are saying. | • Noticing your physical space is one of the ways Regulators will judge you. When the physical space shows well-thought-out systems, order, and functionality, Regulators are at home. | • Show that you are paying attention by following through with what they want.<br>• With their high energy and creative power, sometimes Regulators will give you more information than you can remember at any one time. Don't make the mistake of trying to out-guess them. Simply ask them to repeat themselves, and then show attention by repeating back to them what you heard. |

## Paying Attention to the Energizer

| How You Attention | What Matters to the Person | What You Do |
|---|---|---|
| • You can never give Energizers too much attention. | • Animation and engagement. Paying attention to the Energizer may mean being as animated as they are, and keeping up with their conversation. | • Flatter them (with honest appraisals, of course), or go that extra step to make things look pretty or have a little surprise waiting for them, like an arrangement of flowers or a new coffee cup. |

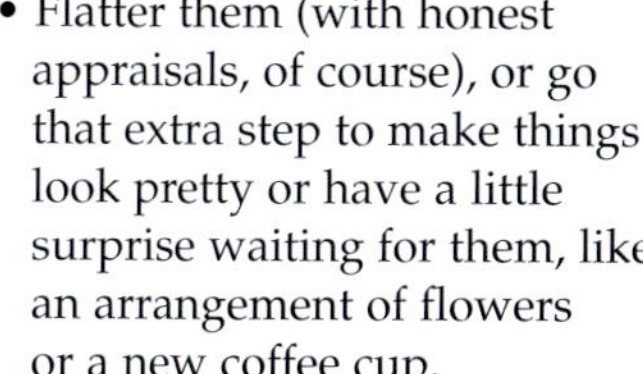

## In the Salon . . .

Andy owned his salon and was proud of the fine staff he hired. They were technically adept and had great people skills. Wendy was his top salon professional. She was frequently asked to style for photo shoots, and top society weddings often featured her work. Recently, however, Wendy had been coming in late and had even missed a very important appointment. Andy feared he would need to fire Wendy. She had not responded to the warnings, and he was nearing the end of his patience.

Andy asked Wendy into the salon office to discuss the situation. He was getting nowhere until he picked up the feeling of despair in Wendy's voice. "Sounds like you are feeling a lot of despair," he said.

"I don't know if it is despair, but it sure feels hopeless," Wendy responded.

"Hopeless?"replied Andy.

"Yes, but I try not to bring my problems to work." Andy encouraged her to talk about her problems if she would like to. Andy suggested a great counselor, and Wendy got the help she needed. Using paraphrasing and repetition, Andy was able to help Wendy get on track and turn her life around. Wendy became an even more loyal employee and opened Andy's first satellite salon a few years later.

**What you listen for depends on what phase of service you are in. Each phase has its own listening requirements.**

## Listening Requirements in the Phases of Service

Each phase in the Service Cycle requires all the skills of listening. If you listen throughout the phases of service, your clients will know they have received the best possible service.

Now that you understand the requirements of effective listening and are aware of the different approaches that each personality style requires, you can begin to see how listening is essential during each phase of the Service Cycle.

### Listening During the Greeting Phase

You can never be sure where your client is coming from unless you really listen. If the client is new, listening during your greeting is even more important. The Greeting Phase generally begins one of two ways—either when your client calls you on the phone, or when you see your client enter the salon or approach your station. One of you will generally say hello first. For this discussion, let's assume that it is you.

It is good practice to ask your client how they are doing as soon as possible. Their response is your first opportunity to use repetition or paraphrasing.

If your client responds that he or she is doing well, you can literally respond by saying, "So, you are doing well?" The client is likely to respond by telling you why he or she is doing well.

If your client doesn't seem forthcoming, you may wish to paraphrase or even interpret. If the client says something along the lines of, "I guess I'm doing OK," you may want to respond by saying something like, "Sounds like you might be having a tough day."

If you are delivering the service, this interaction during the greeting should make the transition smoothly into the Assessment Phase. If you greet a co-worker's client and discover important information about their mood or mindframe, be sure to share it with your co-worker.

### *Listening During the Assessment Phase*

During this phase, you need to be especially alert to the client's nonverbal behavior. Is the client agitated or bored? Is the client excited? Does the client want to talk while you present your ideas?

Listen carefully to the client's opinions. Make sure you convey an understanding of both the facts and feelings. Before proceeding any further with Assessment, let your client know you understand him or her.

Use your repetition, paraphrasing, and other relevant responses to help the client talk about how she felt during and after the last service.

### *Listening During the Agreement Phase*

Of course, it is absolutely essential to listen during the Agreement Phase. How can you tell if you are ready to proceed with your service if there has been no agreement with your client? Clients may not agree, but they might not say so. The way you can be sure you are in agreement is to ask tactful questions to determine their true feelings. Naturally, how you do this will depend on the person's personality style, but it is critical that agreement be reached and that you understand how to proceed with your delivery.

Be sure to ask your client how he or she feels about the plan you are about to execute, whether it is routine or new. Salon professionals who fail to really listen to their clients during the Agreement Phase risk customer dissatisfaction.

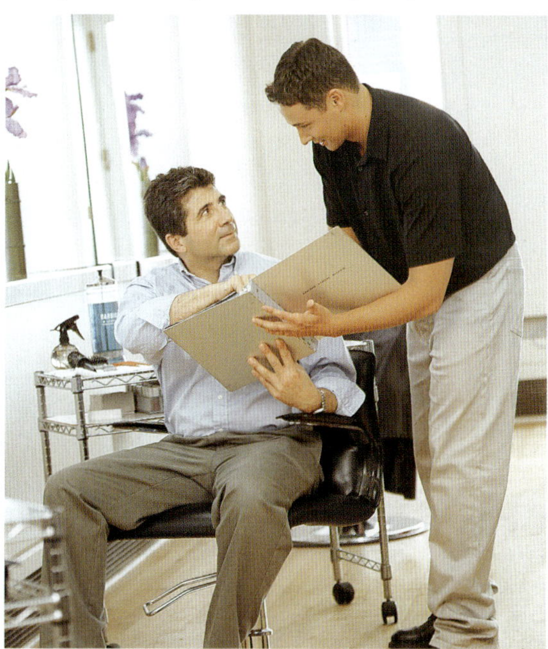

Giving another person your full attention builds rapport.

### Listening During the Delivery Phase

How you listen during delivery depends on the client's personality style. If you are providing nail care or makeup service, you need to listen not only to what the client is saying but also to what he or she may *not* be saying. Making sure you are in agreement during the delivery can be as simple as asking, "Is this what you wanted?" or "Are you comfortable?" Then use your listening skills to respond accordingly.

Listen while keeping your focus on the task at hand for a successful Delivery Phase.

Be sensitive to your client's preference to talk or be silent during the service. Enjoy yourself during delivery. Use your listening skills freely to learn as much as you can about your client.

### Listening During the Recommendation Phase

This phase is all about listening. Ask your clients what types of products they use and what their styling habits are. Listen closely to their response. For the most part, you are using factual listening as you collect quantifiable information on your client's current hair and body care routine.

Be sure to ask clients how they feel about their current products. What are their shopping patterns? What can you do to help them understand the products you offer.

### Listening During the Completion Phase

During the Completion Phase, you discover how well you listened during the previous phases by listening to the answer to this question: "Is the customer satisfied?"

You may have to listen to something you don't want to hear. But, unless you *do* listen and let your client know you have heard them, you could undo all of the other good work you've done. Of course, hearing the client say, "Thank you, it's just what I wanted" is always easier to deal with than dissatisfaction. Dissatisfaction provides challenges to overcome and opportunities for strengthening rapport.

Salon professional responds to her client during the Completion Phase.

After your clients leave, you may wish to write down what they wanted, what they received, and how well they received it. Soon, you will automatically pick up these messages from clients and use the information to improve your listening skills and build rapport.

## In the Salon . . .

During the greeting, Amber asked Courtney how things were going, and Courtney replied that things were tough. To avoid asking a question that might be too personal, Amber remembered her repetitive listening skill and replied, "So, things are tough?" to help draw her client out. Courtney explained that she was worried her daughter might drop out of school. Using repetition again, Amber responded, "Drop out of school?"

Courtney shot back with, "Yes, can you believe it? She got interested in acting and has been doing well in a local theater company. She thinks she'll take off and go to New York and try her luck, waiting tables to make ends meet."

"Really!"Amber said.

Courtney said, "Can you believe it? She thinks she'll make it and doesn't want to waste any more time in school."

From the experience, Amber learned that all most people need is a show of interest and, with a few relevant responses, they will feel understood.

## EXERCISES

1. As you shop, eat at restaurants, or visit your salon, notice how the service provider listens, or does not listen to you. What have you learned about listening as a customer? How will it help you with your own clients?

______________________________________________

______________________________________________

______________________________________________

______________________________________________

2. If you are working on the clinic floor, discuss how well you listened with another student. How well did you listen for facts? For feelings? How well did you pay attention? How well did you respond? What lessons have you learned about listening?

______________________________________________

______________________________________________

______________________________________________

______________________________________________

______________________________________________

## MAIN POINT SUMMARY

Listening is a skill that will be extremely important to you during each phase of the Service Cycle and throughout your career as a salon professional. You must be able to hear your clients' needs, build rapport through listening, and adjust your style of communication to suit your clients' personality types. In this way, your clients become more "real" and more important to you. In turn, you are more able to create satisfied repeat clients who feel that you will listen and understand them.

Rapport is the common thread that unites *Relating with CARE* and *Serving with CARE*. Listening builds rapport quickly. **Factual** listening is used to obtain details and concrete information about your clients, whereas **feeling** listening reveals the underlying meanings and emotions that are often conveyed nonverbally through body language or tone of voice. Different personality types will demand varying degrees of factual and feeling listening. Because people generally listen to and relate to what they value, you must also take into account your own values, which affect how you tend to listen to others.

Three basic requirements define effective listening: **responding, acceptance/ understanding and paying attention.** Your response should acknowledge what the client is saying. Acceptance is a universal need. Your client wants to know that you think their views are valid and that you *accept* what they are saying to you. Paying attention to your clients can be anything from looking at them and nodding when they speak, to bringing them hot tea or making your surroundings more amenable to their mood. .

In the Greeting Phase, your listening lets the client know that they have your full attention. This is a foundation of the rapport that you strive for. Although you will do a lot of talking during the Assessment Phase, you must pay attention to the nonverbal communication and see how the client is reacting to what you say.

During the Delivery Phase, you listen to and remain aware of the client's reactions to the service. In the Recommendation Phase, you need to listen closely to their responses and recommend products or services according to their needs.

Completion is perhaps the most important time to listen, for it is at this point that you determine whether or not your client is satisfied. During Completion, you discover how well you listened to the client throughout the Service Cycle, and how well you have delivered an appropriate service according to what the client said.

## SELF-TEST/REVIEW

1. Name and briefly describe the two types of listening.

   1. ______________________________

   2. ______________________________

2. When you are listening to a client, what is an easy way to make sure that you heard exactly what they meant to say?

   ______________________________

   ______________________________

3. What are the areas of focus for feeling listening?

   ______________________________

   ______________________________

   ______________________________

4. What are the two requirements of effective listening? Give an example of each requirement.

   1. ______________________________

      ______________________________

   2. ______________________________

      ______________________________

5. Acceptance and agreement are the same thing. Explain your answer. Circle One:

   True or False

   ______________________________

   ______________________________

6. Why is it important to show acceptance to your client before offering your own opinions?

   ______________________________

   ______________________________

7. What are three ways that you can show attention to your client?

   1. ________________________________________
   2. ________________________________________
   3. ________________________________________

8. How can you demonstrate to your clients that you are paying attention to them? Give an example for each of the four basic personality types.

   Cooperator:____________________________________

   Analyzer:____________________________________

   Regulator:____________________________________

   Energizer:____________________________________

9. What are two different types of relevant responses?

   1. ________________________________________
   2. ________________________________________

Unit 7

# The Service Cycle

## THE VISION

In Unit 5, you were introduced to the meaning of service and reviewed the four personality styles. In Unit 6, you learned the fundamentals of service, which are valuing service and effective listening. In this unit, you'll learn proven techniques for providing excellent service. These techniques are organized into the Service Cycle, which you first encountered in Lesson 5.1. The lessons in this unit function as a roadmap for a professional service. Each step of the Service Cycle is broken into distinct phases with instructions that guide you through a successful client visit.

### Novice

Novices are learning the Service Cycle. They are beginning to understand that a client visit consists of recognizable phases, and that those phases can be managed in a way that improves rapport. Novices tend to have challenges managing the transition from one phase to another. Because their focus is primarily on technique, Novices are just learning to concentrate on building relationships through excellent service.

### Professional

Professionals understand the Service Cycle and manage each phase as a way to ensure they provide excellent service. For Professionals, each phase of the Service Cycle flows smoothly into the next. They rarely need to think about which phase of the cycle they are in. Because technical skills are second nature to Professionals, they focus on relationships. They use the phases of the Service Cycle to deepen rapport and build long-term relationships with clients.

### Master

Masters move through client visits with grace and ease. The Service Cycle is second nature to Masters. They move so freely from one phase to another that the entire visit seems like a dance. Masters focus on supporting their clients in all facets of their lives. They use their service and relationship skills as a way to help their clients see how beauty, image, and health support their work, family, and overall relationship goals and desires.

## What's Ahead. . .

Each lesson in this unit covers a phase of the Service Cycle. You are introduced to the basic characteristics of each phase and learn specific skills and techniques for serving clients.

After completing this unit of *Serving with CARE*, you will be able to:

- Take a client through each phase of the Service Cycle.
- Use the skills and techniques of each phase to provide excellent service for new and existing clients.
- Focus on building lasting relationships through your ability to provide a positive and memorable experience throughout an entire client visit.

Remember that you were introduced to the Service Cycle in picture form in Lesson 5.1. The following illustration provides a reminder of the phases in the Service Cycle.

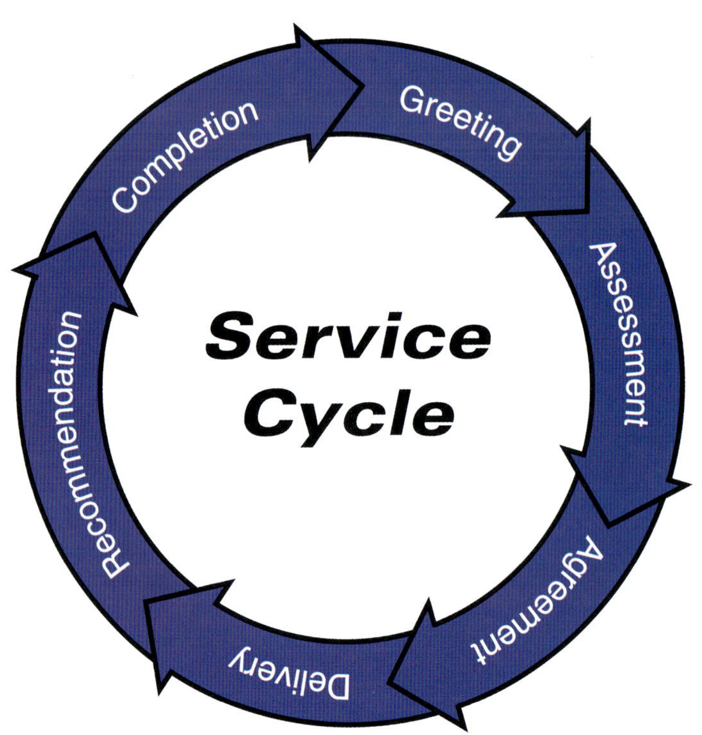


Unit 7: The Service Cycle, consists of six lessons:

Lesson 7.1: Greeting Phase

Lesson 7.2: Assessment Phase

Lesson 7.3: Agreement Phase

Lesson 7.4: Delivery Phase

Lesson 7.5: Recommendation Phase

Lesson 7.6: Completion Phase

Lesson 7.1

# Greeting Phase

Greeting Phase

> **The Greeting Phase consists of Welcome plus Rapport. Your welcome of the client establishes or re-establishes a connection and helps to build rapport.**

## OBJECTIVES

At the completion of this lesson, you will be able to:

- Identify the two components of the Greeting Phase
- Describe the difference between greeting a new client and greeting a repeat client
- Explain how greetings can vary depending on a client's personality style
- Define "hidden agenda" and explain how understanding your clients' hidden agendas can help you serve them better

## WHAT YOU NEED TO KNOW

The Greeting Phase is more complex than it seems. It may begin with a friendly smile, a quick handshake, or a pleasant hello. Although its duration is short, the Greeting Phase is the point at which you welcome your client and begin interaction to establish rapport. Your relationship with a client depends on your ability to establish rapport, so the short and simple Greeting takes on added weight.

The Greeting Phase sets the tone for the entire salon experience. In the Greeting Phase you can establish rapport easily, but it is also the phase where you may fall behind if rapport is not established.

For new clients, the Greeting Phase is an opportunity to show them the salon and its services. For existing clients, the Greeting Phase allows you to catch up on what has happened since their last visit.

Properly engaged, the Greeting Phase establishes initial rapport by providing a first impression between you and your clients. By managing the Greeting Phase effectively, you control the client's first impressions of you and your salon, and ensure that their impression will be positive.

You also have the opportunity to convey your gratitude that they chose you as a salon professional and show that you value both their business and them. Greetings of warmth and acceptance, combined with a hearty welcome, make the client feel at home and help them get oriented to you and the salon.

### Greeting Don'ts

To appreciate the power of a proper Greeting Phase, let's look at the absurdities of Salon Calimité, where service, at best, is an afterthought.

## Salon Calimité. . .

Greeting at Salon Calimité is an insulting experience. When you call for your first appointment, the phone may ring four or five times before it's answered. If the receptionist is busy, you'll get a harried employee in the middle of working with a client. Then you'll be put on hold, only to wait for the receptionist, who's either brusque or spacey.

You make your appointment but don't ask any questions, as you get the feeling that you'll only be a bother. If you're the sort of person who has trouble remembering appointments, you're out of luck. You won't receive a reminder call or postcard.

When you walk into the salon, you're lucky if anyone notices you. The receptionist is either bothered with someone on the phone or chatting with another salon employee (they can hardly be called "professionals" here).

Someone finally notices you and asks, "Do you need anything?" They may page your stylist or they may herd you to the shampoo bowl. Either way, you feel disoriented, not knowing who you are going to see or what is going to happen.

## Greeting Techniques

How you greet clients changes as you gain more experience as a salon professional and as you know your clients better. As you progress in your career from Novice to Professional, and finally to Master, you will naturally shift from focusing on establishing rapport for service and *technique* to focusing on developing a *relationship* during the Greeting Phase.

### Novice Greeting

Efficiency is the watchword for Novices. Focusing on technical service, Novices initially may feel awkward when greeting clients, especially new ones. They tend to see the Greeting Phase as setting up the delivery effectively. As they see repeat clients, Novices begin to develop personal relationships and look forward to seeing and greeting clients again.

In the case of an upset client, the Novice may welcome them in a business-like manner but neglect to ask how they are feeling; a Novice is more likely to be uncomfortable with the perceived confrontation. The cool greeting and weak rapport make the client's problem more difficult to address.

### Professional Greeting

Relatedness characterizes the Professional's greeting. Professionals welcome their clients naturally, with little need to consciously plan what they are going to say or how they are going to say it. They think of their existing clients as friends and greet them in accordance with their personality style and their unique lifestyle and values.

Rapport results easily. Professionals quickly establish the personality style of new clients and naturally take their style into account in their greeting. In the case of an upset client, the Professional likely shows more relatedness, notices and acknowledges the problem, welcomes them, and asks how they are doing.

**After your greeting, clients should feel welcome and comfortable with you as their guide through the salon experience.**

### Master Greeting

The term "grace" characterizes the greeting by the Master salon professional. For Masters, the Greeting Phase can range from a warm, caring reunion to a celebration. Masters also know their clients like they know friends. They are usually very aware of what's going on in their clients' lives and serve as trusted advisors, helping clients achieve both business and personal goals.

The ability of the Master to shift styles is far-reaching and comes naturally. With new clients, Master salon professionals know how to begin learning about a person's life right from the greeting. They can help upset clients come to a resolution easily. In the case of service problems, the Master faces the issue with grace by showing understanding, confidence and compassion. This creates ease and assurance in the client until the situation is corrected.

## Welcome and Rapport

Establishing rapport in the Greeting Phase is the first move of winning the service game. Treat each new greeting as an adventure, an opportunity and a challenge that, when successfully met, will increase your professional satisfaction and success.

The Greeting Phase begins with the first contact your client has with the salon and ends in rapport. Greeting equals welcome and rapport. It may begin with a client's telephone call to make an appointment, or the way clients are received when they walk through the door for the first time. It repeats thereafter each time you see your client again. The quality of that initial contact is critical.

A weak greeting fails to establish rapport. A cranky or indifferent receptionist or unprofessional telephone behavior can build barriers to rapport before you even see the client. If a client does start off on the wrong foot, and you fail to engage in a strong initial greeting, things can easily go from bad to worse. On the other hand, if initial contact is satisfactory, the salon professional's job in the Greeting Phase is easier because the client's first impression is positive. Then the relationship becomes stronger and will tolerate problems better.

A warm, welcoming phrase is useful when beginning your encounter with the client. Experiment with opening greetings to see what works. A friendly, confident greeting is a safe bet with most people. To get new ideas, notice particularly effective greeters at restaurants and other places where you do business and experiment with their style to expand yours.

Your greeting should vary not only by client personality style, but also by their past experience with the salon. Remember that first-time clients feel vulnerable in a new place. Take extra time to introduce them to the salon.

Indifferent Energizer receptionist cares more about her phone conversation than serving clients, much to the distress of the waiting Regulator.

A successful greeting establishes the foundation for successful service.

Whether you are the receptionist or stylist, check with the client after your initial welcome to assess how their day is going and, in particular, how their immediate travel to the salon went. This type of interaction allows them to get possible aggravation, experienced prior to coming to the salon, off their mind. If you fail to check in with your client about their mental state, you may become a casualty of their aggravation.

## SERVICE CHALLENGE

**How do you greet and establish rapport with a client who is obviously in a bad mood?**

**If your client is in a bad mood, it is certainly more difficult to establish rapport, but it is not impossible. Here is where the art of strong interaction comes in. You may ask some questions, or identify with the experience, but don't pry. Just be sensitive to how much they are willing to tell you. Sometimes just a question or two can make the client feel comfortable and they will be more likely to feel that they are in a safe environment where they will be cared for. Their frustration could be something as simple as bad traffic on the way to the salon, a problem they've had at work, or a family dispute. Show concern and allow your client to talk, that may be all that's needed to establish rapport.**

## Greeting the New Client

Put yourself in the first-time client's shoes. Because you are at home in the salon, it is easy to forget the new client's perspective. Think about how it feels to come into a new place, meet new people, and have someone you have never met alter your looks.

Think of your own firsts: the first day at beauty school, your first visit to a new doctor, or a first date. Whether you noticed or not, you probably felt vulnerable and somewhat tense.

Most people feel unsure of themselves in new situations. So may your clients. Your job as a salon professional is to recognize those feelings and put clients at ease. Don't forget that each personality style has a different way of dealing with these feelings. Ways to deal with the uneasiness of new situations can range from the Analyzer's questions to the Regulator's control, the Cooperator's compliance and the Energizer's enthusiasm.

If nothing happens to ease a client's feelings of discomfort and vulnerability, he or she may become dissatisfied and critical. Many complaints and criticisms are born of underlying fears and insecurities. When people feel at ease with themselves and their surroundings, they are much less likely to find fault.

In the Greeting Phase, you have an opportunity to let all clients know that they are welcome, secure, and appreciated. When greeting a new client, you want to go a little further. Greeting becomes a critical "orientation" to the salon and its practices. You have an excellent opportunity to practice style shifting and match the new client's personality style.

First-time clients feel vulnerable and unsure when they enter a salon. Receptionists should be particularly attuned to greeting such clients.

To orient first-time clients to the salon, give them a tour. Walk with them and introduce them to the other salon professionals, indicating the other services they provide. For instance, bring them by the station of the makeup artist, the nail technician, or the masseuse. Some clients don't take advantage of the services because they don't know about them and may not even know how to ask. Don't forget their personality styles and the opportunity for you to practice style shifting.

First-time clients will have a better salon experience when they feel valued and know what to expect. Getting a feel for the "lay of the land" from the start can put your client at ease and make the experience more productive and enjoyable. First-time clients who feel comfortable and welcomed to the salon are more likely to become second-time clients and take advantage of other services and products your salon offers.

## Understanding Client Expectations

Even before clients enter the salon, they have a mental list of the traits they expect their ideal salon professional to possess. They have certain expectations about what their salon experience should be. They also have a catalog of prior negative experiences they may remember.

Few clients walk in and say, "Hello, my name is ________________. I expect an elegant salon with soft lights and soft music. I want to be treated like someone special, and I'm willing to pay well for excellent service."

### In the Salon. . .

After admiring her friend's new hair color, Beth made an appointment with Scott, the master colorist at a new upscale salon. As Beth had never had her hair professionally colored, she was excited to hear what Scott would suggest.

When Beth arrived at the salon, she and Scott spent several minutes discussing how to enhance her look with hair color. They decided that chunky highlights would add dimension and texture to her hair.

During the service, Scott suggested to finish the highlights with a color wash to add vibrant warm tones to her hair. Beth agreed. She was absolutely thrilled with the results of the color.

When Beth received the bill for the hair color service, she was shocked to see the charges were in excess of $150 before tip. She was mortified—this definitely did not fit into her budget—she didn't know what to say. When the receptionist suggested that she make her next appointment to maintain her color, Beth was embarrassed that she could not afford to come back, so she declined and said she would call since she was not sure of her schedule.

Scott lost a new client and potential referrals by not discussing the price of the service in the first place, the price to add on the color wash, and subsequent maintenance costs during the Agreement Phase.

**When a person wants something but has not articulated it, they have a hidden agenda. Determining your client's potential hidden agenda allows you to serve them better, because you will be able to meet their unspoken needs.**

The client's unspoken expectation is called a **hidden agenda**. Hidden agendas are common for all human beings in many situations. It is literally impossible for us to directly express all of our agendas at any given time. A hidden agenda means there is something we want, but don't want to talk openly about.

When we have an understanding of personality styles, we already recognize some of the different things that different people want, but don't directly ask for—their hidden agendas. The Energizer, for example, wants to be appreciated. The Regulator wants control. The Analyzer wants accuracy. The Cooperator wants to be liked. These are hidden agendas that aren't stated directly.

More specifically, the term "hidden agenda" refers to tangible, or more subtle exchange-oriented transactions, such as:

- A politician who wants you to vote for them when they help you.
- A friend who compliments others because he or she wants to receive compliments.
- Someone who offers to come to your house and help you with something because he or she wants to date you.

Your goal is to identify your clients' hidden agendas—the things they seek from the salon experience aside from a good haircut, perm, facial, or manicure.

Some possible hidden agendas are:

- Respect
- Companionship
- Free samples
- Relaxation
- Image advice
- Caring
- An ear for their troubles
- Peace and quiet

Asking questions can help you "read" the agendas that may be hidden behind your client's words, body language, or facial expressions.

By understanding hidden agendas, you'll be better able to fulfill client needs, meet expectations, and manage client relationships.

One common hidden agenda is privacy or confidentiality. Your clients share confidences with you. Take care not to betray one client's confidence with gossip to another. Hidden or not, respect for privacy is an agenda of utmost importance. Maintain the highest ethical standards with all of your clients, and you will reap the rewards of their trust.

## EXERCISE

Think of several people that you know and interact with. Choose at least one person and identify at least three of their different hidden agendas. Be sure that one of those hidden agendas has to do with something they want from you, and that one of the other hidden agendas has to do with a personal desire. Then do the exercise for yourself.

| Name | Hidden Agendas |
|---|---|
| 1. ______________ | a. ______________ |
| | b. ______________ |
| | c. ______________ |
| 2. ______________ | a. ______________ |
| | b. ______________ |
| | c. ______________ |
| 3. ______________ | a. ______________ |
| | b. ______________ |
| | c. ______________ |
| 4. Yourself | a. ______________ |
| | b. ______________ |
| | c. ______________ |

**Greeting repeat clients can be an adventure in human relations, providing an opportunity to interact with a wide variety of people and personalities. Greeting tests your ability to simultaneously maintain rapport with someone in your chair, welcome another, shift styles and re-establish rapport.**

## Greeting the Repeat Client

Every time you see a client, you have a chance to learn more about that person and to develop your relationship.

If you are not the one to provide the reception or initial greeting, do not assume that the client has already been successfully greeted. Take the responsibility for the greeting yourself. You need to do it anyway, even for repeat customers, with whom you must reestablish rapport each and every time they return to your salon.

A successful Greeting Phase and greeting interaction dissolves the distance between you and your client. Sometimes, a simple hello may be enough to re-establish rapport. Other times, you may need to re-establish rapport by extending the interaction and chatting for some time.

## Greeting Each Personality Style

Your greetings, too, can begin through a wide range of welcomes. The establishment of rapport presents you endless opportunities to style shift, especially if you begin by taking your client's personality style into account.

## In the Salon. . .

One world-class Master stylist who provided input into the *People Skills* program spent three weeks a month in Hollywood and one week a month in Chicago. His clientele had been with him for years. Some clients paid top dollar to bring him back from Los Angeles to Chicago each month.

He was truly a Master at style shifting. He welcomed a parade of clients with greetings ranging from warm hugs and sweet welcomes to brusque, efficient service—even occasional greetings that seemed aggressive and rude.

His most impressive talent, however, was not the wide range of behavior that he demonstrated, but the common element of deep rapport and partnership that he established with such a wide variety of greetings and clients.

**Greet the Cooperator in a warm and caring manner and expect them to ask about you.**

## Greeting the Cooperator

For the Cooperator, the Greeting begins with the warm, caring contact of the welcome. Though it is important to show caring with all styles, this is essential with Cooperators. That may mean letting the Cooperators ask questions about your life or you asking about them and their life. In either case, you are establishing rapport and taking the next step in your relationship adventure.

Because the Cooperator is concerned primarily with feelings, you may want to ask, "How have you been?" This question to establish rapport after the welcome is both non-threatening and non-critical, which are two important considerations when dealing with the Cooperator.

### Improper Greeting of a Cooperator

Paul, the stylist, is busy when Georgia arrives. He's not ready to pay attention to her yet. What do you think of his welcome and rapport?

**Georgia:** Hi Paul. How are you doing?

**Paul:** Oh, hi Georgia. Umm, I'm fine. Have a seat. I'm busy right now. I'll be right with you. I'll be finished with this soon.

**Georgia:** Oh, I understand. Take your time.

**Paul:** Yeah. OK.

Paul's welcome is perfunctory and makes no effort to establish rapport with Georgia. He shows no concern for how Georgia may be feeling as she waits. Because Georgia shies from conflict, she doesn't acknowledge how upset she may be with Paul's lack of regard, unlike an Energizer. While Paul's greeting is a problem with all styles, it is particularly harsh for the Cooperator. It may not cause her to quit booking appointments with him now, but it certainly adds to the likelihood of her leaving in the long run.

As a Cooperator, Georgia wants to feel cared about and treated with sincerity. If treated coldly, she will feel hurt but is not likely to mention it—she just won't come back again.

### Proper Greeting of a Cooperator

Here's the same situation with a Greeting that works for Georgia's personality style.

**Georgia:** Hi Paul. How are you?

**Paul:** Hi Georgia. I'm fine. How are you doing today?

**Georgia:** Very well, thanks.

**Paul:** Good, I've been looking forward to seeing you, but I have one thing to finish before we get started. Please have a seat in the chair, and I'll be right with you.

**Georgia:** No problem. Take your time.

In this situation, the outcome may have sounded the same, but chances are that Georgia will feel more acknowledged by the regard Paul showed by asking her a simple question. This greeting will work well with all personality styles.

Energizer salon professional warmly greets a Cooperator client.

**With the Analyzer, remember that time is important. If you are late, acknowledge it as a way to establish rapport.**

## Greeting the Analyzer

It is critical to remember the importance of precision and timing to the Analyzer. If you are behind on your schedule, be certain to acknowledge this to establish rapport.

Of course, that's a good practice regardless of the client's personality style, but it's particularly important for the Analyzer. Analyzer clients will become upset and agitated if you keep them waiting, though they are not likely to say anything.

Because the Analyzer is more concerned with thinking than with feelings, you may want to ask questions more along the lines of, "What's been on your mind today?" The Analyzer is more likely to feel in rapport with this type of question than one about how he or she is feeling. Don't worry if you don't get much of an answer, however, especially if you happen to be an Energizer salon professional. Remember that the Analyzer client will often seem aloof or withdrawn and will provide you with less of the positive reflection that you seek.

### Improper Greeting of an Analyzer

Paul, the stylist, is running late and still has something to finish when Juan arrives. What do you think of his welcome and rapport?

**Paul:** Hi, Juan. I can't believe it's time already. Have a seat. I'm very behind. I'll be with you just as soon as I finish this one thing.

**Juan:** OK.

Juan may say, "OK," but as an Analyzer he probably doesn't like it, especially because Paul made little effort to acknowledge his lateness. Like the Cooperator, the Analyzer wants to avoid conflict. But because Analyzers are concerned with time, Paul's lateness is likely to cause Juan distress. Chances are he will spend his time waiting for Paul by looking at his watch every minute or so.

A salon professional shouldn't take the Analyzer's apparent coldness personally.

### Proper Greeting of an Analyzer

As an Analyzer, Juan is detail and fact-oriented. He likely wants to know exactly what's going on and what will happen. If he doesn't, he feels anxious, though he is likely to express it through silence and withdrawal.

Here's the same situation with a Greeting that works for Juan's personality style.

**Paul:** Hi Juan. It's nice to see you.

**Juan:** Thanks. Same here.

**Paul:** I apologize for the inconvenience. I'm running about 10 minutes late right now. I have a color to apply, and we'll get started as soon as I finish.

**Juan:** No problem. I brought some work with me, and I'll do that until you're ready.

By letting Juan know approximately how long he would have to wait and what was going on, Paul established rapport. He allowed Juan to relax, which will make the rest of the service a more pleasant experience for both of them.

This approach to dealing with lateness works well with all styles. Add an excited statement for the Energizer, an even more acknowledged apology for the Regulator, and a warm personal acknowledgment for the Cooperator.

**Regulator clients want to get right down to business. Make direct eye contact, shake hands firmly, and get started.**

## Greeting the Regulator

Like the Analyzer, the Regulator client is concerned about time. Unlike the Analyzer, they're more likely to enter the salon with a no-nonsense attitude. Cooperator professionals need to pay close attention or face the discomfort of being bowled over by the Regulator's brusque, aggressive manner.

Remember that the Regulator client may want to get right down to business, and it is entirely possible that you will move swiftly through the Greeting to the Assessment, Agreement, and Delivery Phases. They would likely even hit fast-forward to rush through Delivery if they could.

### Improper Greeting of a Regulator

Paul, the stylist, is busy when Anthony arrives. He's running late. Anthony has the receptionist page Paul.

**Anthony:** Paul, you're late, and I'm in a real hurry today.

**Paul:** I know, but I just have one thing to finish, and I'll be right with you. Just have a seat.

**Anthony:** No. We've got to get started now.

**Paul:** I'm sorry, but you'll just have to wait. . .

Here we see the beginning of a control struggle most common with the Regulator. Anthony is not likely to stay, and even if he does, it is likely to be tense. As a Regulator, Anthony wants to feel like he has control over the situation and will have his needs met. Paul has shown no sign or concern to complete the job quickly. He establishes no rapport as a result.

### *Proper Greeting of a Regulator*

As a Regulator, Anthony values action. In this situation, he wants to know that he is respected and the job will get done quickly, or he will likely let his displeasure be known.

Here's the same situation with a Greeting that works for Anthony's personality style.

**Anthony:** Paul, you're late, and I'm in a real hurry today.

**Paul:** Yes, I noticed when I heard the page. I apologize for the inconvenience. Can you give me a few minutes? I'm not quite ready yet, but I've made arrangements for your shampoo to begin while I'm finishing up so we can get right down to work. Is that OK?

**Anthony:** Yes, that works for me, as long as you let the person know I'm in a hurry.

**Paul:** No problem. Let's get started. I'll be finished by the time you're in my chair.

**Anthony:** Good. Let's go. . .

By responding to Anthony's urgency with action, Paul has allowed Anthony to relax in the knowledge that he will be served quickly. Paul has established rapport in a difficult situation.

Stylist and receptionist chat while Regulator client waits to be served.

**Greet the Energizer with enthusiasm and find out how they are feeling and what's new. You may find that you have the widest range of greeting opportunities with the Energizer.**

## Greeting the Energizer

The Energizer may well present the widest range of greeting opportunities. The arrival of the Energizer can be exciting, uplifting, and very challenging.

Remember that the Energizer finds it very important to be liked or appreciated and enjoys liking other people. Remain flexible when greeting the Energizer. They often react much more immediately and strongly than the Cooperator or Analyzer.

In the Greeting Phase, after the welcome, ask the Energizer how they are feeling. This is very useful to establish rapport. The following interaction to establish rapport is generally essential. You may want to ask, "What's new?" If the client has faced an upset before his or her arrival, be sensitive to their need to vent.

### Improper Greeting of an Energizer

Paul, the stylist, is busy when Mary arrives. He's not ready to pay attention to her yet. What do you think of his welcome and rapport?

**Mary:** Hi Paul! How are you?

**Paul:** Oh, hi Mary. Umm, I'm fine. Have a seat. I'm busy right now.

**Mary:** Oh, I can't wait to see how you're going to do my hair for Mary's wedding! I'm so excited.

**Paul:** Yeah. I know. Just have a seat and I'll be right with you.

**Mary:** Well Paul, where is the book with the picture of the style you are going to give me?

**Paul:** I don't know right now. I mean, just have a seat over there and I'll…

**Mary:** Well, I'm important too, you know.

Obviously, Paul hasn't done much to welcome Mary, and rapport is certainly missing. While this greeting would not work well with any style, it is especially grating to the Energizer. Paul wants something and Mary wants something else. Mary's hidden agenda of wanting appreciation is ignored. Worse yet, Paul ignores her repeated attempts to correct the situation.

### Proper Greeting of an Energizer

As an Energizer, Mary is very verbal and fast-acting. She wants to be listened to. She wants to be noticed, appreciated, and respected. If treated with disinterest, she will feel rejected—and may well reject the salon.

Here's the same situation with a Greeting that works for Mary's personality style. It takes almost the same amount of time to provide a much stronger greeting and rapport.

**Mary:** Hi Paul. How are you?

**Paul:** Hi Mary. I'm fine. How about you?

**Mary:** Well, I'm really good. I'm so glad to see you.

**Paul:** Good, I'm glad to see you, too. I can't wait to talk with you. But you know, I've just got to finish this one thing before we get started. Why don't you have a seat in the chair, get ready to fill me in, and I'll be right with you!

**Mary:** Oh, OK. I'm excited to see how you're going to do my hair for the wedding.

**Paul:** Alright. I'm excited, too. I've been planning it and I have the sample design photos with me, but I gotta finish this. It will just take me a minute.

**Mary:** Good! Good, Paul. Great.

**Paul:** OK, I'll be right over.

**Mary:** Thanks.

**Paul:** Great.

Next, you will learn about the second phase of service in Lesson 7.2, *Assessment Phase.*

## EXERCISES

1. Think of a service experience you have had where you felt things went wrong at the Greeting Phase. Describe briefly what happened and how the service professional could have managed the Greeting Phase more successfully.

______________________________________________

______________________________________________

______________________________________________

2. Observe other service professionals in action—designers, waitresses, and store clerks, for example. Study their eye contact, gestures, conversation, grooming and dress. "Grade" each privately in his or her ability to establish rapport, and make notes about their service skills that will be of value to you.

   a. Profession: ______________________________

      Eye contact: ______________________________

      Gestures: ______________________________

      Conversation: ______________________________

      Grooming: ______________________________

      Dress: ______________________________

   b. Profession: ______________________________

      Eye contact: ______________________________

      Gestures: ______________________________

      Conversation: ______________________________

      Grooming: ______________________________

      Dress: ______________________________

   c. Profession: ______________________________

      Eye contact: ______________________________

      Gestures: ______________________________

      Conversation: ______________________________

      Grooming: ______________________________

      Dress: ______________________________

3. Complete the following three Greeting Phase scenarios, describing how you would act and what you would say in each situation with each of the four client personality patterns.

A. You are expecting a new client whom you have not met, and you are running late. The receptionist is away from the reception desk on an errand, and you see someone you do not recognize sitting in the waiting area. It might be your new client. Complete the Greeting Phase:

Cooperator:________________________________________

________________________________________________

Analyzer:_________________________________________

________________________________________________

Regulator:________________________________________

________________________________________________

Energizer:________________________________________

________________________________________________

B. You are running 10 minutes late, working furiously to catch up. Your next client comes out of the waiting area, and walks up to your station frowning. Complete the Greeting Phase:

Cooperator:________________________________________

________________________________________________

Analyzer:_________________________________________

________________________________________________

Regulator:________________________________________

________________________________________________

Energizer:________________________________________

________________________________________________

C. It is pouring rain outside. You hear a squeal of tires in the parking lot and glance out the salon window to see two clients narrowly miss having an accident in their separate cars. Your next client emerges from one of the cars and walks into the salon dripping wet and muttering under his breath. Complete the following Greeting Phase:

Cooperator:________________________________________

________________________________________________

Analyzer:________________________________________

______________________________________________

Regulator:_______________________________________

______________________________________________

Energizer:_______________________________________

______________________________________________

4. Talk about salon professionals you have had who were good greeters. What made them good? List at least three of their personal characteristics or details of their greeting:

______________________________________________

______________________________________________

______________________________________________

______________________________________________

______________________________________________

## MAIN POINT SUMMARY

The first phase of service is the Greeting Phase, and it is your opportunity to establish or reestablish rapport with clients. The Greeting consists of the welcome followed by interaction to establish rapport.

It is important to be aware of clients' hidden agendas, to make a preliminary assessment of their needs, and to allay any fears or concerns they may have.

You can avoid problems later on by establishing what the client's mood and expectations are during your greeting and adapting your approach accordingly. Personality styles offer clues to a client's state of mind and expectations, but it is critical that you listen to what your client is saying (directly or indirectly) and remain mindful of their concerns.

Be aware that the new client will have expectations and needs that differ from those of the returning client. The Cooperator, the Analyzer, the Regulator, and the Energizer all have unique concerns, expectations and hidden agendas that you can anticipate. Your greeting should always express an awareness of these concerns, and begin the encounter by putting the client at ease. This will make the service most productive for everyone and build healthy relationships for the future.

## Greeting Phase Technique Review

| Type of Client | Level of Service | Actions to Take |
|---|---|---|
| **Repeat** | • Same | • Greet as you normally would, according to the client's personality style. |
| | • Modify | • Remind client during the Greeting Phase that you two are planning on refining the client's look. This generates anticipation in the client. |
| | • Makeover | • Greet with anticipation and maybe even delight, depending on the client's personality style. Prepare the client even during Greeting for the results they can expect and the depth of work you both have planned. |
| **New** | • Same | • Greet as you normally would for the first time, according to the client's personality style. |
| | • Modify | • Talk to the client about refining their looks in keeping with their lifestyle only if mentioned by the client. Prepare the client for the Assessment Phase. |
| | • Makeover | • Find out who referred the client for the makeover. Let the client know how the makeover process works, and explain what will happen in each phase in order to put him or her at ease right right away. |

## SELF-TEST/REVIEW

1. What does the Greeting Phase begin and end with?

________________________________________

________________________________________

________________________________________

________________________________________

2. What are two ways to greet a client who is obviously in a bad mood?

   1. ______________________________________

   ________________________________________

   2. ______________________________________

   ________________________________________

3. Complete this equation: W ____________ + R ____________ = Greeting

4. What is a hidden agenda? Give some examples.

   Definition: ______________________________

   Examples:

   1. ______________________________
   2. ______________________________
   3. ______________________________

5. Is the Greeting Phase necessary with repeat clients? Explain your answer.

   ______________________________

   ______________________________

   ______________________________

6. List three things to do or consider when you greet a Cooperator:

   1. ______________________________
   2. ______________________________
   3. ______________________________

7. When greeting an Analyzer, it is critical to remember the importance of

   ______________ and ______________.

8. Since Regulators usually want to get down to business, it is okay to skip over the Greeting Phase with them. Why or why not?
   Circle One:

   True or False

   ______________________________

   ______________________________

9. What are three things to keep in mind when greeting an Energizer?

   1. ______________________________
   2. ______________________________
   3. ______________________________

Lesson 7.2

# Assessment Phase

Assessment Phase

**The Assessment Phase consists of Consultation plus Listening. This is the creative phase, where you learn about your clients and their desires.**

## OBJECTIVES

At the completion of this lesson, you will be able to:

- Describe the Assessment Phase
- Discuss how to assess existing clients and determine if they are ready for a new style
- Demonstrate how to use the New Client Assessment Questionnaire
- Explain how to manage clients' anxiety and resistance

## WHAT YOU NEED TO KNOW

The second service phase, the Assessment Phase, consists of sensitive consultation, in which you ask probing questions to better understand the client's needs and desires. An **assessment** uncovers the information salon professionals need to help clients create a self-image consistent with their lifestyle and, ultimately, their dreams. During an assessment, you probe to identify the client's:

- Likes
- Dislikes
- Dreams
- Lifestyle
- Family background
- Work style
- Past salon experiences
- Self-perception and perception of others

Assessment builds on the rapport you began developing in the Greeting Phase. Thorough, effective assessment eases the way through the remainder of the Service Cycle. This enables you to reach decisions about each client's service program and to propose the proper schedule of services.

Even if the client simply wants the same hair design, nail, or skin care service as the last time, the Assessment Phase includes an update on the person's lifestyle. Most clients will appreciate your interest in their thoughts and feelings. They may also grow to think of you as a trusted advisor and consultant.

## Assessment Don'ts

To appreciate the power of a proper Assessment Phase, let's look at the absurdities of Salon Calimité, where service, at best, is an afterthought.

### Salon Calimité. . .

Salon Calimité employees can hardly be called professionals. Let's refer to them as staff. Nowhere can their unprofessional behavior be better seen than in the Assessment Phase. In routine service, they hardly talk to the client as they point to the chair, treating the customer like an imposition. They are too busy "listening" to the story of each other's last date to do much more than say, "Sit down and let's get started."

On one particularly slow Tuesday, they let the receptionist go to the beach. When Mrs. Johnson arrived, Sandy was sitting in the chair and Marie was doing her nails, while Andrea, Mrs. Johnson's stylist, was redoing her makeup in the mirror.

"Just sit down," Andrea said, as she continued talking about the fellow she'd dated the previous night. Mrs. Johnson was uncomfortable walking through the hair on the floor on her way to the chair, but even more appalling was Andrea's assumption that she knew exactly what Mrs. Johnson wanted. Rather than asking, Andrea sent Mrs. Johnson directly to the shampoo station, without introducing her to Sandy, who performed the shampoo.

The final straw was the rapid questions Andrea asked without allowing time for Mrs. Johnson to reply. Andrea heard "shorter" and promptly cut Mrs. Johnson's hair just like her previous client. Mrs. Johnson was not happy. Andrea's lack of attention showed the worst of the Assessment Phase—but that's the norm at Salon Calimité.

## Assessment Techniques

The techniques you use during the Assessment Phase become more sophisticated as your experience grows. As you progress in your career, you will learn how to ask the right questions to gain the information you need.

### Novice Assessment

Novices are developing the discipline of performing complete assessments. However, they are more likely to duplicate a previous service. Novices ask probing questions in a relatively formal manner, as they are building their knowledge base and learning to make basic connections between needs and lifestyle, such as an easy-care hair design for a busy mother. With existing clients, the Novice is beginning to understand how self-esteem, image, lifestyle, and beauty care can influence one another.

**While all trained salon professionals do makeovers at the most advanced levels, the Assessment Phase results in a total makeover that transforms a client's look, sense of self-esteem and personal image. That's mastery!**

## Professional Assessment

Professionals use the Assessment Phase as a way to go deeper into rapport and support the client's lifestyle through salon care. Professionals conscientiously question new clients to learn the details of their lifestyles and maintenance habits, and use their listening skills to hear the deeper information in the answers. With existing clients, Professionals may easily suggest how changes could support lifestyle. They can make those suggestions because they develop increasingly personal relationships with clients over time and can glean lifestyle changes through the natural flow of conversation.

## Master Assessment

Master salon professionals manage the Assessment Phase with grace and ease. Their understanding of beauty and technique makes them agents of personal transformation. For new clients, Master salon professionals ask about a client's life so naturally that clients may be unaware they are being questioned. Masters know their existing clients intimately and understand how changes in clients' lives should be reflected in their image. At this level, the salon professional gives advice to clients not only on hair, nail, and skin care but also on their self-esteem through a more thorough grasp of total image, including clothes, demeanor, and presentation. The Master professional becomes an ongoing guide for the client on the journey of personal image evolution and the development of self-esteem.

## In the Salon. . .

Judith was wed to her long hair. She grew up in the '60s and '70s in the U.S., when long-haired singer Joni Mitchell caught the imagination of many youths. She thought long hair was important to maintain her femininity.

Judith is a Cooperator-Energizer, and change in this area was particularly difficult for her, as it is for many who identify strongly with the style of a particular time and its cultural icons.

Judith's salon professional, a Master, saw something more. He saw a way to bring out her natural beauty by shortening her hair. During his assessment, he talked to her about a plan to move her toward short hair.

Seeing her discomfort, he recommended that the design he had in mind could be reached in stages over the next year. She could gradually get used to shorter hair, and stop along the way, if necessary. This Master designer did not secure her agreement for the entire makeover, but by the time they had worked for a year together, Judith wore her short platinum hair with pleasure and pride.

Cooperator salon professional shows Energizer client different looks while assessing her style.

## Conducting an Assessment

Many salon professionals acquire consulting skills naturally and easily. Most of those attracted to the salon profession are, after all, "people people." Others need to practice consulting with people. Just as your technical skills improve over time, with practice you can improve your communication skills—including the art of consultation.

Assessments can range in length from a few words with a regular client to an in-depth consultation on the first visit.

Between an experienced salon professional and a long-time client, the Assessment Phase might seem minor. It can be as short as, "What are we going to do differently today?" What is not seen behind that simple, straightforward question are the years of successful consultations.

Take time in this phase of the Service Cycle. You might want to book an extra time slot for first-time services. Listen carefully to your clients' opinions. Make sure you understand both the facts and their feelings. Really get them talking. Because you might also be doing a lot of talking during the Assessment Phase, be especially alert to the client's nonverbal behavior to see how they are reacting to what you are saying.

Before proceeding, let your clients know that you understand and accept them. The rapport you establish by using your listening skills during the Assessment Phase will be invaluable in the remaining phases of the Service Cycle.

To fully understand the Assessment Phase, it helps to understand the three ways salon professionals consult with clients. They serve as:

1. Service consultants
2. Product consultants
3. Image consultants

Ask questions to find out your client's likes and dislikes.

All salon professionals, at every level of professional development, serve in those three consulting capacities. The difference is in the degree of skill and the years of experience that a salon professional brings to the task.

## 1. Service Consultant

All salon professionals, from Novice to Master, serve as a styling and service consultant, whether they do nails, skin and makeup, or hair. Even when simply maintaining a client's existing look, you are a service consultant. You owe it to your client to assess their needs and share your knowledge with them.

Service consultants ask clients about the history of their service, what they have liked the best, and when they have been disappointed. They also discuss services that clients need for maintenance.

As a service consultant, you are learning more about clients' tastes and maintenance habits and gathering information you will need in later phases of the Service Cycle to determine what will best serve your clients. After learning about the client's habits, for instance, you may recommend during the Completion Phase that clients re-book sooner in order to maintain their look.

## 2. Product Consultant

One of the major mistakes that salon professionals make, from Novice to Master, is failing to discover what products the client is using and what care techniques the client uses at home. Use the "New Client Assessment Questionnaire" at the end of this lesson to determine your client's product and maintenance habits. Do clients buy product because of convenience, price, or the chemical qualities of the product? Knowing the answers to such questions allows you to satisfy your client during the Recommendation Phase.

Remember that during the Assessment Phase, you are not selling products but rather gathering the information may help you make recommendations later.

Consulting with clients on products is one of the most valuable services a salon professional can offer.

### 3. Image Consultant

At its highest level of mastery, the Assessment Phase provides a challenge to literally transform a client's life and self-image. When you work collaboratively with clients to transform their total image, you serve as an agent of change in their lives.

Some image consultants involve clients by having them look for images they like and clip photos from magazines. You can also use style books to come up with ideas and possibilities. For example, Pivot Point's *Design Forum* provides a constantly updated resource for fashion, hair, and makeup styles

Keep in mind that many clients have difficulty seeing themselves as beautiful or glamorous as the photos in *Design Forum*, but they can realize their full potential if guided sensitively and expertly.

The woman below, a Cooperator, had little idea of the beauty and grace she could exude. In her waiting room photo, she has the pleasant but somewhat shy look of the Cooperator. After her makeover, she comes across as much more powerful and confident.

Many salon professionals who are image consultants work with entertainment and sports stars, corporate executives, and political leaders. However, that isn't the only audience for image consulting. You can make a tremendous difference in the appearance and attitudes of anyone. That's what Master professionals are able to achieve.

The Energizer below was willing to listen to his salon professional's assessment. The result is a clear win: a flexible style that can work in a wider variety of situations and events.

You may need to nudge your clients a little to bring out aspects of their personality that they may not display on their own. The client here often shows the harried Analyzer and Regulator aspects of her personality style. In her makeover, the designer brought out the softer, more professional side of her two personality styles.

Don't be afraid to bring in salon professionals who specialize in areas other than your own for their opinion when doing an image assessment.

## In the Salon . . .

Paul Glick

The late Paul Glick, who helped originate the *People Skills* program, was a master at the Assessment Phase. For instance, on one occasion he interviewed a television personality who was new to the Chicago scene. Paul sensitively discussed the man's receding hairline and how he was attempting to cover it with long, bushy hair.

Paul's rapport with this man was very strong. Paul talked with him about how his hair hid his strongest features, such as his jawline. Paul said he wanted to focus the look on the man's face.

In the end, the man gladly took the risk of having his hair cut to three-quarters of an inch. He walked out of Paul's salon radiant and self-confident. It is no wonder that the list of personalities visiting Paul continued to grow, ranging from Princess Diana to Oprah Winfrey. Additionally, Paul had a column in the *Chicago Sun Times* newspaper and a radio show. He also made numerous television appearances.

Eventually, Paul quit cutting hair altogether so that he could further develop his image and presentation business. He spent the final years of his life working as an artist in Santa Fe, New Mexico, where he reaped the fruits of a most remarkable career in the salon industry. All these possibilities await you too. Although you may not wish to attain the level of professional service that Paul reached, you most certainly would be thrilled to touch your clients in such meaningful ways.

**Applying your consultation skills helps you build trust and rapport with clients. Along with listening carefully, consultation skills will put you on the road to mastering Assessment.**

## Consultation and Assessment

Sensitive consultation helps put your clients at ease and gains access to valuable information. Consultation consists of asking careful, probing questions to improve your understanding of each client. You listen factually and with feeling, using the skills for effective listening: responding, acceptance/understanding, and paying attention.

From the first moment you ask a client what he or she would like in the Assessment Phase, you are learning consulting skills. Consulting skills are service skills that aim to uncover what the client wants.

Consulting skills begin with rapport and understanding. The more you ask clients what they want and how they feel about your work, the more they see you as their consultant. The depth to which you can take clients will vary with your ability to listen and build trust.

Your mastery of people skills and your skill in paying attention to personality style, lifestyle, and image building form the foundation for your consultation skills.

Overcoming physical, emotional, and mental boundaries, as well as knowing your client's comfort zone are critical Assessment Phase skills.

## *Overcoming Boundaries*

Consultation helps you overcome boundaries between you and your clients and allows you to understand each other more completely, but it must be done in a way that doesn't appear to violate a client's sense of privacy. Boundaries between people can be physical, emotional, or mental.

**Physical boundaries** include the distance two people stand from each other. In some cultures, people require less space around them than in other cultures. Some people prefer to maintain more physical distance and refrain from physical contact, except with close friends.

**Emotional boundaries** define limits of personal sharing and expressing. If you push too hard, you may prevent clients from opening up and sharing their feelings.

**Mental boundaries** are the attitudes, perceptions, and prejudices that divide people. Watch carefully that you do not initiate conversation in any areas such as politics, religion, gender and race. If a client starts a conversation that involves any of these topics, be more of a listener and keep the conversation professional. This means you should try not to engage or give your opinion, but stay neutral. There are plenty of friendly ways to participate in conversation without crossing the line. A client who strongly disagrees with a sensitive subject may be as close as the next chair, and may be offended.

## *Crossing into the Comfort Zone*

Not all people have the same physical, emotional, and mental boundaries. The "distance" we maintain between ourselves and others is called our comfort zone.

With strangers, we are more likely to maintain a larger comfort zone, keeping more distance between us. We let friends come closer. Being in rapport helps decrease the physical, emotional, and mental distances between you and others.

As a member of a personal service profession, you are often allowed to cross into comfort zones that others may not be allowed to cross into. Some clients will tell you things they tell no one else. Remember, you have the right to set your boundaries, too. If a client veers into a conversation that makes you uncomfortable, gently change the subject.

Analyzer clients may be uncomfortable with even the tamest suggestions made by the Energizer salon professional.

Be aware of the responsibilities that result from crossing into the comfort zones of others. Your actions, behavior, and attitude will help maintain a delicate balance of friendly professionalism. Once clients feel accepted as they are with close friends and family members, they will tend to cross some boundaries. It is up to you to keep a comfortable professional relationship.

## SERVICE CHALLENGE

**How do you and your client react when you cross too far into your client's comfort zone?**

**You may get physically closer than your client likes or ask more personal questions than they are comfortable with. When this occurs, some people withdraw, while others might get angry. As a nervous reaction, some clients may actually talk more when they become uncomfortable.**

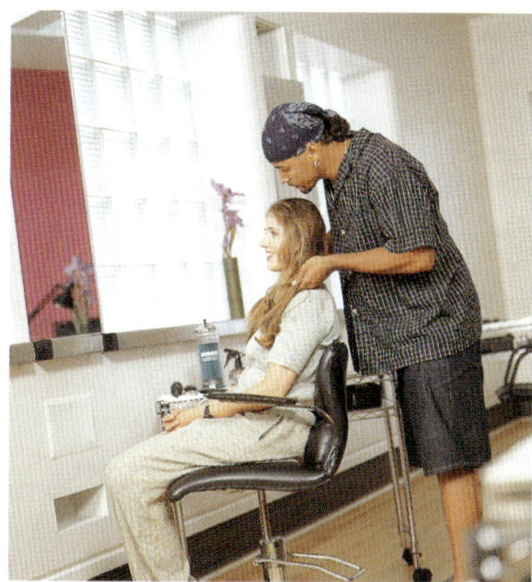

**Observe your clients carefully. Be in tune with their signals. Respect their limits. It may help to think about your own limits and how you react when someone crosses, uninvited, into your comfort zone.**

**If you do cross into their comfort zone and cause discomfort, withdraw, keep working and observe. This may be sufficient. If you feel the need to, do not hesitate to apologize.**

## Assessing a New Client

The Assessment Phase is particularly important with new clients. This is the first opportunity you will have to learn about their unique needs, wants, and concerns. Aside from the initial greeting, it is also your first chance to discover their personality style and begin building rapport. Take your time, and try to learn as much as possible about them and their lifestyle so you can plan the best course of action.

**Use your knowledge of the personality styles to listen to your clients during the Assessment Phase.**

Listen to your client. Make sure that you understand the facts and their feelings by using repetition and paraphrasing. If you approach the Assessment Phase with the goal of establishing and maintaining rapport, the client will tell you everything you need to know in order to serve them well.

Many designers make the mistake of never learning important facts. They may create a wonderful style for the client, but when the client cannot maintain it at home, the client may become disillusioned and never return to the salon.

Cooperator clients often respond well to a friendly but firm approach. Cooperator clients are not as likely to change styles and tend to be slow in considering new options. It may take several visits to complete an assessment.

## Assessing the Cooperator

| Personality Style | Common Challenges | Overcoming Challenges |
|---|---|---|
| **Cooperator** | • Tends to be less verbal. | • Make an extra effort to get Cooperator clients talking. |
| | • Most likely to go along with a change for which they are not ready. | • Remember that it may take several visits to make a change. |
| | • Likely to be slow in considering options and making decisions. | • Watch to make sure your client is not overwhelmed by your questions. |

Analyzer clients tend to be the most conservative and least likely to change. Move slowly and maintain rapport with Analyzer clients by covering details. Be prepared for questions.

## Assessing the Analyzer

| Personality Style | Common Challenges | Overcoming Challenges |
|---|---|---|
| **Analyzer** | • Tends to be less verbal. | • Make an effort to get the Analyzer talking, but don't push. |
| | • Generally want to consider all options. | • Move slowly in order to maintain rapport. |
| | • Detail-oriented. | • Try to provide as many details as you can about each new service. Say why certain options are preferable, based on specific hair, nail or skin needs. |
| | • Wants to know why. | • Be prepared to answer a variety of questions once you get your Analyzer clients talking. |

Regulator clients tend to want to remain in control. Ask what they want, listen carefully, and maintain a professional demeanor. In assessing Regulator clients, plan for timely service. Ask what they want, and use your listening skills so you can deliver.

## Assessing the Regulator

| Personality Style | Common Challenges | Overcoming Challenges |
|---|---|---|
| **Regulator** | • Efficient, timely service is generally of the essence. | • Strike a balance between thorough planning and efficiency. Regulators generally require less detail than Analyzers. |
| | • Tends to want to remain in control. | • Ask what they want. Use your listening skills to draw out their fullest expectations.<br>• Ask about their previous salon experiences, both good and bad. Those experiences tell you what they perceive as essential for satisfaction and what to avoid. |

Energizer clients may be your most exciting clients during the Assessment Phase. They can be the most fun of all of your clients. But they will talk about option after option. Allow their creativity to flow, but help them decide by moving more slowly and directing them.

## Assessing the Energizer

| Personality Style | Common Challenges | Overcoming Challenges |
|---|---|---|
| **Energizer** | • Tends to be full of possibilities and ideas. | • Help them to establish lifestyle needs as basis for changes. |
| | • Enthusiastic about an idea initially, but may feel remorse about it later on. | • Encourage Energizer clients to think about flamboyant color changes or other drastic styles between visits, rather than making a spontaneous decision. |
| | • Assessment may seem to never end. | • Allow Assessment to take place over several visits, and go with the client's flow! |

**Analyzers, Cooperators, and Regulators are likely to be your most routine clients. Be sensitive to the client's thoughts and feelings during a routine assessment and don't pressure them to make a change they are not ready for.**

### *Using the Personality Styles as a Guide with New Clients*

The Assessment Phase presents unique challenges and opportunities when you are dealing with a client for the first time. Not only do you need to learn enough about their needs and desires to form a plan, but you also have to uncover their personality style and determine how you can best maintain rapport throughout the remaining phases.

When you go through the "New Client Assessment Questionnaire" (it appears at the end of the lesson) with your client, listen for clues that might suggest a primary or secondary personality style. Once you start to sense a personality style, use that information to improve your assessment of the client.

Establishing rapport at this stage is critical because you gain the credibility you may need to establish mutually rewarding rapport. It will also be invaluable should problems arise with any aspect of service.

## *Existing Clients — Routine Assessment*

As a salon professional, you will encounter many clients who want basically the same style or service every time. It may be that their lifestyle requires them to have an unchanging, conservative style. Or maybe they have found what works for them, and they don't want to risk dissatisfaction with something new.

Whatever their reasoning, you should always be sensitive to the thoughts and feelings of routine existing clients. Be careful not to pressure them into making a change that they are not ready for. But do not assume they want exactly what they received in the past.

Keep in mind that you are still assessing the client's wants and needs. The Assessment Phase for routine clients, at minimum, consists of asking about their experience with the service from their previous visit.

You can ask something as simple as, "What service would you like me to do today?" That's a good way to find out if they want to stay with the same or try something new without putting any pressure on them.

With regular clients, you may want to say something like, "So, would you like the usual?" That lets them know you remember what they have liked in the past and that you are willing and able to recreate the same.

### *Analyzers and Regulators — Routine Assessment*

Typically, Analyzers and Regulators are most likely to be routine clients.

- **Analyzers** are often conservative and may be unwilling to depart from a proven service. Ask, "How do you think the last service worked for you?"

- **Regulators** may not have the time to learn about the upkeep of a new hair or nail design, or their lifestyle at work or home may not allow for much style change. Ask, "Was the last service effective at work? At home?"

Still, you may want to ask an occasional probing question during the Assessment Phase to let clients know that they have other options. By maintaining rapport with routine clients, you can sense which questions you should ask and how often you should ask them.

**Assessment that leads to a major change can be a most rewarding part of the salon experience. You begin to develop looks that support your client's lifestyle. Be sure to talk about how the client and others may react to the change.**

### *Cooperators and Energizers — Routine Assessment*

Cooperators and Energizers can also be routine clients.

- **Cooperators** might stay with the same style or service because they are not risk-takers and are not sure how a new change will make themselves or others feel. Ask, "How did you feel about the last design?"
- **Energizers** with a radical change may like the way it makes them feel and the compliments they get from others, so they may decide to keep the new look for several salon visits. Ask, "How did other people like the last look?"

Although you may have more flexibility for suggesting new options with routine Cooperator and Energizer clients, don't try too hard to change their minds or feel disappointed if they want to stay with their existing image.

## *Existing Clients — Major Change Assessment*

Some existing clients will want to change services from time to time. Others may want to try something different with each visit to the salon. Oftentimes, clients aren't exactly sure what type of new service they are looking for; they just know that they are ready for a change. Maybe they just need a subtle change, or maybe they are in the mood for something radically different.

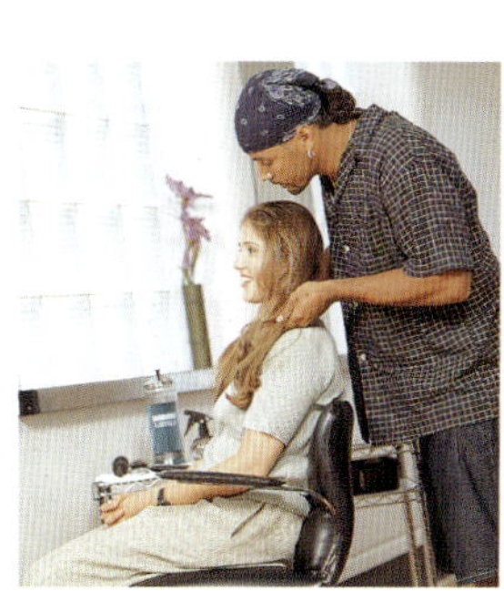

### Three Steps to Achieving a Successful Major Change Assessment

A major change assessment for existing clients will go smoothly if you follow these three steps in your assessment:

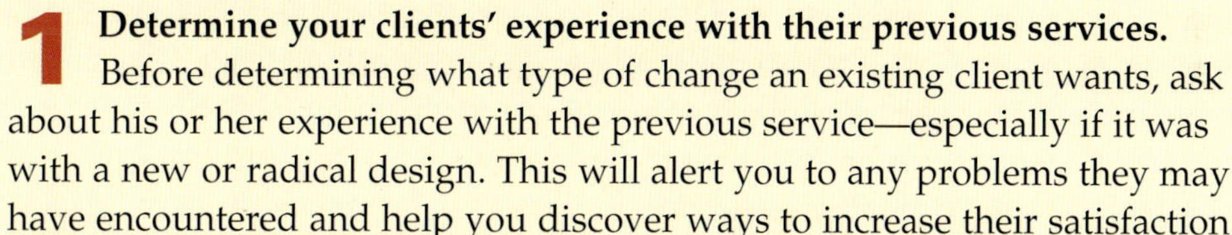

**1 Determine your clients' experience with their previous services.** Before determining what type of change an existing client wants, ask about his or her experience with the previous service—especially if it was with a new or radical design. This will alert you to any problems they may have encountered and help you discover ways to increase their satisfaction.

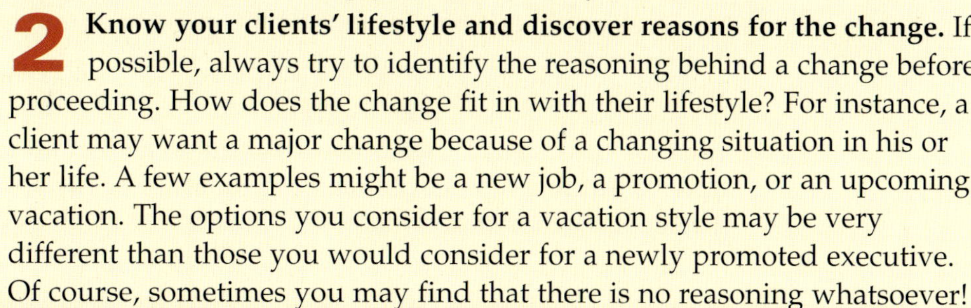

**2 Know your clients' lifestyle and discover reasons for the change.** If possible, always try to identify the reasoning behind a change before proceeding. How does the change fit in with their lifestyle? For instance, a client may want a major change because of a changing situation in his or her life. A few examples might be a new job, a promotion, or an upcoming vacation. The options you consider for a vacation style may be very different than those you would consider for a newly promoted executive. Of course, sometimes you may find that there is no reasoning whatsoever!

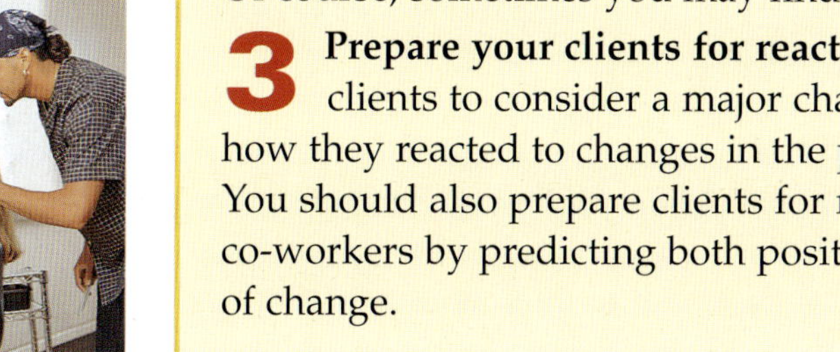

**3 Prepare your clients for reactions.** When you are helping existing clients to consider a major change, it is important to keep in mind how they reacted to changes in the past, both physically and emotionally. You should also prepare clients for reactions from their friends, family, and co-workers by predicting both positive and negative experiences as part of change.

**When you begin assessing clients, it helps to have a list of questions. Salon professionals sometimes make the mistake of never learning the facts about their clients' lives. The New Client Assessment Questionnaire helps you avoid that mistake.**

The Assessment Phase is your opportunity to discover exactly what type of changes your clients have in mind and to come up with some ideas of your own for discussion as well. It is also your opportunity to advise clients on what will make them look their best.

That may mean questioning your clients' initial desires. Suppose that a client has seen a different hair design on one of her friends, and she wants her hair to look exactly the same way. However, you know that your client's hair will not respond well to that type of style or treatment.

Based on this knowledge, you should politely educate your client and suggest an alternative that might look similar and work better. Similarly, if a client has struggled with a major color change or a drastic hair-length reduction in the past, you will definitely want to consider these emotions before proceeding with a potentially upsetting style change.

Make sure you ask clients how their previous design worked and why they want a change. In addition to helping you discover potential problems, it is a good way to let them know that you remember their previous visit. Almost all clients will feel special when they realize you haven't forgotten about them! Maintaining files for your clients will help remind you of important service details that you might otherwise naturally forget.

To aid your understanding, use the "New Client Assessment Questionnaire" to build a total hair and body care profile of your clients. When repeating a style or with a returning customer, you may be able to do it automatically throughout the Service Cycle, but never forget the final review. This form is your best reminder.

## New Client Assessment Questionnaire

The New Client Assessment Questionnaire is a powerful tool for assessing the salon service and product needs of new clients. These questions help you draw information from your clients that you can use to improve rapport and the quality of service.

Novices may find it helpful to read the questions from a form, but try to demonstrate your sincere interest in the clients' answers by maintaining eye contact throughout the consultation and by using your listening skills.

You may also want to make notes as you go along and keep them in the clients' files for future reference. Be ready to rephrase or further explain any question the clients do not understand.

## New Client Assessment Questionnaire

Name________________________________________

Personality Styles________________________________

Phone Work____________Home____________Cell__________

Marital Status_______Spouse's Name____________________

Childrens' Names__________________________________

Occupation______________________________________

Interests_______________________________________

E-mail________________________________________

### Lifestyle

Tell me some things about your life and work styles that will help me evaluate your salon needs.

How do you take care of your hair now?

________________________________________

What do you like best about your hair?

________________________________________

What kind of changes, if any, would you like to make?

________________________________________

________________________________________

________________________________________

What is important to you in caring for your hair? Nails? Skin?

________________________________________

________________________________________

________________________________________

## Image

What image would you like to project on the job? At home? In your social life?

______________________________________________

______________________________________________

What kind of look or image do you want to achieve here today?

______________________________________________

______________________________________________

## Salon Experiences

What are your likes and dislikes about salons? Salon professionals?

______________________________________________

______________________________________________

______________________________________________

What was one of your best salon experiences? Why?

______________________________________________

______________________________________________

______________________________________________

What was one of your worst salon experiences? Why?

______________________________________________

______________________________________________

______________________________________________

Why did you leave your last salon, and why did you choose ours?

______________________________________________

______________________________________________

Do you have any reservations or concerns about hair, nail, or skin care that we should explore before we begin? If so, what are they?

_______________________________________________

_______________________________________________

## Hair Care

How often do you shampoo your hair?

_______________________________________________

Do you use a separate conditioner? Yes____ No____

Do you use a combined shampoo/conditioner? Yes____ No____

How often do you use a separate conditioner?

_______________________________________________

Do you use any special-purpose shampoos, such as for dandruff, damaged hair, or chemically treated hair? If so, what types?

_______________________________________________

_______________________________________________

What brand of shampoo do you use, and why?

_______________________________________________

What brand of conditioner do you use, and why?

_______________________________________________

Do you use any finishing products? Yes____ No____

If so, what kinds and for what purpose?

_______________________________________________

_______________________________________________

_______________________________________________

_______________________________________________

| Finishing Products | Reason for Use |
|---|---|
| Hairsprays | |
| Styling Gels | |
| Mousse | |
| Pomade | |
| Others | |

How often do you generally replenish your hair care products?

## Nail Care

How often do you do your nails at home?

How often do you have a manicure or pedicure done by a professional?

How often do you change the color of your nails?

How many different colors of nail polish do you own?

Do you have a favorite brand? Yes____ No____

If so, what is it?________________________________________

Do you use any other nail products? Yes____ No____

If so, what kinds?

________________________________________

________________________________________

________________________________________

## Skin Care

| Do you have oily skin? | Yes____ | No____ |
|---|---|---|
| dry skin? | Yes____ | No____ |
| combination? | Yes____ | No____ |

Do you have any skin conditions we should know about?

If Yes, please describe:

________________________________________

________________________________________

Describe your use of makeup:

________________________________________

________________________________________

How important is skin care to you and what's the most important part of your skin care routine?

________________________________________

________________________________________

________________________________________

What other skin care products do you use?

________________________________________

________________________________________

________________________________________

## EXERCISES

1. How do you know when an existing client is ready for a major change? Should you leave it entirely to the client, or should you suggest a change? How should you suggest changes for each of the four personality styles? Discuss in class.
2. Use the New Client Assessment Questionnaire with three friends, family members, or students. Discuss your experience with each person in class. What differences did you notice between the personality styles?
3. Working with a group of classmates, create a role play for the following scenario: A client has seen a different style on one of her friends, and she wants her hair to look exactly the same way. However, you know that your client's hair will not respond to that type of style or treatment. How do you respond to the client? What influence does the client's personality style have on your response if the client is a Cooperator? An Energizer? Discuss in class.

## MAIN POINT SUMMARY

The second phase of service is the Assessment Phase, and it consists of a sensitive consultation with clients and requires listening to their wants. Using the New Client Assessment Questionnaire as a guide, you can determine the client's likes and dislikes, lifestyle and workstyle, past salon experiences, and their perception of their own image. Make sure that your client articulates his or her needs, and that you have a common understanding of what those needs are.

Consultation builds upon the rapport that you establish in the Greeting Phase. At this stage, it is important to be aware of your client's comfort zone regarding physical, emotional, and mental boundaries, and to learn how to be sensitive to these boundaries.

With Cooperators, your emphasis should be on getting them to talk freely and openly. With Analyzers, you must be ready to move slowly and maintain rapport. Regulators respond best to timely, efficient service, but you should listen carefully to understand their full expectations. Energizers often require a longer assessment or even an ongoing assessment, and they may need you to help them with their decision-making.

New clients will take longer because you will be analyzing their responses and collecting data into the New Client Assessment Questionnaire. You are establishing the foundation of strong rapport. Existing clients will be easier to assess due to your existing rapport, but you should certainly still *really listen* even during a *routine* assessment.

For a *major change* assessment, it is important to determine the client's reasons, hesitations, reservations, and experiences with the last service. Once you determine and accept the reasons for the change, prepare the client for the outcome and reactions.

## Assessment Phase Technique Review

| Type of Client | Level of Service | Actions to Take |
|---|---|---|
| **Repeat** | • Same | • Conduct a simple assessment to see how the last service worked, according to the client's personality style. |
| | • Modify | • Conduct a more thorough assessment, referring back to the questions you asked during the client's initial visit. You may begin by saying you had some other ideas to discuss. |
| | • Makeover | • Conduct a thorough assessment, keeping in mind all you know about the client from your relationship with him or her. You may even work to convince the client to try your ideas or simply trust you, depending on the depth of your relationship with the client. |
| **New** | • Same | • Conduct a simple assessment to find out how the client generally uses salon services, according to the client's personality style. |
| | • Modify | • Ask probing questions as you normally would on a first-time assessment. Make suggestions based on the client's answers. |
| | • Makeover | • Your experience in dealing with a wide range of people should influence your recommendations. Your ability to build rapport and let the client talk is critical. |

## SELF-TEST/REVIEW

1. The Assessment Phase consists of ______________________________ and ______________________________.

2. Consultation is the key to establishing ______________________ with clients.

3. Name the three ways salon professionals consult with clients.
   1. ______________________________
   2. ______________________________
   3. ______________________________

4. How do salon professionals use materials like Design Forum during the Assessment Phase?
   1. ______________________________
   2. ______________________________
   3. ______________________________

5. List the one thing that consulting skills seek to uncover.

______________________________________________

6. Name the two elements that consulting skills begin with.

   1. ______________________________________________

   2. ______________________________________________

7. Comfort zones are the ______________, ______________, and

______________ boundaries we place between ourselves and others.

8. When dealing with existing clients, the two types of assessment are:

______________________ and ______________________

9. Name the three steps to achieving a successful major change assessment.

   1. ______________________________________________

   2. ______________________________________________

   3. ______________________________________________

Lesson 7.3

# Agreement Phase

Agreement Phase

The Agreement Phase consists of Planning plus Anticipation. You narrow options, create a plan, and anticipate any problems.

## OBJECTIVES

At the completion of this lesson, you will be able to:

- Present a service plan in language a client can understand
- Explain how to avoid the three areas of conflict that arise when clients are not sufficiently informed of the service options
- List the five steps of alignment

## WHAT YOU NEED TO KNOW

Once you have completed the assessment of your clients' needs through consulting and listening, you are ready to shift into the third phase: the Agreement Phase. The Agreement Phase flows naturally out of the Assessment Phase. Dreams, possibilities, and desires revealed during the assessment are firmed up in the Agreement Phase. This is when you sort options, make service recommendations, and secure your client's partnership in the service.

The Agreement Phase is often overlooked. Two primary problems occur when this happens. First, an inadequate assessment leads to a weak agreement. Second, a good assessment is performed, but the agreement is incomplete and fails to establish rapport. The Agreement Phase is perhaps the most exciting and challenging of the phases when doing makeovers or revisions to a client's look.

Maintaining rapport is critical to ensure that agreement is complete and clients are not surprised during or after the delivery. An easily understood service program or plan that fulfills the client's needs will maintain rapport, create loyalty, increase service use, and assure satisfaction.

By helping clients explore their needs and creating a customized image program, you become more than someone who cuts hair, does nails, or tends to skin for a living. You become a total image consultant. You can guide clients to unimagined beautiful looks as your expertise becomes more valuable than the specific services you provide.

You will be paid not only for your technical skills but also for your:

- Vision
- Ability to transform image needs and desires into satisfying beauty solutions
- Positive influence on your clients' self-esteem

### Agreement Don'ts

To appreciate the power of a proper Agreement Phase, let's look at the absurdities of Salon Calimité, where service, at best, is an afterthought.

## Salon Calimité . . .

If the Agreement Phase even occurs at Salon Calimité, it goes something like this: "How about this?" You know it isn't a real question and you're going to get "this" whether you like it or not.

You may be able to take things into your own hands and review style options on your own as you wait. But you generally find that the magazines are months old and the style books are left over from two or three years ago. So much for discussing and agreeing on a current style.

Unfortunately, that's only a foreshadowing of what is to come in the Delivery Phase.

## Agreement Techniques

At the highest levels of mastery, the techniques salon professionals use during the Agreement Phase allow them to use their creativity and see an image of the clients that they could never imagine without expert help. Top salon professionals have developed the ability to help clients see that image, even if agreement takes years.

### Novice Agreements

The Novice salon professional initially has difficulty distinguishing the Assessment Phase from the Agreement Phase. Mainly, they work to maintain rapport. With new clients, agreement generally consists of obtaining the clients' agreement on details like the length of bangs or sideburns. As Novices cultivate deeper relationships with repeat clients, they learn to establish trust and discuss a wider range of service options, as well as learn how to plan multi-visit style changes.

### Professional Agreements

For the Professional, the Agreement Phase flows naturally from the Assessment Phase. With new clients, the Professional uses the information from the assessment to create and discuss options. The Professional then reviews a plan, and obtains the clients' explicit agreement. The Professional senses when clients are unsure, despite what they may say, and makes sure clients understand and agree with the program. With existing clients, the client and Professional are so in tune that agreement is often implicit from the assessment conversation. The Professional begins to make longer-term plans for image and transformation.

**Your job in the Agreement Phase is to help your client envision themselves after the service and secure their agreement with the plan, especially if you are doing a total makeover.**

## *Master Agreements*

At the Master level, salon professionals are most skilled at reflecting their clients' dreams and desires through image and presentation. Masters are skilled in presenting their vision so that clients understand and agree that even the most radical change can fit their lifestyles. A Master salon professional may also build a long-term plan and work with clients over a long period to achieve it. The Master senses how far clients are willing to go during any visit. The Master works simultaneously at multiple levels with grace.

### In the Salon . . .

As we saw in the previous Assessment lesson, Judith's long hair was important to her and her sense of self. It represented her femininity and was a deep part of her self-concept.

Here is what happened during the Agreement Phase, which took two years.

The salon professional listened intently to her image history, uncovered her past of being overweight, and discovered how her hair was symbolic of her ideals. They considered alternatives and looked at style books, and with superb listening skills, the stylist helped Judith see the possibilities of a new, more open image. They planned for the new image to evolve slowly.

The Master designer began by taking off four inches, and Judith's look was much airier and brighter. By the end of two years, her hair was only a few inches long and platinum blonde! She loved it, and she loved herself.

The designer did his job. He helped Judith to become more secure in her femininity. He accomplished the transformation in Judith's image in a dynamic, flexible way that fit her personality style while maintaining her agreement. Don't be surprised if, when repeated in subsequent visits, assessment and agreement lead to ongoing adjustments as they did in Judith's case.

## Understanding Agreement

Contrasting the Agreement Phase with the preceding Assessment Phase can give you a clearer understanding of agreement and how it flows directly from assessment.

During the Assessment Phase, you:

- Gather information
- Consider alternatives
- Engage your client in the adventure of self-expression

During the Agreement Phase, you:

- Sort through and consider the alternatives
- Secure the clients' agreement to a service program that fulfills their needs
- Agree on a plan
- Anticipate potential problems
- Face the challenge of fulfilling your clients' expectations

**What clients want when they arrive and what they want after the assessment may be very different.**

Another way to think of the transition from assessment to agreement is to visualize two funnels with the wide ends touching one another. The first funnel is the Assessment Phase, where you start with the clients' existing style and generate a widening flow of ideas and alternatives.

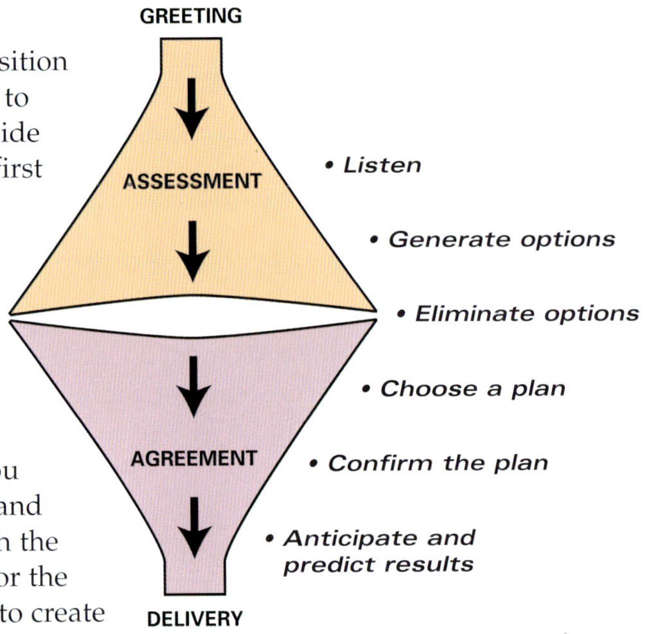

GREETING

ASSESSMENT

AGREEMENT

DELIVERY

- *Listen*
- *Generate options*
- *Eliminate options*
- *Choose a plan*
- *Confirm the plan*
- *Anticipate and predict results*

As you move to agreement, the flow reaches its peak volume. During the Agreement Phase, you funnel the flow into a narrower and narrower channel until you reach the specific look your client desires or the course of action you will follow to create that look.

In short, the Agreement Phase consists of narrowing the mass of alternatives generated in the Assessment Phase into a workable plan.

In routine services, the assessment may be a simple question, "The usual?" and the agreement can be even shorter, "Yes, please." Even this brief encounter expands possibilities with a question and narrows them with a response.

### *Setting a Plan*

In the Agreement Phase, it is important for you and your clients to fully envision what you plan to do and the possible outcomes.

Changes in color, hair length, or treatments like perms can be upsetting to clients if they haven't been prepared for the results. Even seemingly subtle changes in nail color or makeup shade can have an unsettling effect, especially when long-standing looks and habits are changed.

Do not assume that what you anticipated and discussed in the Assessment Phase is sufficient. Your clients may have imagined something totally different than what you meant. The most perfect look is worthless if it is not what they wanted, expected, or was told they would receive. Also, remember that changing looks may mean shifts in wardrobe, exercise, job, marital status, and many more lifestyle areas.

## *Five Steps of Alignment*

Through the Agreement Phase, you strive to reach **Alignment** with your clients. Alignment occurs when the client and the salon professional are moving together with a focus upon the same goal and both have an understanding of services to be delivered.

What clients want when you first sit down together, before the Assessment Phase, may be very different from what they want after talking with you and listening to your recommendations. That's why the Agreement Phase is so critical.

In order to align and agree on a plan, follow these five steps:

1. Review the assessment
2. Eliminate options
3. Choose a plan
4. Confirm the plan
5. Anticipate and predict results

### *Step 1: Review the Assessment*

During your assessment conversation with the client, you gained a sense of your client's likes, dislikes, desires, lifestyle, and work style. Possibilities for different styles and looks developed as you talked about how your client leads his or her life.

Review the ideas you came up with during the Agreement Phase and begin to explore options. This may be done as you finish the Assessment Phase or during another appointment. If you looked at photos, magazines, or color swatches, for instance, take another look at them. This step bridges assessment and agreement.

When agreeing on a long-term plan to change a client's image, write an outline of the long-term image plan. Give a copy to your client as a reminder.

Your review should be fun, open, and creative—and should solidify what you learned during the assessment. As you explore options, you can zero in on your final recommendations by using your empathic, feeling, and factual listening skills to better understand your clients' preferences.

### Step 2: Eliminate Options

In this step, you narrow your final selection down to acceptable options. Perhaps one option was too conservative, another too flamboyant.

Here you demonstrate how well you listened during the Assessment Phase, by eliminating options as unacceptable even before your clients do.

Some possibilities will be excluded temporarily but incorporated into a long-term image development plan, as was the same with Judith in the example on p. 281. Write an outline of your client's long-term image development program, keeping the original in the client file and giving the client a "reminder" copy.

It is possible at this stage that a client will feel uncertain or even disagree with you. For example, your client may want a curly perm, but you see that the client's hair is currently too fragile and over-processed. Here you must summon all your CARE skills to gently dissuade the client, which can be particularly difficult with Energizers who have fallen in love with the latest look. If the client persists in wanting a style you disagree with, you will do well to focus on making sure they understand the problems you are able to predict. See Step 5, *Anticipate and Predict.*

- Use the mirror.
- Use pictures.
- Use your listening skills.

### Eliminating Options Exercise

### Advising All Four Personality Styles

Write a brief dialogue with a client, showing how you would handle advising each of the four personality styles to defer the perm option temporarily until his or her hair is in better condition.

**Cooperator** ______________________________

______________________________

______________________________

**Analyzer** ______________________________

______________________________

______________________________

**Regulator** ______________________________

______________________________

______________________________

Energizer ______________________

______________________

______________________

## In the Salon . . .

Technical jargon—terms that have meaning to salon professionals but are not in the clients' vocabulary—could confuse and muddy the plan, or simply be off-putting if clients don't understand them.

The reason for avoiding the use of technical jargon is that false agreement can result. Clients may not know what they are agreeing to but may nod in agreement rather than ask questions, particularly if the client is a Cooperator. Many people are uncomfortable with what they do not know, and they are reluctant to ask questions that might display their ignorance.

The Energizer, for instance, may be more interested in the result, and the Regulator may be impatient with the lack of action. The Analyzer, on the other hand, might enjoy learning these kinds of details, so use your best judgment, but err on the side of using less technical jargon.

**Clarify the plan with objective, not subjective, words. Make sure all meanings are clear.**

### Step 3: Choose a Plan

Choose the course of action. This should flow smoothly from consideration and elimination of options. This can be as simple as identifying an appointment time or as elaborate as outlining a long-term strategy for moving a client from straight and long to short and curly hair.

State your recommendation based on your mutual perspective, how you will proceed, and what outcome clients can expect.

To ensure alignment on the plan between you and your clients, you should define or generally avoid using the technical terms of the salon profession. Those terms may be comfortable to you, but they can be mysterious to your clients.

## EXERCISE

Translate the following technical words and phrases into plain language, and explain fully what you mean.

| Term | Definition |
|---|---|
| **Hair** | |
| • Volume | ____________________ |
| • Graduation | ____________________ |
| • Weight line | ____________________ |
| • Partial Perm | ____________________ |
| • Weaving | ____________________ |
| **Skin** | |
| • pH | ____________________ |
| • Exfoliation | ____________________ |
| • Hydration | ____________________ |
| **Nails** | |
| • Nail Bed | ____________________ |
| • Fill-in | ____________________ |

> **Your knowledge of the personality styles gives you a potent tool for ensuring that you are in alignment with your client.**

### *Step 4: Confirm the Plan*

When clarifying the plan, make it as concrete, objective, and observable as possible. Use any tools that you can to help clients visualize the outcome:

- Create a nail color selector by securing pre-polished tips to a piece of cardboard with the wide side of the nail tip extending beyond the cardboard. This allows the client to place the tip over her nail to see the color next to her skin.
- Demonstrate shorter hair length in the mirror by folding and arranging the hair.
- Show photos of a style on someone with similar facial structure.
- Develop a computer image or summon your art skills to draw a sketch.

In complex plans, you might even ask clients to repeat what you proposed as they understand it. That lets you know whether they truly understood and visualized the outcome and whether they are excited by it.

Now is the time to ensure your success. As you head toward the Delivery Phase, make sure you're not setting your clients up for disappointment and yourself for failure. Take into account the differences in personality styles and attitudes and strive to reach agreement with each.

### *Step 5: Anticipate and Predict Results*

Always anticipate problems. It can save you much headache and heartache. Even a routine service should include the reminder to watch and report any discomfort, such as concern that the hair is too short or the color isn't right. With more radical changes of style, the client's and their family's reactions to an image change should always be predicted and anticipated. As the saying goes, "An ounce of prevention is worth a pound of cure."

With more complex changes, predict everything from the discomfort of a perm to the time the procedure will take. Anticipate problems with colors, chemicals, and more. This prediction and anticipation gives you the foundation for good rapport even in the face of severe service problems.

Salon professional pulls back Cooperator client's hair, seeking her agreement for the new design.

**Cooperators tend to be uncomfortable with change, but may go along with your recommendations to please you. With the Cooperator, make sure you stay in rapport.**

## Agreement with Each Style

Taking personality styles into account when reaching agreement is particularly important when working with Cooperators or other clients who are likely to have reservations about changes.

### Reaching Agreement with Cooperators (Steps 1-4)

Agreement may come most easily with Cooperators, but be aware of their compliant nature. Cooperators may go along with you simply to please you. It is entirely likely that they will not tell you about some personal circumstance that would influence the decision.

Remember that Cooperators will be reluctant to change. Change can lead to uncertainty, and Cooperators generally seek to avoid uncertainty.

Unlike Energizers, who may be willing to change makeup, hair colors, and hair length with the season, Cooperators have a cautious nature that makes them less likely to shift. If a Cooperator does change rapidly, it will most likely be a result of the relationship built with either the salon professional or a peer group.

*Critical variables in reaching agreement with Cooperators are:*

- Relationship
- Risk-reduction
- Avoidance of description and even conflict in the Cooperator's other relationships

Salon professional takes a slow, thoughtful approach in seeking agreement with an Analyzer client in order to maintain rapport.

**Analyzers respond best to precision and facts. Don't rush their Agreement Phase, and remember that, style-wise, they are likely to be your most conservative clients.**

## *Reaching Agreement with Analyzers (Steps 1-4)*

In the Agreement Phase, Analyzers are similar to Cooperators in that they are not as likely as some to change styles and may remain passive. Remember their aversion to risk and their preference for hearing compelling reasons before taking action. Analyzers will be more likely to change if they don't care about their image or see an advantage.

It is not uncommon for Analyzers to have a more conservative presentation. Analyzers are less likely than the other personality styles to want to stand out and be noticed. As a result, they are more likely to prefer a look that helps them blend in. They are also more likely to be sensitive to cost when it comes to clothing or additional services that they may perceive as luxuries.

In general, Analyzers speak more slowly and require that you move more slowly in order to maintain rapport with them.

*Critical variables in reaching agreement with Analyzers are*:

- Precision
- Good reasons
- A more thoughtful, slow approach

Salon professional works efficiently to reach agreement with a Regulator client in order to assure that the client is served and the professional is protected.

**With Regulators, anticipating problems is critical to securing agreement. You may need persistence and diplomacy if you seek to change a Regulator's image.**

## *Reaching Agreement with Regulators (Steps 1-4)*

Regulator clients may not have patience for the slower, more methodical ways in which Cooperators or Analyzers reach agreement. Don't be fooled by this impatience. You must still complete all steps of agreement. It is critical that you learn to efficiently complete the Agreement Phase with Regulators in order to assure that you are serving them well and protecting yourself.

Regulators tend to be like Analyzers in their inclination toward conservative dress. When they do dress in more outgoing ways, it tends to be bold. Changing a Regulator's established image can take persistence and diplomacy. You may need to suggest a change over several visits, particularly one that may not fit a Regulator's conservative image. Regulators generally need a good, strong, practical reason for image changes. As you build trust and rapport, Regulators start to relax and become more open to change.

Once you reach an agreement with a Regulator, be sure to anticipate any problems. Regulators do not like surprises and tend to be concerned with control. When you suggest a change, you are taking them out of their comfort zone. They have less control, but are more likely to experience the world anew.

*Critical variables in reaching agreement with Regulators are*:

- Persistence
- Practicality
- Anticipation of problems so there are no surprises

Salon professional works on agreement with an Energizer until her response is enthusiastic.

Try to keep Energizers focused on the plan without boring or irritating them with details. Talk about how others will like a new

## Reaching Agreement with Energizers (Steps 1-4)

Reaching agreement with Energizers can be easy, but getting it done systematically may be difficult. Energizers often dislike going over details, especially when they are excited about a new look. If you do not reach full, complete agreement, you may be setting yourself up for trouble if there are problems later on.

It's crucial to make sure your client is aware of possible difficulties and risks, and that they are aware of how others may perceive a style or a change. Join Energizers in their enthusiasm, but temper it with good planning when necessary.

The fact that a person is an Energizer doesn't mean that they favor radical images, or that they have lifestyles that permit them to change their look with each visit.

*Critical variables in reaching agreement with Energizers are*:

- Enthusiasm
- Firm grounding in reality
- A focus on the reaction of others

Any change can be threatening or upsetting to clients, so it's best to prepare them to anticipate the outcome. Make sure you cover the actions you and your clients can take if the service turns out wrong.

## Anticipating Problems with All Personality Styles (Step 5)

No matter what the scope of service or change you and your clients agree upon, you likely have embarked on an adventure that will open up new possibilities for them. It is critical that you complete the Agreement Phase by anticipating and identifying potential problems so that you can maintain rapport with your clients—and protect yourself—if those problems arise.

In short, anticipate results and predict both positive outcomes and possible problems with all clients, but especially with Energizers and clients receiving radical makeovers.

Any alteration of a person's presentation, or image, can seem threatening both to the client and to people who are accustomed to seeing your client in a certain way. Predicting problems goes hand-in-hand with anticipating solutions. If you have predicted the possible reactions, and discussed solutions, your voice is more likely to resonate in your clients' head when what you predict happens. If your prediction was about a problem, your client's trust in your makeovers will eventually grow.

After discussing the problems of a change to short hair, the client agrees to the change.

Anticipating problems is especially important when you are delivering a new service, such as color, a shorter cut, or a perm. These services have high variability, and it is important, first of all, to inform clients of the risks and to discuss your **contingencies**—the actions or alternative plan you and your clients can take if the service doesn't turn out as expected

As you anticipate potential problems, consider the following three areas:

1. Relationship
   - How will others in the client's life react to a change?
2. Psychology
   - How will the client react to the change?
   - What help does he or she need to reach a positive reaction to the outcome?
3. Physical realities
   - How will the change fit in with the client's personal and work lives?
   - Will the client be able to care for his or her own hair?
   - What new styling tools and products will be required to maintain the style?
   - Can the client use these proficiently?

**Your ability to handle your clients' fears and feelings marks your emergence as a true professional.**

## Discussing Contingencies

It isn't enough to simply predict what could go wrong. It's also critical to discuss contingencies.

Salon professionals who face the discomfort of discussing contingencies consistently find that these discussions increase client confidence.

Make contingencies as specific as possible for each service you perform. With a new skin treatment for instance, discuss what you can do should his or her skin redden or flush. Inform your client that it is only temporary. Talk about what you can do if a hair color shade isn't right or what the client can do if scalp irritation develops as a result of a chemical treatment.

For major changes, make sure your clients know they can call you and discuss their reactions. This may also be a good time to review any policies your salon has for clients who feel dissatisfied with the results of a service.

## The Agreement Phase Challenge

The challenge of the Agreement Phase consists of reviewing the assessment and discovering the feelings and attitudes that have made the client maintain his or her hair, skin or nails in the same way year after year. You must be sure you:

- Travel the sensitive territory of personal feelings and self-esteem. ("I always felt my skin was my best feature, and I never wanted to wear makeup.")
- Traverse the route of a spouse's or friend's idea of what is appealing. ("My husband hates short hair on me.")
- Encounter the roadblocks of simple avoidance. ("I never knew exactly what would look good, and I never trusted anyone else to tell me, so I took the easy way out by doing nothing.")

Your ability to handle such deep-seated feelings gently and with understanding is the mark of your entry to the Professional level.

One final caution about the Agreement Phase: Stay within your limits! If you know a client would be suited to a particular cut or chemical service, but you don't feel you are the best person to handle the service, be mature and wise enough to refer the client to another professional in your salon—an action that should win you the respect of your client and co-worker alike.

In Lesson 7.4, *Delivery Phase*, you will learn how to stay in rapport as you deliver the technical service.

## EXERCISES

1. Write a long-term image development plan for changing a client from short, bleached hair to mid-length hair with heavy highlights. How would you plan the change for each of the personality styles? Assume that your client is a professional woman.

   **Cooperator**

   ______________________________

   ______________________________

   **Analyzer**

   ______________________________

   ______________________________

   **Regulator**

   ______________________________

   ______________________________

   **Energizer**

   ______________________________

   ______________________________

2. Create an Agreement Phase skit that role-plays the following situations, and discuss in class:
   - Energizer salon professional seeking agreement on a perm from an Analyzer client.
   - Cooperator salon professional seeking agreement on a highlighting service from a Regulator client.

## MAIN POINT SUMMARY

The Agreement Phase flows directly from the Assessment Phase. During the Agreement Phase, you should sum up what was discovered in the Assessment Phase. Focus attention on goals, needs, and a plan of action. A good plan can enhance your position by increasing the value of your service and thereby increasing client loyalty.

Eliminate options based on client needs and preferences. Choose a plan of action and explain it in non-technical terms. Confirm the plan with them, and use any visual aids you need. It is important that you confirm that the clients fully understand what you are proposing, so encourage them to explain the plan to you in their own words.

Pay close attention to the tendencies of the CARE personality types during the Agreement Phase:

- Cooperators may be quick to agree, but be certain that they fully understand the plan. Be aware that the Cooperator's tendency to avoid conflict may complicate matters.
- Analyzers generally require a precise, thoughtful, and deliberate approach. Be patient, but be prepared to encourage the decision-making process.
- In the case of Regulators, you may need to be persistent. Take extra care to anticipate and explain any potential problems or difficulties.
- Energizers generally appreciate enthusiasm on your part, as well as anticipate the reactions they will get from their new style.

The Agreement Phase is not complete until you have anticipated problems and discussed contingencies with the clients. Although you may initially find this difficult to do, it will increase client confidence in your technical abilities and increase the level of loyalty they feel toward you. It will also improve manageability in the event that any problems should arise by defining a course of action ahead of time.

## Agreement Phase Technique Review

| Type of Client | Level of Service | Actions to Take |
|---|---|---|
| **Repeat** | Same | • Ask whether the client agrees to do the same style, noting the client's personality style. |
| | Modify | • Make sure the client understands any changes you propose. Use your knowledge of the client to decide on the level of detail with which to review agreement. |
| | Makeover | • Review your plan at the level of detail you know your client needs. Make sure that your client understands how other people may react to the changes in appearance. |
| **New** | Same | • Ask whether the client agrees to keeping the same style, but note any variations you may make as a result of your technique, and keep in mind the client's personality style. |
| | Modify | • Be thorough in explaining the changes you suggest and obtain the client's complete agreement. Review the plan and explain each change and how it will improve the client's look. Make sure the client agrees to all changes in order to avoid surprises. |
| | Makeover | • A makeover with a new client requires a complete explanation of and agreement to all changes and possible reactions, both on the part of the client and on the part of others. You may want to ask about particular family members, business associates, or others in order to help the client prepare for reactions, both positive and negative. |

## SELF-TEST/REVIEW

1. What are the main differences between the Assessment Phase and the Agreement Phase?

______________________________

______________________________

______________________________

2. Why is the Agreement Phase so pivotal to the service process?

______________________________

______________________________

______________________________

3. List and describe the five steps of alignment in the Agreement Phase.

1. ____________________

____________________

____________________

2. ____________________

____________________

____________________

3. ____________________

____________________

____________________

4. ____________________

____________________

____________________

5. ____________________

____________________

____________________

4. List the key considerations for obtaining agreement with each of the four personality styles.

**Cooperator**

______________________________________________

______________________________________________

**Analyzer**

______________________________________________

______________________________________________

**Regulator**

______________________________________________

______________________________________________

**Energizer**

______________________________________________

______________________________________________

Lesson 7.4

# Delivery Phase

Delivery Phase

The Delivery Phase consists of Partnership plus Action. You work together with your client as you deliver service, creating a conversation that can flow between the technical and the personal.

## OBJECTIVES

At the completion of this lesson, you will be able to:

- Balance technical skills and people skills
- Use non-technical language to maintain rapport during services
- Discuss the four obstacles to partnership
- Demonstrate communication skills using the conversational style appropriate to the client's needs and personality style
- Inform clients about each procedure before it occurs and offer maintenance tips

## WHAT YOU NEED TO KNOW

The Delivery Phase should seamlessly integrate techniques of professional service and rapport. During the first three phases of the Service Cycle, you primarily used your people skills, while drawing upon your technical skills for assessing service needs and recommending the proper action. Now your technical skills with hair, nails or skin are ready to be used in full force as you deliver on the plan.

At the same time, however, you must also shift your people skills into an even higher gear in order to maintain and build rapport and partnership with your client as you provide your service. Even after receiving explanation of the process, some clients may feel uncomfortable during a procedure. People frequently are afraid, for instance, that you will cut their hair too short, and almost as frequently, they do not say anything about it.

By using your people skills, you can develop a partnership with your clients that makes them feel they can tell you what they like and don't like. Through conversation, salon professionals also learn how their clients lead their lives, share common concerns, learn about each other's interests, and discuss the events of the day.

### Delivery Don'ts

To appreciate the power of a proper Delivery Phase, let's look at the absurdities of Salon Calimité, where service, at best, is an afterthought.

## Salon Calimité. . .

Delivery at Salon Calimité is a lesson in managing uncertainty from a client's point of view. Salon employees pay little attention to you, the client. They generally converse with one another, with only a glance at you now and then.

As a client, you are never really sure what you will end up with. Stylists will carry out your instructions however they see fit, assuming they have even asked for them. As a client, if you see too much hair falling on the cape, and you have the nerve to mention it, the stylist will likely say, "Don't worry. It will look just fine."

If you have questions about how to maintain your style at home, you won't receive much instruction. "Do what I'm doing" is a typical response. You might also be admonished with this, "You come here to get expert styling. If you need it done again, you'll have to make another appointment."

You realize you took a gamble and probably lost. You figure it can't get any worse . . . but it does.

## Delivery Techniques

The Delivery Phase provides the greatest block of time for the professional relationship to develop. Initially you likely will spend much of the Delivery Phase working on your technical skills. When your technical skills become second, however, you will start to focus more on building relationships with clients and to develop the art of conversation.

### Novice Delivery

The Delivery Phase can be especially awkward for the Novice salon professional, who focuses mainly on developing technical skills. With both new and existing clients, Novices tend to either use silence while they work or keep their clients talking. Both techniques allow Novices to put most of their attention on the technical details, rather than on the relationship. Novices do well to point out technical details and ask questions about client preferences as a way of maintaining rapport during the Delivery Phase.

### Professional Delivery

To Professionals, technical skills are second nature. This leaves room for a wide range of interaction and conversation. When serving new clients, Professionals ask questions about the client's life or interests and sense when the client is uncomfortable with a question or topic. The conversation flows naturally between topics of general interest and service delivery. Professionals determine further what the client needs and wants to know about the details of service delivery and home maintenance. Professionals also maintain rapport with clients as they move through other salon services during a visit. They are still learning about the variety of ways to serve clients as they add to their knowledge about people, style, professional, and social issues.

### Master Delivery

Drawing from their rich background and experience, Masters display a full range of conversational techniques and tailor their interaction to each client's interests and personality. A Master can easily talk with a corporate officer about business, advise a model on her hair color, or entertain a bored housewife. When the client visits multiple salon professionals during a single visit, the Master keeps in touch with the client. If an upset client calls or returns, the Master quickly assesses the situation and resolves the problem, all while maintaining rapport with the client who is currently receiving service.

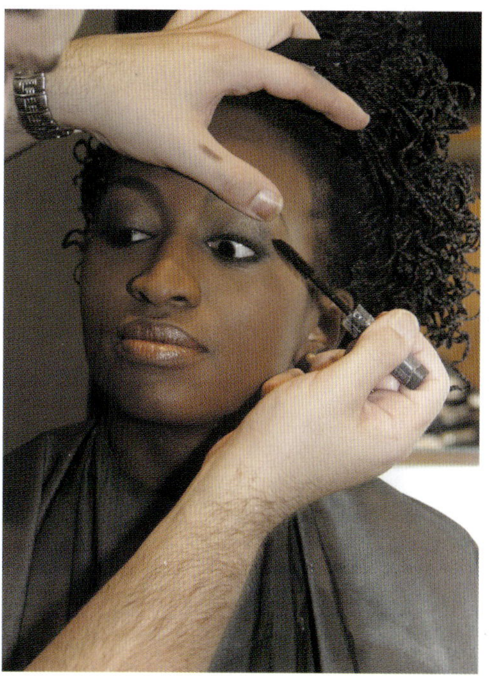

Clients can feel very vulnerable in the salon. Stay attuned to those feelings and talk about them as a way to deepen rapport.

## Breaking Rapport During Delivery

The rapport you worked so hard to build in the first three phases can be broken quite easily due to neglect in the Delivery Phase, resulting in an unsatisfying Completion for both salon professional and the client. Salon professionals, especially Novices, tend to break rapport during the Delivery Phase by:

- Becoming so engrossed in their work that they don't pay attention to the client.
- Working so automatically that their minds wander outside the client partnership.
- Engaging in conversations with others in the salon while forgetting the client.

Clients, for their part, may have the most difficulty remaining in rapport while trying to follow what you are doing.

### Warning Signs

Throughout the Delivery Phase, watch for clues or warning signs in the client's expressions or body language that tell you rapport is at risk, including:

- Fidgeting
- Blinking back tears
- Holding breath
- Frowning
- Tensely gripping the arms of the chair

- Scratching at the hairline or touching perm rods
- Unusual silence or chatter
- Redness in the face or neck area (this could be an allergic reaction to a substance or an indication of nervous tension)

## In the Salon. . .

Hector is a Master salon professional giving a cut to his client, Joseph, for the first time. Hector knew that Joseph, as an Analyzer, would not be quick to talk. During the Assessment Phase, Hector had suggested that Joseph change his image but he had not gotten Agreement yet.

As a result, Hector obtained Joseph's agreement by asking very specific, literal questions such as, "How long do you want it on the sides?"

Having feared he would be asked questions related to his fashion preferences, which he would have difficulty answering, Joseph relaxed during Delivery Phase. As Hector cut, continuing to ask specific questions, Joseph suddenly joked, "It'd be nice if you could add it to the top so it won't look so thin up there."

Hector smiled. He had found Joseph's main concern—his sensitivity toward his thinning hair. They again discussed changing Joseph's image. Hector recommended shorter interior lengths which would make the top look fuller.

This time Joseph agreed. Hector had won his trust by talking to him during the Delivery Phase in a way he could hear.

Had Hector simply cut as he wanted, Joseph may have felt that his thinning hair would be all the more apparent, as he saw his fine top hair falling onto his smock. Hector had maintained rapport and reached the perfect balance between his technical skills and people skills.

**Check in with your clients from time to time, especially if they act in a way that leads you to believe they are upset.**

### *Addressing Warning Signs*

When warning signs appear, stop for a moment and gently ask your client a few questions. You might even softly rest your hand on the client's shoulder. Take care not to use language that could be upsetting:

- A simple "Are you feeling comfortable?" will achieve the same results in a more gentle way than asking, "Is this burning you too much?"
- Ask the client what he or she is thinking or feeling.
- Apply the technical skills and knowledge that you have acquired to inform and calm your client.

Keeping the client informed puts the client at ease.

## *Informing and Involving*

During the Delivery Phase, keep the client informed about what you're doing and why you're doing it. Remind the client of the plan that you agreed upon and how each step you accomplish fulfills part of that plan. You should also be coaching your client on maintenance practices.

Use non-technical language that the client can comprehend, and explain any unfamiliar terms. Even when doing nothing new, keep the client informed of your actions. This helps generate the rapport for a strong service delivery partnership between the two of you.

## REMEMBER

**In the Assessment Phase, you should have interviewed the new client to discover the problems they experienced in their previous salon visits. Noting their fears during the assessment allows you to address and minimize those fears during the Delivery Phase.**

**Be sure to check in with your client from time to time. A Master salon professional senses when to ask a client how he or she feels about the service.**

**Because clients are often afraid to express their concerns, don't wait for them to tell you when something is wrong. Ask them. Be alert to warning signs of physical and emotional discomfort.**

**Keep the client informed and involved. Remember that the biggest complaint clients make is that the stylist cut their hair too short and didn't listen. Keeping them involved, especially before making a major change, can avoid such a crisis.**

There is an art to weaving technical and service-oriented communication into the more free-flowing conversation that typically takes place in the Delivery Phase of service. Even in the case of Regulators and Energizers, who may not seem interested, make it a point to keep them involved.

The following table shows the level of involvement each style tends to prefer during Service Delivery Phase.

## Delivery Phase Involvement Preferences

| Personality Style | During Service Delivery Phase. . . |
|---|---|
| Cooperator | • May be satisfied with simply maintaining rapport. |
| Analyzer | • Likely wants to know what's going on and what you are doing. |
| Regulator | • Generally doesn't want as much detail as the Analyzer but frequently prefers to be included in the process. |
| Energizer | • May not want detail on what you are doing but wants to hear how the style will look and may want suggestions and other ideas as you go. |

Most clients appreciate hearing your technical expertise and styling tips as you go along. It is in your best interest to share that information because clients who were never advised on how to maintain the style at home may stop thinking of you as a trusted salon professional. Remember that you are working as a presentation coach, and your client may need to hear maintenance and care tips many times before these tips stick in their mind.

Here are examples of helpful remarks that will take the mystery out of personal care maintenance for your clients:

Take a few seconds when necessary to make sure the client understands what you are doing—especially in the back of the head where the client can't see.

- "When you blow dry your hair, hold the brush at this angle."
- "To achieve this degree of volume, use a round brush like this one."
- "Apply a top coat of clear nail polish every few days to help prevent your nail color from chipping."
- "Use a good moisturizer on your skin every day after cleansing."

Some clients are indifferent to this kind of education and others feel like they are already adequately skilled and prefer silence instead. There is nothing wrong with asking clients if they enjoy learning about the services or if they prefer silence or other interaction.

It is also a good idea to take an "attitude check," particularly if the style change is dramatic: "Well, Carla, we just saw six inches of hair fall to the floor. As you can see, there's plenty left, but how does it feel right now?"

Your alertness and attention during the Delivery Phase will tell you how to proceed. The following table gives some suggestions for coaching and educating clients, based on their personality style.

### Delivery Involvement Challenges

| Personality Style | Common Challenges | Overcoming Challenges |
|---|---|---|
| **Cooperator** | • Cooperators are often passive and won't always ask you for an explanation of techniques. | • Don't wait for Cooperators to ask questions; show you care by taking time to explain each step. |
| **Analyzer** | • Although they may sit silently, Analyzers usually appreciate if you explain each step slowly and in some detail. Once you begin an explanation, they may ask follow-up questions. | • Without getting too sidetracked, try to be as detailed as possible with your Analyzer clients. Analyzers usually like it if you use more technical language, but make sure to define each term you use. |
| **Regulator** | • Regulators usually like to feel that they are in control, so they might not like receiving instructions from you or might try to tell you what to do. | • Listen to suggestions or corrections from Regulators, but don't be afraid to politely explain the advantages of your own technique. Ultimately, they will appreciate knowing the best method so that they can be in control of their style at home. |
| **Energizer** | • Energizers are often excited about their own ideas, so they may have a hard time listening to a detailed explanation or staying focused. | • Try to have fun when you are educating your Energizer clients. Be conversational. If you are interrupted, look for a smooth way to transition back to explaining the current step. |

## Maintaining Partnership

Through the previous three phases, you worked hard to build a partnership with your client. Your work culminated in a partnership agreement by the end of the Agreement Phase, and now your job is to fulfill your part of that agreement. Be careful to keep the new partnership strong and to avoid the following common obstacles:

- Overstating results; making promises you can't keep.
- Neglecting clients.
- Ignoring client's feelings.
- Believing the myth that you have to be a "performer".

Notice how the Regulator client grips the arm of the chair. How would you make the client feel more at ease?

**The art of conversing while providing salon services can be one of the most satisfying parts of the profession. Use the Delivery Phase as a chance to improve both your conversation and listening skills.**

*Overstating Results.* When you exaggerate by saying something you don't mean or making promises you cannot keep, you undermine your credibility. Remember that it will be very difficult to regain your client's trust once it is broken by a false promise or an insincere remark. Your professional reputation is of great importance.

*Neglecting Clients.* When you neglect or ignore your clients, you are indirectly telling them that you think they are unimportant, which endangers any partnership. Neglect takes many forms, such as:

- Socializing with other salon professionals and clients to the exclusion of your current client.
- Answering the phone and talking unnecessarily.
- Becoming absorbed in your own thoughts and ignoring your client.

*Ignoring Client's Feelings.* Brushing off a client's worries by responding with such phrases as, "Don't worry," "You shouldn't feel that way," or "Trust me," may be the easy way out for you, but they're also an easy way to break your partnership with the client.

When clients perceive that you aren't listening or don't care about their feelings, they are likely to quietly withdraw or complain, thereby breaking the partnership. You won't even know it happened until it is too late.

***Believing the "Performer" Myth.*** Another obstacle is the misconception that good salon professionals are "performers." They feel they have to be "on" for an audience. This can lead to false gaiety, stretched smiles, forced conversation, and overly dramatic behavior.

Although entertaining is one of the four conversational techniques discussed in the following section, being entertaining should come naturally and be appropriate for the personality style of the client. Consider which personality styles are not so interested in being entertained.

## Engaging in Conversation

During the Delivery Phase, you have a wonderful opportunity to become a trusted advisor. You can serve in many ways. You can:

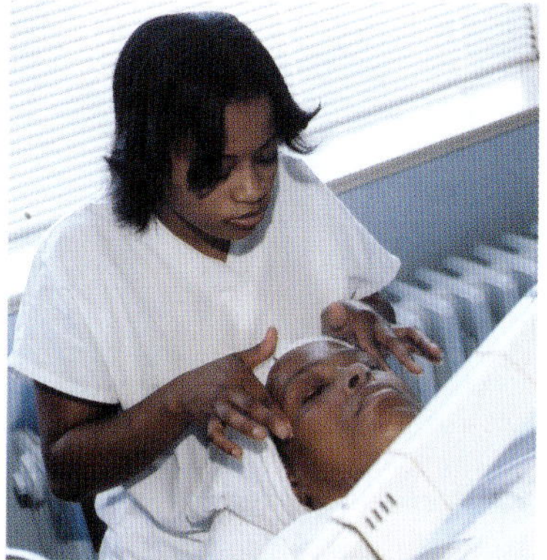

Being "in tune" with your client's feelings increases your rapport during the Delivery Phase, even if you aren't talking.

- Provide an uplifting influence for those who are down.
- Listen to those who have few outside contacts.
- Advise those with image improvement needs.
- Direct client to resources they might not know about, and much more.

When you engage in rapport-building conversation, the Delivery Phase becomes much more enjoyable for both you and the client. Your relationship grows with repeated rapport. The extent of your communication skills and your ability to choose the right conversational style for each client both show the degree of your mastery in the Delivery Phase and add to your career and life fulfillment.

Do not forget that conversation is most likely to suffer in the Delivery Phase. During that time, the salon professional can become distracted by other salon professionals or clients, or become too engrossed in his or her work. Additionally, many salon services require the client and salon professional to be apart from one another for long periods of time—while skin treatments or color and perms are processing, for example.

Your ability to engage in conversation during any phase of the Service Cycle increases your clients' trust.

It is particularly important during the Delivery Phase to remember the Service Cycle within the Service Cycle. After each interruption or separation from your client, greet the client anew. Then, assess the situation, renew the conversation, re-establish agreement, and make sure rapport is ongoing. This can be a swift interaction. Top professionals are keenly sensitive and re-engage smoothly and efficiently.

During times of separation, such as during chemical processing, clients may feel ignored, and they are often hesitant to ask questions for fear they are bothering you. They had your undivided attention during the Greeting, Assessment, and Agreement Phases. Now they may be left alone, sometimes for up to 30 minutes. A sensitive salon professional with good people skills will check in periodically, to make sure the client is all right and doesn't need anything.

You don't need to talk to maintain contact and focus on the client.

In a salon with high-quality service programs and a teamwork environment, all staff are focused on maintaining rapport with the client. Staff members are alert to any developing problems, and everyone takes responsibility for their successful resolution. This is the ideal service atmosphere, where every salon professional is concerned about every client—not just the person presently occupying his or her station. In such an environment, everyone benefits.

## Conversational Approaches

There are four basic conversational approaches that you can use with your clients during the Delivery Phase. No conversation completely matches any of these. But by mastering the four styles, you will increase your requisite variety. This means you will have flexibility in service, which leads to even greater rapport. They are:

1. Active conversation
2. Passive conversation
3. High interaction
4. Low interaction

The table on the next page describes each approach.

## Four Conversational Approaches

| Approach | Consists of. . . |
|---|---|
| Active Conversation | • The salon professional initiates most of the conversation topics and dialogue. This approach often works best with passive clients—Cooperators and Analyzers. |
| Passive Conversation | • The salon professional mostly listens or responds, using occasional responses and encouragement to continue drawing the client out. This approach often works best with assertive clients—Regulators and Energizers. |
| High Interaction | • The salon professional maintains the client's attention with a high level of exchange. This may mean amusing statements or actions, or it could mean interested probing or sharing stories. This approach can work with all four of the personality styles. Regulators and Analyzers are likely to appreciate sharing while feeling-oriented Cooperators and Energizers may appreciate being entertained more. Be sensitive to your clients. If they don't laugh at your jokes or appear entertained, then they probably prefer to have more involvement in the conversation by sharing their thoughts with you. |
| Low Interaction | • This approach builds rapport with select clients and should be used sparingly. However, some clients, especially Analyzers, may prefer uninterrupted relaxing or thinking during the Delivery Phase. Remember, respectful silence can be perceived as ignoring clients or as a sign that you dislike them. Watch for signs that indicate your client's comfort level to silence. A relaxed body posture or engaged reading are clues that clients are comfortable. |

## SERVICE CHALLENGE

**What will you do when your client seems steadfastly committed to silence, even when you are asking for information to serve them better?**

What will you do when you have a client who is uncommunicative?

**Your decisions in the face of challenges like this will help you achieve your highest potential with people skills. With the client who prefers silence, many salon professionals need to overcome their fear of rejection in order to maintain rapport and continue keeping the client abreast of the service.**

**It is not uncommon for a long silence to pass. Remember that the silence itself can be a key element of rapport with certain people.**

> **When you achieve mastery as a salon conversationalist, you will be able to converse about most any subject. You may lack knowledge on the subject but you will know how to question and to learn.**

## Conversational Challenges

What you say and how you say it is important. As a salon professional, you face the challenge of staying engaged with a wide range of people and conversing on a wide range of topics while maintaining a professional demeanor.

Conversational challenge can be most apparent when you face the client who wants to talk about things you don't want to hear or who wants to hear things from you that you don't want to talk about.

Remember to stay in your own personal conversation comfort zone. Some topics of conversation such as religion and politics are challenging, particularly for Novice salon professionals, and some should be avoided all together. Gossip and demeaning conversations are unprofessional and should be left out of the workplace.

The table below lists topics that are likely to require highly skilled conversationalists to be handled in a professional manner. This is not a hard and fast list of rules, but guidelines for you to feel your way to higher rapport. Remember that you can use your listening skills here and need not express your opinion on everything. Simply seeking to understand your client may be sufficient.

### Challenging Conversational Topics

| Topic | Risk |
|---|---|
| • The cost of things—cars, houses, etc.—and how much money people make | • The wide range of wealth and emotions around money |
| • Details of illnesses or hospital care | • Not being ready to listen empathetically. |
| • Your love life, or your client's love life | • Risks embarrassment and need to backtrack |
| • Religion | • Risks conflict of opinions |
| • Politics | • Risks conflict of opinions |
| • Your opinions of the salon, if they are not favorable | • Makes you look unprofessional |
| • Unfavorable discussion of your former place of employment | • Makes you look unprofessional |
| • Rumors that affect someone's reputation | • Makes you look unprofessional |

You should not always expect your client to be forthcoming, especially on sensitive topics. Remember that you could be losing a potential ongoing client if you are oblivious to their feelings and thoughts.

Despite your efforts to avoid topics about which you or your client are likely to have strong, even conflicting feelings, many clients will launch into such subjects anyway. Even though they started it, do not allow yourself to be drawn in beyond your comfort zone.

If you can maintain rapport and deepen the relationship, that's fine. To be safe, take the passive conversational approach. Avoid any display of disapproval or impoliteness:

- If you don't offer an opinion, eventually the client will go on to a different topic.
- If not, wait for an opportunity and politely change the subject yourself.
- Later in your career, when you reach the Professional and Master levels, these topics may offer a basis for deep rapport and friendship.

Remember, too, that drawing the client's attention to some aspect of the service is always a useful, effective way of avoiding unpleasant or unprofessional topics of conversation.

Whatever conversational approach you decide to take, base both the content and feeling on your determination of the client's personality style and needs. Although no one can really know what topics another person enjoys, look at the following table and see how it fits your experience.

**As your career progresses, you will also know which clients you can discuss business with, which ones you can discuss personal matters with, and which ones prefer silence.**

## Conversational Topics by Personality Style

| Personality Type | Personality Style | Conversation Content/Feeling |
|---|---|---|
| **Cooperator** | • Children and family activities<br>• How much friends will like the new hairstyle<br>• Feelings | • Warm and unhurried speech<br>• Soft voice |
| **Analyzer** | • The weather<br>• His/her job<br>• Practicality of new hairstyle<br>• Facts about new style or current topic | • Slow and deliberate speech<br>• Non-threatening voice |
| **Regulator** | • His/her job responsibilities<br>• Efficiency of new style<br>• Facts about new style or current topic | • Firm and confident speech<br>• Calm and controlled voice |
| **Energizer** | • His/her activities<br>• Style and fashion<br>• How great the new hairstyle will look and feel | • Bright and lively speech<br>• Energetic voice |

## REMEMBER

**Experiment and discover what each individual really cares about. Play with the speed and tempo of the conversation, as you learned in Lesson 4.2 in *Relating with CARE*. Remember that rapport is the aim. Practice your style shifting until you have it.**

In Lesson 7.5, *Recommendation Phase*, we'll explain the importance of giving your clients advice on product use and purchase.

## EXERCISES

1. Write your own list of challenging conversational topics and risks. Share this list with your classmates.

2. Write or role-play a script for a short conversation you would have while cutting a client's hair. Your client is a friendly Energizer who has been coming to you for years and who has always praised your technical work. You are cutting her hair very short for the first time, so she may tend to get a little fussy during the Delivery Phase. Because Energizers usually accept change better than others, your biggest problem in this conversation could be saying everything you'd like to say about the style because your client would rather talk about her personal life and activities.

   The conversation should contain five client comments and five salon professional responses, followed by a comment or question. Use your imagination and your knowledge of the Energizer personality in creating this dialogue.

3. Write a conversation you would have with a new Analyzer client who is not talking. You want to draw her out a little bit without scaring her away. Refer to the Conversational Topics by Personality Style table on p. 311 to give you some ideas about topics of discussion. Again, give both the client and the salon professional at least five turns each.

4. Write what you would say and do in the following situations:

*Client is silent when you talk.*

*Client tells dirty jokes and you are offended.*

*Client talks non-stop about things that don't interest you.*

5. Identify at least one conversation with high rapport you had while receiving service at a restaurant, salon, or other business. What did you like about it?

______________________________________________

______________________________________________

______________________________________________

6. Identify at least one poor conversation you had while receiving service at a restaurant, salon, or other business. What made it a poor conversation?

______________________________________________

______________________________________________

______________________________________________

## MAIN POINT SUMMARY

One of the most important things to accomplish in the Delivery Phase of service is to maintain rapport with the client. While you are busy executing the plan that you and the client agreed upon in the Agreement Phase, your technical skills will naturally come to the front, and your people skills will tend to recede in the face of the technical challenges.

It is extremely important at this point to shift them into an even higher gear. The client needs you to guide them through the experience. There are no absolutes when it comes to the flow of conversation between you and the client, so you must learn to read the client and the situation and respond accordingly.

In general, keep clients informed of what you are doing and why, and give them tips on how they can best care for and style their new look on their own. Take into account the different kinds of information and conversation they will expect from you. You want to avoid the following obstacles to the partnership you have established: overpromising or exaggerating, neglecting clients, ignoring clients' feelings, and believing that you must be a "performer."

This is your opportunity to deepen the rapport with your client, to serve as advisor, and to explain the technical side of your craft. Be aware of the various conversational styles—active, passive, high interaction, and low interaction—and how these different approaches might work with the different personality styles.

Also know which topics to avoid, based on whether they are appropriate for a professional relationship and your skills as a conversationalist. And remember, have fun—it's easier to establish and maintain rapport when you are enjoying yourself.

## Delivery Phase Technique Review

| Type of Client | Level of Service | Actions to Take |
|---|---|---|
| **Repeat** | Same | • Maintain rapport and conversation, according to the client's personality style. |
| | Modify | • Keep your client informed, especially if your modification makes major changes, such as taking off six inches of hair or changing hair color. Keep track and ask about client's reactions to the service. |
| | Makeover | • Maintain high-quality rapport throughout the delivery, especially because the client will likely visit several professionals. If the change takes place over multiple visits, remind the client why he or she made the change at the level of detail needed for the client's personality style.. |
| **New** | Same | • Maintain rapport and conversation, according to the client's personality style. Ask about the client's life as a way to get to know him or her better. |
| | Modify | • Explain what you are doing at a level of detail for the client's personality style. If you make a major change, say something about it. Ask about the client's reactions, especially if he or she seems nervous. Your confidence and reassurance can put the client at ease. |
| | Makeover | • Your client may feel vulnerable with new people and new procedures, moving from one salon professional to another. The client will appreciate your presence and direction, whether they express discomfort or not. That attention builds rapport, as does your conversational ability. |

## SELF-TEST/REVIEW

1. Fill in the blanks: Delivery Phase = ______________________________ +

   ______________________________.

2. Once you have completed the first three phases of service, you can put away your people skills and concentrate on your technical skills instead.
   Circle One:

   True or False

3. List the six warning signs that indicate that your clients might be physically or mentally uncomfortable during the Delivery Phase.

   1. ______________________________

   2. ______________________________

   3. ______________________________

   4. ______________________________

   5. ______________________________

   6. ______________________________

4. Name the four obstacles to a good partnership with your client.

   1. ______________________________

   2. ______________________________

   3. ______________________________

   4. ______________________________

5. Which of the following is a problematic element of good conversation?

   ____ A. A feeling of being liked

   ____ B. Being able to express oneself

   ____ C. Getting "caught up" on neighborhood gossip

   ____ D. Uncovering beauty opinions

   Why?

   ______________________________

   ______________________________

   ______________________________

   ______________________________

6. List the four approaches to conversation.

1. ______________________________
2. ______________________________
3. ______________________________
4. ______________________________

7. Put a check beside any of the following that would be a questionable comment for a salon professional to use during a conversation with a client.

____ A. "Do you play any sports on a regular basis?"

____ B. "I'm a Democrat, but I'm not voting for him. He's a jerk!"

____ C. "I really liked that comedy. Did you see it?"

____ D. "How much money does your husband make?"

____ E. "How long have you lived there?"

____ F. "Do you have any children?"

____ G. "I'm so fed up with this boring town."

Why are the ones you checked questionable?

______________________________

______________________________

______________________________

______________________________

______________________________

______________________________

8. List three topics or questions you would like to use to help establish high-quality rapport with any client.

1. ______________________________
2. ______________________________
3. ______________________________

9. Write four questions of your own that would be safe, appropriate, and effective conversation openers with a new client during the Delivery Phase. Write a different question that is most likely to work well for each of the four personality styles.

   Cooperator Question: ______________________________

   ______________________________

   ______________________________

   Analyzer Question: ______________________________

   ______________________________

   ______________________________

   Regulator Question: ______________________________

   ______________________________

   ______________________________

   Energizer Question: ______________________________

   ______________________________

   ______________________________

10. Low interaction is the best conversational approach to use with a client you have difficulty relating to.
    Circle One:

    True or False

Lesson 7.5

# Recommendation Phase

Recommendation Phase

In the Recommendation Phase, you listen and collect data on your client's product use, then make appropriate recommendations.

## OBJECTIVES

At the completion of this lesson, you will be able to:

- Explain the importance of the Recommendation Phase
- Demonstrate how to serve clients by assessing their product use and making recommendations where appropriate
- Identify buying traits of each personality style
- Use the Recommendation Phase form to determine the products clients use

## WHAT YOU NEED TO KNOW

The Recommendation Phase is often the most overlooked phase of the Service Cycle. It can be an afterthought, because some salon professionals don't view sales as a part of service. That can make the Recommendation Phase awkward and challenging, especially for Novice salon professionals. Cooperator and Analyzer salon professionals may also find this phase difficult because of their low-risk perspective.

In the Recommendation Phase, you:

- Review the hair, nail, and skin care products and services your clients use and need.
- Use your professional experience to help them determine whether they are using the best products for their hair and body characteristics.
- Tell them about the quality and convenience of using your salon's products.
- Recommend where they can buy a truly superior product that they need but that is not sold by your salon, or see if your salon can carry it.

### Recommendation Don'ts

To appreciate the power of a proper Recommendation Phase, let's look at the absurdities of Salon Calimité, where service, at best, is an afterthought.

## Salon Calimité. . .

Recommendation is not a service to the client at Salon Calimité. If salon employees discuss products and services at all, they do it out of obligation to the salon, not to clients. Salon employees can sound like pushy salespeople or unthinking robots when talking about products and services available through the salon.

As a client, you either wonder about the products used at the salon or you feel captive to a bad commercial. In either case, your need for information on products and services that will help you maintain your look goes ignored. Plus, you end up making another trip to the drugstore to pick up items you could have bought at the salon.

## Recommendation Techniques

The Recommendation Phase provides the opportunity for salon professionals to serve as their clients' primary source of hair and body care knowledge, whether or not these clients buy products from the salon. Clients should know when they have a convenient source of high-quality products that serve their needs available for purchase right in their salon.

### Novice Recommendation

The Novice discusses the products he or she uses during the Delivery Phase and as a convenience, suggests that the client buy the products while paying for the service. Product conversations can be awkward for the Novice at first. Novices are still learning about product chemistry and benefits and generally don't venture too far beyond the products they have used. Novices should take as many classes as they can. The more they learn, the better they can sort the facts from the hype in product sales.

### Professional Recommendation

Professionals begin to see product conversations as a whole new way of providing service to the client. Professionals feel confident about hair texture, color, and other issues. They know the products and tools of their trade. Product conversations are smooth because they are well-integrated into Delivery Phase conversations. Professionals seamlessly take the next step after delivery and review all of their clients' hair, nail, and skin care products and services, commenting on their quality and proper use. Their clients generally accept their guidance and benefit from the convenience of buying at the salon.

### Master Recommendation

Master salon professionals are generally their clients' total beauty, fashion, and image consultants. Master salon professionals smoothly involve themselves in the selection, purchase and use of their clients' salon products and services, whether or not the salon sells those products or provides those services. You know you are a Master when your client wouldn't think of using any kind of hair, nail, or skin care product without consulting you first.

### Why Recommend Products and Services

You serve your clients better through your product and service recommendations. As a salon professional, you have a greater understanding of salon products than most of your clients.

Your knowledge can greatly aid them in maintaining an appearance that improves the quality of their lives, both professionally and personally. You can also serve clients better by saving them an often frustrating shopping trip.

As always, when you serve your clients better, you serve yourself better. Becoming proficient at the Recommendation Phase improves your career success by helping your salon increase its retail sales and thus its profits.

Because your recommendation is often critical to the sale of products, salon owners often give professionals a percentage of the retail sale as earned income. This additional income can be significant.

Learn the art of Recommendation, and you will not only help your clients, but you will also maximize your earning potential.

## Determining Product Use

You will develop your own style for the Recommendation Phase if you begin diligently providing this phase of service to every client. Many Professional and Master-level salon professionals integrate their recommendations into the Delivery and Completion Phases. Novices have a harder time seeing how products are an important part of service because they are so focused on Delivery.

Review product use and benefits as a way to provide additional service to your clients, in addition to increasing salon revenue.

**Master the art of the Recommendation Phase, and you'll at once serve your clients better and increase your income.**

## In the Salon. . .

Ray's first client of the day is Colleen. She is a district manager for a large retail chain, which requires her to travel extensively throughout the Midwest. During her last appointment, Ray had created a dramatic color change for Colleen, taking her dark hair to a light, cool blonde.

As Ray waits for Colleen, he is expecting to hear how everyone raved over her new look. Instead, when Colleen arrives, she immediately informs Ray that she is dissatisfied with the way her color held. "If I can't depend on the color holding, I would like to return to my natural dark color," she says.

Ray's first instinct is to tell her that even though the color didn't hold, it still looks fabulous. Instead, he analyzes her hair and agrees that the soft blonde shade had become slightly brassy.

Ray asks Colleen what type of shampoo and conditioner she is currently using, especially when she travels. Colleen states that she generally uses the shampoo that the hotels provide but does not always condition her hair.

"Because you travel, your hair is probably exposed to hard water, which can cause discoloration," Ray explains. He recommends that she maintain her color between salon visits by using a violet-based, color-enhancing shampoo in order to eliminate the undesired warm tones in her hair.

Colleen takes the recommendation of the color-enhancing shampoo. On her next visit, Ray is thrilled to hear how everyone raved about Colleen's hair color.

Use this formal step of the Recommendation Phase to determine the products your clients use and the way they use them. You can then discuss the convenience and quality of salon products as your clients maintain their look at home.

Many salon professionals lose credibility and fail to serve by ignoring products, tools, or services. They miss a great opportunity to talk about about the products used during the Delivery Phase and then fail to reinforce product recommendations later on.

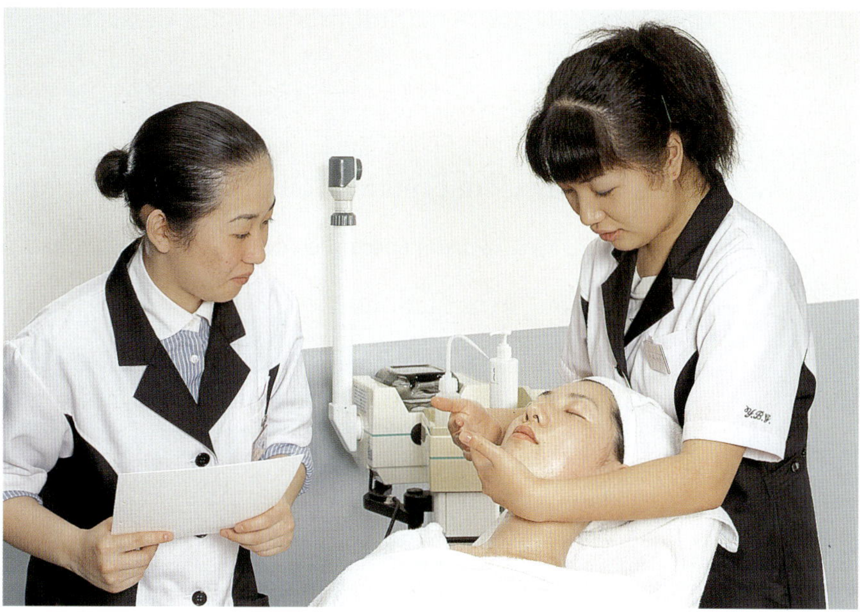

Make sure you understand how your clients care for their hair, skin and nails. Some clients may not think of your salon as a potential source of their salon-care products.

When you wait until clients are on their way out the door, some clients may perceive that you only gave them a required sales pitch.

Indeed, many salon professionals feel they are "pushing" the salon's retail lines if they talk about product. If you feel that way, you must not understand the great service clients can receive. Unless your salon doesn't carry the product your client needs, why not buy it from you? Research on clients shows that they often appreciate the help and convenience. Many clients actually get home without product and are upset that they forgot to pick it up.

If you really want to fully serve, you must alter your attitude about sales. Start thinking of the salon's retail section as an convenience or service for the client, not an inconvenience.

**As a salon professional, you have much greater knowledge of products and services than your clients. Use that knowledge help them know what products work best for their hair, skin, and nail characteristics.**

Every single one of your clients at least buys shampoo. For many clients, the small price difference between the salon and other stores is well worth it.

Remember with the rapid pace of today's business and society, many clients find it inconvenient to go to stores to buy hair and body-care products. Don't underestimate the service you provide for your clients when you offer your advice and recommend products.

## *Influencing Product Selection*

Go into a store today and look at the products available. A typical store may have an entire aisle, with hundreds of choices, devoted to shampoo and conditioners alone.

**Each personality style has different buying habits. Learn what each personality style values when making buying decisions and speak to those concerns.**

Within each category, you find products distinguished by:

- Price
- Scent
- Hair or skin type (fine, normal, oily)
- Treatment formulations (permed, colored, tinted)
- Special "salon" formulations

Given the number of choices, don't expect your clients to know what they need. As a salon professional, you should learn as much as you can. You should be your clients' best guide to product selection and use.

As you ask your clients about the products they use, make sure you find out the reason why they use each product. Frequently, it will be force of habit. At that point in the conversation, you learn more about what makes your client "tick" which, in turn, leads to greater rapport and increased opportunities to serve.

You'll find that some clients pay no attention to what they use on their hair. The purchasing decisions of other clients are influenced by price, convenience, advertising, celebrities, friends, and other sources that have no relationship to the unique qualities of their hair, nails, and skin or their lifestyles.

And that's where the opportunities lie to serve. You can guide your clients toward products that fit them best, thereby increasing your value to the client.

Note that Cooperator and Energizer clients may be more open to your suggestions than Analyzer and Regulator clients. The Analyzer and Regulator will require more facts and explanations of product benefits.

## Influencing Services

As you discuss products, refer back to the client's habits, as listed in the "New Client Assessment Questionnaire," in order to discuss services.

- Does the client use home finishing products, such as mousse, pomade or hair gel?
- How does the client care for his or her nails or skin?

If you don't know, ask again. Your client would be better served by taking advantage of the other services that your salon offers.

The following table provides guidance on discussing product and service selection with each of the personality styles.

### Product and Service Buying Traits

| Personality Style | Buying Traits and Actions |
|---|---|
| **Cooperator** | • Likely to be influenced by friends, co-workers, celebrities and advertising.<br>• Likely to care about how pleasing a product will make them look.<br>• Focus on guiding product selection but be aware that the Cooperator client may buy something to please you, so don't push products on anyone, especially Cooperator clients. |
| **Analyzer** | • Most likely to be influenced by cost and convenience.<br>• Likely to care about features and formulation and less likely to pay attention to branding.<br>• Focus on the specific benefits of a product and, if possible, other facts, such as how it can save money by lasting longer. You can also focus on the time it saves to buy in the salon while they are already here. |
| **Regulator** | • Likely to be influenced by purchasing convenience and the time it saves to buy in the salon.<br>• Likely to care about branding.<br>• Focus on the benefits of how a product allows them to achieve a more finished look in less time on their own. |
| **Energizer** | • Likely to be influenced by advertising and trends they read about in magazines. They like to sizzle more than other styles.<br>• Likely to care about how a product improves their looks.<br>• Present benefits as with other styles, but you can talk about "newness" and "trendiness." Also focus on beauty benefits. |

Remember that selling products and services is not the highest purpose of the Recommendation Phase. It's only the starting point on the way to becoming your client's total image consultant.

In Lesson 7.6, *Completion Phase*, you will learn about the final phase of the Service Cycle.

## EXERCISE

Review the New Client Assessment Questionnaire you filled out in Exercise 2 in Lesson 7.2. Focus on the product and services questions and discuss or role play Recommendation Phase conversations. What did you learn about yourself as a service provider? As a consumer?

______________________________________________

______________________________________________

______________________________________________

______________________________________________

______________________________________________

______________________________________________

______________________________________________

______________________________________________

______________________________________________

## MAIN POINT SUMMARY

During the Recommendation Phase, you evaluate the client's current hair and body care and make suggestions for improvements. This phase can run the entire gamut from simply suggesting usage of new products to serving as a comprehensive image consultant to your clients. The range of service that you provide will depend on your level of expertise and on the client's level of need.

Many inexperienced salon professionals fail to fully serve clients because they feel an initial discomfort with this phase. They have difficulty with making "sales pitches" to clients. Because of this, they fail to fully assess the client's hair and body care habits and aids.

In reality, however, the opportunity to examine what products your clients use and what new products might better achieve the result they desire, is the one that most clients greatly appreciate. Likewise, clients will appreciate your technical expertise and the opportunity to take care of all their hair and body care needs in one convenient stop.

Take your cue from the client when determining the level of service that they need and what approach will best meet their need. Once again, the different CARE personality styles can guide you.

## Recommendation Phase Technique Review

| Type of Client | Level of Service | Actions to Take |
|---|---|---|
| **Repeat** | Same | • Ask your client how products you have recommended are working and whether any more products are needed. Keep in mind your client's personality style. |
| | Modify | • Ask your client how the products you have recommended are working and whether they need any more. Suggest any other products based on modifications you have made. |
| | Makeover | • Explain which new products are required to maintain the makeover. Talk about the products used in the salon and find out if the client uses anything similar. Make recommendations based on what the client uses now and needs to maintain the new look. |
| **New** | Same | • Ask the client what products he or she uses and why they selected them. Discuss whether those products are the best to maintain his or her appearance. |
| | Modify | • Ask the client what products he or she uses and how they were selected. Assess whether those products are adequate to maintain their clients's appearance and explain which other products are required, especially if they are unfamiliar to the client. |
| | Makeover | • Ask the client what products he or she uses and assess his or her ability to maintain the new look. The client will most likely need additional products. Make sure you discuss the reasons why they are needed, especially if your client has never used these products before. |

## SELF-TEST/REVIEW

1. The sole purpose of the Recommendation Phase is to make money for the salon through retail sales of products to your client.
   Circle One:

   True or False

   Briefly explain your answer.

   ______________________________________________

   ______________________________________________

   ______________________________________________

   ______________________________________________

   ______________________________________________

2. Match the appropriate Recommendation Phase approach to the CARE personality types:

____ Cooperator

____ Analyzer

____ Regulator

____ Energizer

A. Focus on the specific benefits of a product and how it will save money by lasting longer because it requires less quantity or because it saves time to buy in the salon while they are already there.

B. Focus on guiding product selection but be aware that the client may buy something to please you. Don't push products on these clients.

C. Focus on "newness" and "trendiness," but do not insult your client's intelligence with an "everybody's using this" pitch. Also focus on the beauty benefits.

D. Focus on the benefits of how a product allows them to achieve a more finished look in less time, on their own.

3. Write the first sentence of your approach for starting the Recommendation Phase conversation with each of the four personality styles.

**Cooperator**:

______________________________________________

______________________________________________

**Analyzer**:

______________________________________________

______________________________________________

**Regulator**:

______________________________________________

______________________________________________

**Energizer**:

______________________________________________

______________________________________________

Lesson 7.6

# Completion Phase

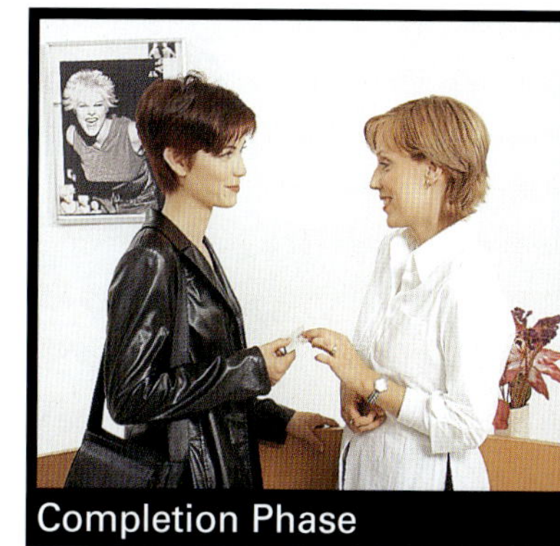
Completion Phase

The Completion phase consists of Review plus Acknowledgment. Achievement and success are the results you want.

## OBJECTIVES

At the completion of this lesson, you will be able to:

- Discuss the critical elements of the Completion Phase
- Demonstrate how to review your clients' salon experience to determine their level of satisfaction
- Re-book clients before they leave the salon.
- Say genuine goodbyes to your clients, taking into account their personality styles, and ensure that they look forward to their next visit
- Be sensitive to client dissatisfaction and know how to turn the situation around with tact and diplomacy

## WHAT YOU NEED TO KNOW

The Completion Phase brings the Service Cycle to an end and a beginning—it leads full circle into the Greeting Phase of the next appointment. Even though it may seem like your work is done, you're really at the most critical phase of the Service Cycle.

The way you handle the Completion Phase often determines whether or not your client returns and refers others. When done properly, the Completion Phase assures that you get another chance to experience the six phases of service with the client, because he or she will re-book before leaving the salon.

The objectives of the Completion Phase are:

- Review the services to make sure the client is satisfied
- Acknowledge and solve any problems
- Confirm the details of home maintenance and care
- Help the client select the correct retail products
- Review and set appointments for other services such as skin, nails, perms, etc.
- Secure a firm appointment for the client's next salon visit
- Say goodbye to your client and wish them well

### Completion Don'ts

To appreciate the power of a proper Completion Phase, let's look at the absurdities of Salon Calimité, where service, at best, is an afterthought.

## Salon Calimité . . .

Clients look forward to the Completion Phase at Salon Calimité because, by the time it comes around, they are ready to leave. Salon employees allow clients to view the final style with an expectation of praise. They are not interested in reviewing the client's experience or hearing about problems.

When it comes time to say goodbye, an employee at Salon Calimité is most interested in receiving his or her tip. The nature of the goodbye the client receives it dependent on the amount of the tip, rather than a genuine interest in the client.

Salon employees generally forget to ask the client to re-book. But it hardly matters. Most clients don't want to return. Salon Calimité is a business of walk-ins and walk-outs.

## Completion Techniques

In the Completion Phase, salon professionals review the overall service and assess the satisfaction of the client. This phase solidifies the relationship and partnership between salon professional and client, ending with a warm goodbye as the client faces a major event or the business of daily life. For the clients who have made major changes in their appearance, salon professionals prepare them for the challenges of presenting a new image to the outside world.

### Novice Completion

Novice salon professionals initially worry about client's reaction to their work and may want to avoid the review. They often spend much of the Completion Phase relieved to have made it through the Delivery Phase unscathed.

As they develop and gain confidence in their work, they relate to the client more and more with pride, knowing they have helped someone present their most positive face to the world. They thank the client and begin to learn the art of re-booking and leaving one client while greeting the next. Novices frequently feel flustered when clients have problems with the work performed, in those cases, often seek the aid of more experienced professionals or managers.

### Professional Completion

Professionals feel confident that they have made a difference in another person's life. They review any service details as a natural part of saying goodbye. They genuinely want to hear about discomfort, worries, and problems. They also help each client remember to schedule another appointment before leaving the salon and remind clients to purchase products they expressed interest in. professionals handle complaints about problems with grace and know how to respond to most difficult situations. They also have mastered the art of leaving one client while greeting the next.

### Master Completion

Masters are aware of the multiple facets of their client's lifestyle, from general activities to immediate directions. They use the Completion Phase as an opportunity to wish them well. They know how to tailor their goodbyes so that each individual leaves feeling complete. Masters know the appropriate degree of familiarity to show their clients, whether to help them out of the chair or maintain reserve, for instance. Masters focus on the person as they are leaving, assuring that the details of re-booking, product sales, and problem resolution flow easily from their relationship with the client.

## Reviewing Services

In the Completion Phase, you review what you did and find out whether your client liked it. Also check to make sure any other service you and your client agreed upon was accomplished.

The following table provides a list of questions you should be able to answer before you say goodbye to your client.

### Completion Phase Review Questions

| Objective |
| --- |
| • Are all the services complete? |
| • Did you meet your client's expectations? |
| • Is there anything else your client needs to know about home maintenance? |
| • Have you discussed products for home use, such as nail polish or other finishing products? |
| • Are other services scheduled? |
| • Is your client satisfied with the entire salon experience? |
| • Is there anything you need to correct either now or later on? |

Completion Phase is the time for you and your client to enjoy the results of your creative partnership.

If you didn't complete everything or your client is not satisfied, then offer alternatives. Maybe you can take care of it on the spot. Maybe you can schedule another appointment to complete a service. Or maybe you can offer a complimentary service, if that's your salon's policy.

Now we'll look at the parts of the Completion Phase:

- Re-booking
- Saying goodbye
- Tipping

**Re-booking your clients before they leave the salon is the critical goal of the Completion Phase.**

## Re-booking or Scheduling the Next Visit

Re-booking is the core goal of the Completion Phase. Many clients have not formed an allegiance to a particular salon. They may have enjoyed working with you and like the result, but if you don't complete the session with a new appointment, you can't be certain you'll see the client again.

If you don't schedule them, they may go elsewhere. Clients say they are generally frustrated when they forget to re-book and consider your reminder a valuable service.

Indeed, most clients don't think about their next visit as they leave the salon unless you or the receptionist asks them to re-book. If they think of it after they leave, they will likely put off making the call until they notice in the mirror that their hair looks bad. Then they'll call in a rush and see if they can get an appointment. Repeat clients appreciate having their appointments booked just as much as new clients.

For a well-organized, service-oriented salon, reminder calls and postcards often serve as a useful bridge between the Completion Phase of the last visit and the Greeting Phase of the next. If done well, reminders can generate excitement for the client.

Receptionist hands client a card noting her next appointment.

**Wish your client well, especially if they are off to an event. The art of saying goodbye is enhanced when you can finish with one client while greeting the next.**

If your clients are unsure about their schedule, suggest that they go ahead and schedule, then cancel if their scheduled time does not work. This saves forgotten service and unnecessary phones calls for all.

As always, take the personality style of your client into account when you schedule another visit. The following table shows some broad re-booking guidelines for each personality style.

### Re-booking Traits

| Personality Style | Traits and Actions |
|---|---|
| Cooperator | • Less concerned about time but dependable.<br>• Probably has appointment book handy.<br>• May have some difficulty deciding when to come in next.<br>• Gently suggest a time. |
| Analyzer | • Precise about time.<br>• Likely has appointment book or hand-held computer ready to make the next appointment.<br>• Will likely re-book—if for no other reason than to take care of a task as early as possible.<br>• Suggest an exact future appointment time. |
| Regulator | • Leads purposeful life and is concerned about timing.<br>• Likely has appointment book handy for re-booking<br>• Will appreciate having a routine schedule of standing appointments. |
| Energizer | • Tends to be the most difficult to re-book on the spot because timing is not a primary concern.<br>• May not have an appointment book on-hand or may not have one at all.<br>• Will likely be unconcerned about re-booking.<br>• Make a follow-up phone call, or have the receptionist call, to get the next appointment scheduled. |

## Saying Goodbye

Many successful salon professionals views their clientele as an extension of their friendship network. They get a sense of fulfillment when saying a warm goodbye, and know that they can look forward to seeing that client again.

Wish your client well as the Completion Phase winds to a close, especially when your client is going off to a party or some social event—wish them well and hope that they have a good time.

If you have not already started with your next client, you may want to end the Completion Phase by sending your client off with a warm goodbye while walking them to the door. If you have started with your next client, you face the challenge of graciously thanking your last client while maintaining contact with your current client.

With Analyzer and Regulator clients, you may want to make your goodbye quick and without touching, while Cooperator and Energizer clients may extend their goodbyes longer than you wish.

Don't be surprised if Regulator and Analyzer clients, the thinking-oriented personality styles, seem to want a quicker goodbye. The Completion Phase can seem awkward for the Analyzer, who may appear reticent, and the Regulator, who may be perceived as brusque. Both personality styles tend to be concerned about their schedules and will most likely feel invaded by any sort of touch.

With Cooperator and Energizer clients, however, you can usually be much more demonstrative if that fits your personality style and the closeness of your relationship with your client. The following table provides guidance on ways to say goodbye to each personality style.

## Ways of Saying Goodbye

| Personality Style | Traits and Actions |
|---|---|
| Cooperator | • Frequently finda it difficult to say goodbye because of orientation to people—likes to extend the goodbye by chatting.<br>• Appreciates a warm goodbye.<br>• Don't rush but lead toward closure.<br>• Tell them how others will like their new look. |
| Analyzer | • Generally likes crisp goodbyes.<br>• Not often demonstrative and may be awkward and seem reticent.<br>• Increase comfort with a simple goodbye and acknowledgment. |
| Regulator | • Focused, often busy and in a hurry.<br>• May seem brusque.<br>• Be direct in your goodbye and don't dawdle. |
| Energizer | • May want to chat and find it difficult to finish, especially if rapport is high.<br>• Needs to be appreciated.<br>• If the relationship supports it, tell them how great they look. |

Tailor your goodbye to both your client's personality style and the depth of your relationship with him or her.

## Tipping

The Completion Phase is also the time when many salon professionals receive a tip. It can be an awkward moment.

Consider the situation from the client's point of view. You are beginning to work with your next client, and your last client comes up to hand you a tip. For some people, especially Cooperators and Analyzers, who don't like to call attention to themselves, that's an awkward situation. These kind of people may feel more comfortable leaving their tip in an envelope at the front desk.

At the same time, making it easy for a client to leave the tip with you personally gives you one last chance for a personal connection and a reward for your service. Both methods are acceptable for salons that allow tipping.

Now let's look at the Completion Phase in action, first with a Novice stylist and then with a Master.

Cooperator salon professional and Regulator client say goodbye after a successful cut.

**Your listening skills are critical during the Completion Phase.**

## Losing a Client in the Completion Phase

Christopher had followed each phase of the Service Cycle and prepared to finish with his client, Naomi. His rapport was strong. Delivery proceeded without difficulty. The conversation was pleasant and rewarding. He finished on-schedule, and gave Naomi the hand mirror, and swung her around so she could see the style from all sides.

Christopher watched Naomi examine the style. He was satisfied—it had turned out as he had visualized. Both client and designer said nothing for a minute, then Christopher spoke up.

**Christopher:** Everything okay, Naomi?

**Naomi:** Um, yes, Christopher. It's fine, thank-you.

**Christopher:** Well, I just saw my next client come in. You've been a delight to serve today, Naomi. The receptionist will help you schedule your next appointment. Thank you.

**Naomi:** You're welcome.

Naomi got her coat and went up to the reception desk. Just then, the receptionist got a very lengthy call. It gave Naomi time to think about her bill and decide she really didn't want to spend any more on retail products that day. The receptionist forgot to ask her about her next appointment, so Naomi figured she would just call later.

Sooner or later every salon professional has a dissatisfied client. How will you handle it?

Ten weeks later, to his surprise, Christopher found Naomi's name on his monthly report of inactive clients. She should have been in for her color touch-up appointment a month ago, Christopher thought. Wondering what happened, he gave her a call at her work number.

**Christopher:** Hi Naomi, it's Christopher Newman of the Paris Salon.

**Naomi:** Hello Christopher, how are you?

**Christopher:** I'm fine, but I was wondering why we haven't seen you in 10 weeks. You seemed so pleased with your color design. I was expecting to see you for your touch-up and cut a month ago.

*Naomi was silent for a moment, then she took a deep breath, seeming to gather courage before she spoke.*

**Naomi:** To tell you the truth, I was pleased with the way it looked when I left. But after 2 weeks it appeared very dry and the color faded. Then, the next day I noticed color stains on my forehead and on the nape of my neck.

**Christopher:** Naomi, I'm shocked and very, very sorry. Why didn't you call?

**Naomi:** I tried to call that Saturday, but the salon phone was always busy. I went out of town on a business trip the next night; I was desperate for help because it looked so bad, so I made an appointment at the salon in the hotel where I was staying.

**Christopher:** I see. What did the designer tell you?

**Naomi:** Well, I hate to repeat it. Basically, she felt my color had been overprocessed and my designer should have known that.

**Christopher:** Naomi, I hate to contradict another professional, but I had no indication there was a problem with your color. I would have appreciated the chance to make it up to you. I would have conditioned and refreshed your color at no charge that very week, if I had known. One last question: How did you shampoo and condition your hair at home?

*Naomi gave Christopher the name of two popular over-the-counter products she used.*

**Christopher:** Naomi, both of those products are very alkaline. Even though they say they are for chemically processed hair, my experience has been that they destroy the condition of color-treated hair. Why didn't you use the products we discussed?

**Naomi:** Christopher, I really have to get back to work. I didn't buy the products you recommended because your receptionist was too busy to help me, and I got to thinking that I really did not have enough money that day. I'm sorry, but I believed the hotel designer, so when I got home I made my next appointment at a salon of my co-workers. I've been very happy there so far. Thanks for calling. Goodbye.

Naomi hung up before Christopher had a chance to say goodbye—goodbye to hundreds, maybe thousands of dollars in future service revenue and referrals.

That situation illustrates the importance of the Completion Phase as the vital finishing touch to your efforts. Even when you do everything right from Agreement through Product Recommendation, ignoring the Completion Phase may mean that all the time and skill you have already invested may prove to be wasted.

What did Christopher do wrong? He really didn't do anything wrong. He is simply guilty of not doing some things right. Let's rewrite the same salon situation, with a successful Completion Phase.

## Gaining Client Loyalty in the Completion Phase

**Christopher:** There, Naomi, we're finished. Let me get this cape off and hand you the mirror. Take a few moments, then tell me honestly what you think.

*Naomi takes the hand mirror and swivels around, examining the style carefully.*

**Naomi:** Well, Christopher. It's a lovely design. I guess I am just getting used to less hair on my shoulders, but more around my face.

**Christopher:** It's definitely a change from your old image, Naomi. Your straight, center-parted hair gave your magnificent face a long, thin look. We've allowed your hair to showcase your facial structure.

**Naomi:** I'm sure you're right, Christopher. I'll take time to get used to the new me. I'll know better by the way others react to it. Believe me, my business associates won't pull any punches.

**Christopher:** I'd be willing to bet you get rave reviews. Excuse me a moment, Naomi. Don't go away. I see another client has just walked in, and I want to tell him I'll be a few more minutes. You keep looking and make sure you ask me all your questions before you go home. I want you to be satisfied. Be back in a minute.

*Christopher walks over to the waiting area, and greets his next client warmly, making sure the client can wait five or 10 more minutes while he finishes up with Naomi. The client is agreeable and picks up a magazine while he waits. He returns to the station, where Naomi is looking at her hair and touching it gently.*

**Naomi:** There are so many layers in it now, are you sure I'll be able to style it like you did?

**Christopher:** Just remember what I showed you with the round brush. And remember to hold the layers up and dry underneath the hair, for fullness. You can touch up the front with a curling iron.

**Naomi:** Okay. I guess that's all.

**Christopher:** Do you remember the products we discussed to maintain the condition of your hair?

**Naomi:** Gosh, I tried to listen, but I got confused. What did you say they were again? I hate to keep you when you have a client waiting.

**Christopher:** It's okay. Remember what I said about the drugstore shampoo you're now using? It has high pH, which means it is alkaline, and that may dry your hair. This is an excellent shampoo. (*Christopher takes a professional product off the shelf.*) Now, this red bottle contains the finishing and detangling product you want to spray on after you've shampooed and towel-dried your hair. Work it through with your fingers, then style as usual.

**Naomi:** I don't rinse it out?

**Christopher:** No, and it can be used daily. This third bottle is the conditioner I used on your hair today. Remember the apricot smell you commented on? Well, this is it. Use only a little in the palm of your hand, after you've shampooed, twice a week. Leave it on three or four minutes, then rinse it out completely. Here, I'll write it all down on this paper for you. Just don't tape it inside the shower!

**Naomi:** (*Laughing*) Okay, I'll take all three. And while I'm here, I'll take that styling brush, too, I don't have one.

**Christopher:** Good choice. All our styling tools are 25 percent off this week. Now remember the importance of your re-touch visit. I'd like you to book it now and I think it should be in approximately four weeks.

**Naomi:** Okay, Thursday, the 29$^{th}$, exactly four weeks from today, 6 p.m.

**Christopher:** (*Reaching over and looking at the book.*) It's available. (*Speaking to the receptionist.*) Claire, please book Naomi for a color re-touch, deep conditioning and a cut. We'll need an hour. (*Turning back to the client.*) Naomi, Claire will give you a card with the date on it as a reminder. But in the meantime, if you have any difficulty at all, call me. Please. Some clients have questions about managing new designs. I'll be happy to help you get the hang of it. You can come in some morning before work, and we'll style it together.

**Naomi:** Christopher, thanks for everything. I'll see you in four weeks.

**Christopher:** Thank you, Naomi. I wish I could be a fly on the wall in your office when you go into work tomorrow. I'd love to see all those heads turn!

**Naomi:** I'll tell you all about it when I see you again. Goodbye, Christopher. I'm really very pleased.

**Christopher:** Goodbye Naomi. (*Turning to his waiting client.*) Mr. Johnson! Hello again. And thanks for waiting, I do apologize for keeping you.

**Mr. Johnson:** No problem, Christopher.

One service is successfully completed and the next service begins.

## EXERCISES

1. Work through the following analysis of the story of Christopher and Naomi. Examine and discuss what Christopher did right in the second situation and for future business by studying the table below, which breaks the Completion Phase scenario into review and acknowledgment parts. Notice how Christopher and Naomi reviewed the service and acknowledged each other's review.

| Review | Acknowledgment |
|---|---|
| The designer gave his client time to get used to the look and the opportunity to express her feelings. Part of the reason she needed time was because most clients see themselves differently from how others see them. The designer immediately saw the style as perfect for the client's face. The client was not used to so much lift and fullness and was having a hard time accepting it. | The designer acknowledged his client's feelings and offered an explanation why she felt that way. |
| The client expressed concerns about not knowing how to style her hair. | The designer acknowledged her concerns. |

| **Review** | **Acknowledgment** |
| --- | --- |
| The designer reviewed techniques for styling hair at home. | The client acknowledged the advice. |
| The designer asked the client about her understanding of the products needed to maintain her hair. | The client admitted she was unsure what to use. |
| The designer took the time to go over the products, and write a brief description of how they should be used and when. | The client accepted the advice and purchased the products. |
| The designer repeated the importance of a visit within four weeks to check the condition of her hair and the client's satisfaction. | The client agreed and made a firm appointment. |
| The designer offered assistance in case problems arose in the interim. | The client thanked him and confirmed she was satisfied. The designer acknowledged her comments and thanked her. They parted in rapport, and the next Greeting Phase began equally well. |

2. Write or role play goodbye scenarios for each of the four personality styles.

**Cooperator**

______________________________________________

______________________________________________

**Analyzer**

______________________________________________

______________________________________________

**Regulator**

---

---

**Energizer**

---

---

## MAIN POINT SUMMARY

The last phase in the Service Cycle is the Completion Phase, and it is crucial because it often determines if the client returns.

Your objective in the Completion Phase should be, first of all, to review the service and determine the client's level of satisfaction. This is your opportunity to acknowledge and solve any problems that may have arisen. Next, confirm any suggestions you made for home care or product selection. Finally, schedule his or her next appointment and say goodbye.

Your ultimate goal in this phase is to re-book a satisfied and happy client. You want to create loyal clients who return again and again. Significantly, even clients who genuinely appreciate and enjoy your service may not automatically form an allegiance to your salon. It is vital that you take the initiative in scheduling the next visit.

Once again, knowledge of CARE personality types can be quite useful. Cooperators are less concerned with time but are often quite dependable, so you should gently suggest a time that is convenient. You may have to lead the Cooperator to closure and give them a warm goodbye as they depart. Analyzers are more concerned with timing and would appreciate setting an exact date and time well in advance, and a quick and simple goodbye should do nicely.

Regulators are likewise concerned with timing but may have a disdain for details and prefer that you set standing appointments that are automatically scheduled, well in advance. A direct goodbye works best, and you should anticipate some degree of brusqueness. Energizers are often most difficult to re-book. You may need to make a follow-up call, and goodbyes may be quite chatty.

## Completion Phase Technique Review

| Type of Client | Level of Service | Actions to Take |
|---|---|---|
| **Repeat** | • Same | • Say your normal goodbye and re-book your client, according to their personality style. |
| | • Modify | • Review the service to make sure everything is complete. Wish your client well with the new look and make sure he or she schedules any required maintenance visits. |
| | • Makeover | • After checking whether all the details of the makeover are complete, make sure the client schedules any maintenance visits and understands home maintenance. Congratulate your client on the new look, and compliment according to your client's personality. |
| **New** | • Same | • Say goodbye according to the client's personality style and suggest that he or she re-book. Make sure you give the client your business card. |
| | • Modify | • Be extra professional in your review of the service, taking care of any remaining details. Make sure the client understands home maintenance and the reason behind any required maintenance visits. Wish the client well with the new look and follow up with a call. |
| | • Makeover | • Take extra care in making sure all of the services are complete. Review what you did and why, at a level of detail the person needs. Cover home maintenance, the need for maintenance visits, and the reasons behind them. With radical changes, the client may look unsure. Ask how the client feels about the new look and spend extra time if required to send the client off with more confidence. Follow-up calls may be in order here. |

## SELF-TEST/REVIEW

1. The core goal of the Completion Phase is: ______________________________.

2. Why is it so important, even with satisfied clients, to schedule the next visit?

______________________________________________________________________

______________________________________________________________________

______________________________________________________________________

______________________________________________________________________

3. Briefly contrast how you might say goodbye to a Regulator with how you might say goodbye to an Energizer.

4. Give an example of a situation in which a busy, time-constrained client might appreciate the opportunity to re-book while they are at the salon in the Completion Phase. What might have happened if they'd not been given this opportunity to re-book?

5. Explain the importance of reviewing the service and acknowledging the client's concerns during the Completion Phase. How does this relate to your listening skills?

Unit 8

# Service Development

## THE VISION

In Unit 5, you learned the fundamentals of service—you learned what service is and what it is not. You learned about values and effective listening in Unit 6, and in Unit 7 you covered the Service Cycle. For each phase of the Service Cycle, you learned precise techniques and skills for building rapport by providing excellent service. Now you'll wrap up your study of service by learning follow-through techniques to develop your business over the long term. Service is a lifelong journey. You'll get off to a great start by reviewing each skill and technique in each phase of the Service Cycle and deciding how you will put those techniques and skills into practice.

### Novice

Novices rarely follow-through after a client visit. They are still learning the connection between service and sales and are in the the beginning stages of developing a regular clientele. They generally rely on the salon to generate new clients for them. If they follow-through with a client, it is generally a friend or family member. Novices who are focused on developing their careers pay attention to service quality and evaluate their performance with individual clients, often in consultation with a more experienced salon professional. They also review their own actions and develop their own standards of service based on which behaviors please clients.

### Professional

Professionals pay a good deal of attention to developing a long-term clientele and use a wide variety of techniques to follow-through and keep in touch with clients. They regularly make follow-up phone calls and send thank-you notes to new clients.

Professionals also review their service with each client and discuss challenges with other salon professionals. They maintain a file on each client and refer to that file before and after each visit. Before the visit, they review notes from previous visits for client comments and aspects of service the Professional might want to improve upon. After the visit, they note any problems they want to work out or points to remember on the next visit. Professionals have clearly defined service standards of their own and keep them up-to-date.

### Master

Masters know that sales and service are intricately linked. They follow-up with clients—particularly first-time clients—as a regular part of their service routine. Like Professionals, they maintain files on their clients. Masters, however, also have clients that they know like family members. They note important events in their clients' lives—such as birthdays and anniversaries—as a matter of course. Masters have well-established standards of service, which they keep up-to-date by training Novices and Professionals on the finer points of business and service development.

## What's Ahead. . .

This unit is designed to provide an introduction to salon service development by presenting the link between sales and service. The lesson in this unit provides the basic techniques of follow-through and service evaluation required to build an ongoing clientele. After completing this unit of *Serving with CARE*, you should be able to:

- Make follow-up phone calls that clients appreciate.
- Send appropriate thank-you cards for each of the four personality styles.
- Evaluate your performance after each client visit and note areas you need to improve upon for their next visit.
- Set your own standards of service by looking at the component parts of each phase in the Service Cycle and listing the specific behaviors you will take to meet that standard.

*Unit 8: Service Development, consists of one lesson:*

**Lesson 8.1: Service Follow-Through, Evaluation, and Standards**

Lesson 8.1

# Service Follow-Through, Evaluation, and Standards

> The best way to build your business is to provide outstanding service. Remember: Service is selling.

## OBJECTIVES

At the completion of this lesson, you will be able to:

- Describe techniques for retaining clients, such as: writing reminder cards, thank-you notes, and making follow-up calls
- Complete your own Service Standards Worksheet

## WHAT YOU NEED TO KNOW

Congratulations! You have almost completed your journey through the Service Cycle. Now it's time to review what you've learned by envisioning how you are going to put your knowledge of service into action.

First, we will look at some service techniques that build your client base. Next we will evaluate how well you're doing. Then, we'll set standards for service and how you practice it in the salon.

### Serving is Selling

The most basic sales technique for building your client base is retaining clients you already have. This activity can be summed up in one word: Serving. By serving fully, you keep clients you have and they refer others.

If a client appreciates both your work and your relationship with them, you will likely find that person's family, friends, and co-workers among your clients as well. You are then selling by serving.

Follow-through is one of the most powerful service-oriented business-building sales techniques you can practice. By following through, you are extending your relationship with the client beyond the Completion Phase in a way that helps ensure you get another chance at the Greeting Phase.

Following are some techniques that help you retain clients by extending your relationship with them.

**Appointment reminder cards, follow-up calls, and thank-you cards show clients you care. They are among the easiest ways to build the goodwill that makes clients return.**

## Make Follow-Up Calls

Few salon professionals make follow-up calls, even in problem situations that may demand it. A client with a first-ever perm, for instance, would likely feel an extra degree of comfort after getting a call from a designer who wants to make sure everything was okay. Few things would impress a first-time client more than a call from either the designer or the receptionist asking how they liked their perm, nails, or facial.

By calling your clients to make sure they are happy, you get a second chance to address any problems that they might not have mentioned during the Completion Phase. Your call will make them feel important. The following table gives some ideas on how to follow-up with the different personality styles. Remember that most people have no one pure personality style, so your focus should be on enhancing rapport.

### Follow-Up Call Characteristics

| Personality Style | Follow-Up by Asking. . . |
|---|---|
| Cooperator | • How others liked the style and look |
| Analyzer | • Whether they had any difficulty with any details related to maintenance |
| Regulator | • Whether it's met their expectations for look and maintenance |
| Energizer | • How it looked and what kind of attention the style attracted |

## Send Thank-You Cards

Make it a habit to send a thank-you postcard to every new client. Your cards should appeal to all styles. You might even experiment with different cards for different personality styles. The following table provides some possibilities.

### Thank-You Card Possibilities

| Personality Style | Card Preferences |
|---|---|
| Cooperator | • Tends to respond to a friendly, warm design with a personal touch |
| Analyzer | • Generally responds best to something more formal and business like, and generally dislikes "cutesy" touches |
| Regulator | • Often prefers a fine, elegant card with hand-written address |
| Energizer | • Generally likes bright, bold designs and needs an appointment reminder |

In all cases, hand-addressing the envelope adds a personal touch to the card. Your client will notice that you took the time.

## Expanding Client Services

As you build your own clientele, remember that you are also responsible for the overall success of the salon and its other professionals. Once you have established a relationship with a client and they consistently return, it's your responsibility to see that they take advantage of your salon's other services.

The trend in the salon industry is to provide an increasingly wide range of beauty and spa services. The most effective way to build business for each salon professional is to introduce clients to a wide range of salon services. Better service, consistently delivered to the client, means success for the whole salon.

As you get to know a client, you will recognize additional ways that the salon can serve them:

- Provide a service that clients do themselves. For example, if a client mentions doing her nails, introduce her to your salon's nail technician with whom she may get a better manicure with less trouble.
- Provide a service the client is unfamiliar with. If a client talks about feeling stressed, offer to introduce him or her to the professional who provides facials or massages.
- Provide your male clients with services that they may think of as women's services, such as manicures or facials.

As you develop your level of contact and relationship with your clients, you'll know what they need and how to ask. At that point, you'll simply be providing greater service—and selling all the while.

**Service, like any skill, must be practiced. To gauge your performance, complete the Client Evaluation Worksheet for every client after each visit.**

## Evaluating Your Service Quality

The *Serving with CARE* program is a guide to providing excellent service, but it only works when you consistently put it into practice with all of your clients. The client evaluation form is intended to help you do this.

It helps you to practice your customer service skills and provides a system to ensure that clients are satisfied. It gives you a method to establish your starting point as well as gauge your progress.

Arranged according to the phases of the Service Cycle, the Service Checklist and Client Evaluation Worksheet help you evaluate your performance for each client over multiple visits.

Follow these guidelines with the Service Checklist and Client Evaluation Worksheet to enhance your service skills:

- Have copies of the form available.
- Complete the form after a client's initial visit.
- File the completed form for future reference.
- Before the client's next visit, check to see what areas needed improvement, and keep those in mind.
- Complete the form after the next visit and see what improvements you made and where you might still be lacking.

**If you are diligent, you can use the forms to keep statistics on repeat clients.**

## Service Checklist and Client Evaluation Worksheet

Client Name ______________________________

Client Personality Style ______________________________

The Service Checklist helps you make sure that none of the Service Cycle steps were missed during a client's visit. The Client Evaluation Worksheet allows you to rate your own performance during the service. As an evaluation form, it allows you to rate each aspect of your service. Both forms help you keep a better overall vision of your service ideal and how it develops as you progress to a Master salon professional.

| | Visit 1 Date | | | | Visit 2 Date | | | | Visit 3 Date | | | |
|---|---|---|---|---|---|---|---|---|---|---|---|---|
| | Exceptional | High-Quality | Medium | Below Average | Exceptional | High-Quality | Medium | Below Average | Exceptional | High-Quality | Medium | Below Average |
| **Greeting** | | | | | | | | | | | | |
| • How Well Did I Assess and Treat Client According to Personality Style? | | | | | | | | | | | | |
| • What was my Quality of Eye Contact? | | | | | | | | | | | | |
| • What was the Level of Client Comfort? | | | | | | | | | | | | |
| • What was my Level of Rapport? | | | | | | | | | | | | |
| **Assessment** | | | | | | | | | | | | |
| • Degree of Getting to Know Client | | | | | | | | | | | | |
| • Depth of Lifestyle and Values Assessment | | | | | | | | | | | | |
| • Range of Understanding Client Needs | | | | | | | | | | | | |
| • Depth to Which I Appreciated Client Desires and Motivations | | | | | | | | | | | | |
| • Degree I Showed Caring for Client | | | | | | | | | | | | |
| • What was my Level of Rapport? | | | | | | | | | | | | |

| | Visit 1 Date | | | | Visit 2 Date | | | | Visit 3 Date | | | |
|---|---|---|---|---|---|---|---|---|---|---|---|---|
| | Exceptional | High-Quality | Medium | Below Average | Exceptional | High-Quality | Medium | Below Average | Exceptional | High-Quality | Medium | Below Average |
| **Agreement** | | | | | | | | | | | | |
| • Quality and Range of Plan Created with Client | | | | | | | | | | | | |
| • Degree of Alignment with Client | | | | | | | | | | | | |
| • Level to Which I Communicated Plan in Understandable Terms | | | | | | | | | | | | |
| • Quality of Agreement | | | | | | | | | | | | |
| • How Well did I Anticipate Problems | | | | | | | | | | | | |
| • What was my Level of Rapport? | | | | | | | | | | | | |
| **Delivery** | | | | | | | | | | | | |
| • Did I Develop and Maintain Partnership with Client? | | | | | | | | | | | | |
| • Quality of Conversation with Client | | | | | | | | | | | | |
| • How Well Did I Keep Client Informed of What I Did? | | | | | | | | | | | | |
| • Did I Describe Products Used to Client? | | | | | | | | | | | | |
| • How Well Did I Discuss Techniques for Home Maintenance with Client? | | | | | | | | | | | | |
| • What was my Level of Rapport? | | | | | | | | | | | | |

| | Visit 1 Date | | | | Visit 2 Date | | | | Visit 3 Date | | | |
|---|---|---|---|---|---|---|---|---|---|---|---|---|
| | Exceptional | High-Quality | Medium | Below Average | Exceptional | High-Quality | Medium | Below Average | Exceptional | High-Quality | Medium | Below Average |
| **Recommendation** | | | | | | | | | | | | |
| • How Thoroughly Did I Assess First-time Client's Product Usage? | | | | | | | | | | | | |
| • How Well Did I Discuss Future Product Usage with Client? | | | | | | | | | | | | |
| • When Appropriate, Did I Make Product Recommendations to Client? | | | | | | | | | | | | |
| • How Well Did I Recommend Products from Multiple Service Areas? (Hair, Nails, Skin) | | | | | | | | | | | | |
| • What was my Level of Rapport? | | | | | | | | | | | | |
| **Completion** | | | | | | | | | | | | |
| • How Well Did I Review Service with Client? | | | | | | | | | | | | |
| • How Well Did I Correct Problems? | | | | | | | | | | | | |
| • How Well Did I Determine Whether Client Likes the Result? | | | | | | | | | | | | |
| • How Well Did I Thank the Client? | | | | | | | | | | | | |
| • How Well Did I Re-book the Client? | | | | | | | | | | | | |
| • What was my Level of Rapport? | | | | | | | | | | | | |
| • Did the Client Return? | | | | | | | | | | | | |

**Complete a Service Standards Worksheet to translate the concepts in *Serving with CARE* into your daily salon performance. You set the standards you want to achieve and identify the behaviors that will make it happen.**

## Setting Your Service Standards

To ensure that you provide a consistently high level of service, it helps to translate the concepts you learned in *Serving with CARE* into specific behaviors. That's the purpose of the Service Standards Worksheet we are about to introduce to you.

The form is designed for Novice salon professionals, but Professionals and Masters may find it useful for self-examination as well as for reinforcing existing habits and discovering any gaps in their client relationship skills.

You might want to present your Service Standards Worksheet along with your resumé when you seek a salon job. It will show prospective employers that you care about how you treat clients—a critical concern in the salon business today. It will also give you a way to assess the fit between you and the employer.

Salon owners, in fact, consistently report that they have difficulty finding beginning stylists who appreciate client service and who are skilled in working with people. The Service Standards Worksheet is designed to give you an edge by preparing to show salon owners:

- How you will present yourself in the salon and to clients?
- How you will manage each phase of the Service Cycle?
- How you will behave in relationships with customers?
- What you will do to handle problems?
- How you will retain existing clients?
- What you will do to gain new clients?
- How you will perform as a salon employee?

## Service Standards Worksheet

Now let's look at the Service Standards Worksheet. When complete, the worksheet lists:

- Actions you take with clients in the salon.
- Your standards for those actions.
- The behaviors you will exhibit to make the standard real. (You might want to actually photograph salons and situations that reflect your service standards and ideals).

But what is a "standard"? This definition of *standard* from *Webster's New World College Dictionary* serves our purposes: "a level of excellence, or attainment, regarded as a measure of adequacy."

A standard, in other words, is the level of performance you intend to be measured against. It's your vision of how you want to perform as a professional in a given area.

Here's how it works:

The Service Standards Worksheet is divided into sections that cover material presented in the *Serving with CARE* lessons. Each section contains these columns:

- Behavior and Service Area
- Standard(s) for Action
- Behavior to Achieve Standard

### Behaviors and Service Areas

Under each section, the first column lists Behaviors and Service Areas. All of the Behaviors and Service Areas listed in the worksheet are discussed in the course.

### Standards for Action

The second column is the area where you write your standard for that action. In writing your standards, think about how you like to be treated and use that as a guide for writing your own standard and the accompanying behaviors. Consider these questions:

- What is my ideal in this area?
- What behaviors do I want to display?
- What do I want my clients to experience as I perform that action?
- What would someone look at to see whether they had the experience I desired?

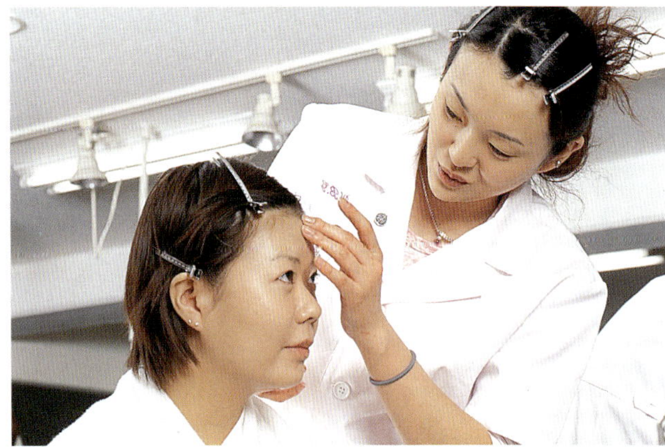

Remember as you work with your fellow students that you are practicing your standards of service as well as your technical skills.

How you write the standard depends on your personality and professional desires.

For instance, one area of your image as a salon professional is your choice of wardrobe. You may decide that your manner of dressing should set a fashion example for your clients. You may write your standard for dress like this:

- I will dress in creative, fashionable, yet professional clothes that are neat and clean.

Or maybe you decide you want your dress to match the environment of your salon. In that case, you would write your standard for dress like this:

- My dress will be conservative or flamboyant to match that of my salon's main clientele, whether professional, business casual, fashionable, or sporty.

Both are valid standards. Both can be measured. Where appropriate, include in your standard why you chose the standard. For example, in discussing your dress you might add, "To communicate respect and appreciation to my clients and co-workers."

### *Behavior to Achieve Standards*

In the third column, you list the behaviors necessary to make your client experience your standards. Consider this question:

- What do you need to do in order to achieve the standard?

For the standard of fashionable dress, you need to keep up with fashion trends. Your behavior may be to:

- Review fashion magazines monthly.
- Discuss my dress with my boss and colleagues.
- Pay attention to current street fashion.
- Notice how people dress on popular TV shows.

In order to match the environment of your salon, your behavior may be to:

- Review employee manual for dress codes.
- Observe how top stylists dress.
- Analyze my closet to locate appropriate wardrobe.

It may seem basic and maybe even tedious. But taking the time to picture yourself in each area of your professional performance will pay in both career and client success. You are building a vision for your future. It provides an initial map to mastery and will help you to operate a cut above the others. What will your standard be for filling your Service Standards Worksheet out?

What will you do to make sure you know current fashion trends in order to advise your clients?

## Service Standards Worksheet

This worksheet contains the standards for service I have developed during the *People Skills: Serving with CARE* course. As a salon professional, I uphold the highest standards of client service and care. This worksheet specifies the standards I hold and the behavior I exhibit to make those standards a daily reality in serving my clients.

### My Standards

| Behavior and Service Area | Standard(s) for Action | Behavior to Achieve Standard |
|---|---|---|
| **My Dress** | | |
| | | |
| | | |
| **My Hair Care** | | |
| | | |
| | | |
| **My Makeup** | | |
| | | |
| | | |
| **My Attitude** | | |
| | | |
| | | |
| | | |
| | | |

## My Standards for My Workspace

| Behavior and Service Area | Standard(s) for Action | Behavior to Achieve Standard |
|---|---|---|
| ***My Neatness*** | | |
| | | |
| | | |
| ***My Cleanliness*** | | |
| | | |
| | | |
| ***Availability of Tools*** | | |
| | | |
| | | |
| ***Maintenance of Tools*** | | |
| | | |
| | | |

## My Standards for Listening

| Behavior and Service Area | Standard(s) for Action | Behavior to Achieve Standard |
|---|---|---|
| *Factual Listening* | | |
| | | |
| | | |
| *Feeling Listening* | | |
| | | |
| | | |
| *Paying Attention* | | |
| | | |
| | | |
| *Accepting* | | |
| | | |
| | | |
| *Repetition* | | |
| | | |
| | | |
| *Paraphrasing* | | |
| | | |
| | | |

## My Standards for Greeting

| Behavior and Service Area | Standard(s) for Action | Behavior to Achieve Standard |
|---|---|---|
| Read Client Personality Style | | |
| | | |
| | | |
| Shake Hands | | |
| | | |
| | | |
| Make Eye Contact | | |
| | | |
| | | |
| Make Clients Feel Comfortable | | |
| | | |
| | | |
| Create Rapport | | |
| | | |
| | | |
| Show New Clients Around the Salon | | |
| | | |
| | | |
| Explain Salon Policies to New Clients | | |
| | | |
| | | |

## *My Standards for Assessment*

| Behavior and Service Area | Standard(s) for Action | Behavior to Achieve Standard |
|---|---|---|
| ***Get to Know the Client*** | | |
| | | |
| | | |
| ***Assess Lifestyle and Values*** | | |
| | | |
| | | |
| ***Understand Client Needs*** | | |
| | | |
| | | |
| ***Appreciate Client Desires*** | | |
| | | |
| | | |
| ***Understand Client Motivations*** | | |
| | | |
| | | |

## My Standards for Agreement

| Behavior and Service Area | Standard(s) for Action | Behavior to Achieve Standard |
|---|---|---|
| *Create Plan with Client* | | |
| | | |
| | | |
| *Become Aligned with Client* | | |
| | | |
| | | |
| *Communicate Plan in Terms the Client Understands* | | |
| | | |
| | | |
| *Agree on Plan* | | |
| | | |
| | | |
| *Anticipate Problems* | | |
| | | |
| | | |
| *Provide Contingencies for Problems* | | |
| | | |
| | | |
| *Develop Partnership with Client* | | |
| | | |
| | | |

## My Standards for Delivery

| Behavior and Service Area | Standard(s) for Action | Behavior to Achieve Standard |
|---|---|---|
| *Converse with Client* | | |
| | | |
| | | |
| *Keep Client Informed of What I'm Doing* | | |
| | | |
| | | |
| *Discuss Techniques for Home Maintenance with Client* | | |
| | | |
| | | |

## My Standards for Product Recommendation

| Behavior and Service Area | Standard(s) for Action | Behavior to Achieve Standard |
|---|---|---|
| *Discuss Product Usage with Client* | | |
| | | |
| | | |
| *Make Product Recommendations to Client* | | |
| | | |
| | | |
| *Recommend Products from Multiple Service Areas (Hair, Nails, Skin)* | | |
| | | |
| | | |

## My Standards for Completion

| Behavior and Service Area | Standard(s) for Action (why) | Behavior to Achieve Standard |
|---|---|---|
| Review Service with Clients | | |
| | | |
| | | |
| Correct Problems | | |
| | | |
| | | |
| Determine Whether Client Likes the Result | | |
| | | |
| | | |
| Thank the Client | | |
| | | |
| | | |
| Re-book the Client | | |
| | | |
| | | |
| Relay Client Feedback to Others in Salon | | |
| | | |
| | | |
| Follow-up with Client After Service | | |
| | | |
| | | |

## *My Standards for Career Development*

| Behavior and Service Area | Standard(s) for Action | Behavior to Achieve Standard |
|---|---|---|
| ***Maintain Polite, Professional Phone Manner*** | | |
| | | |
| | | |
| ***Show up on Time*** | | |
| | | |
| | | |
| ***Stay on Schedule*** | | |
| | | |
| | | |
| ***Help Out Fellow Employees When Needed*** | | |
| | | |
| | | |
| ***Follow Salon Policies and Procedures*** | | |
| | | |
| | | |
| ***Set Goals with Supervisor*** | | |
| | | |
| | | |

## EXERCISES

1. Fill out the "Client Evaluation Worksheet" for each of your clients. Rate yourself honestly as a way to review and reinforce your developing people skills.

2. Write thank-you cards to send to first-time clients (even in the clinic). Write a classy thank-you, a humorous thank-you, a sincere thank-you, and a business-like thank-you. When choosing a style, consider your personal style and what is appropriate for individual clients. Think of additional thank-you card possibilities, and decide which clients you would send to each.

3. Make follow-up calls to your new clients. Ask them how they like the results of the service and whether they have any questions or problems with home maintenance. What kind of results did you get? Discuss in class.

4. List the service businesses you use and the ways they follow up, such as thank-you cards and follow-up calls. Think of businesses you use and instances in which you receive thank-you notes. What do you like about them?

## MAIN POINT SUMMARY

Building your business for the long-term means expanding your client base. Retaining existing clients while you continue building your clientele will help you accomplish this.

Providing excellent service is the surest way to retain clients. In the final analysis, it is your relationship with the client and the way you provide service—rather than technical expertise—that keeps them coming back.

To retain clients, it is critical that you re-book before they leave the salon. Without follow-up, even the most satisfied and loyal clients may not return. Hectic modern life often forces us to change plans on the spur of the moment, and a great client without an appointment may simply find it more convenient to go elsewhere. Remember the follow-up techniques and which ones are most effective with the different CARE personality types.

The concepts you've learned in *Serving with CARE* are a starting point toward providing excellent service and growing your business. Use it to provide stellar service to all of your clients. The Client Evaluation Worksheet, organized according to the Service Cycle, can be an excellent gauge of your developing service relationship with each and every client.

## SELF-TEST/REVIEW

1. What are the two basic activities that allow you to grow your client base?

   1. ______________________________

   2. ______________________________

2. In general, your technical abilities will suffice to retain and gain clients.
   Circle One:

   True or False

3. Briefly describe a scenario in which a satisfied client—who has not been re-booked—does not return and is not retained.

   ______________________________

   ______________________________

   ______________________________

   ______________________________

4. Write a couple of short thank-you sentences for each of the four personality styles.

   Cooperator: ______________________________

   ______________________________

   ______________________________

   Analyzer: ______________________________

   ______________________________

   ______________________________

   Regulator: ______________________________

   ______________________________

   ______________________________

   Energizer: ______________________________

   ______________________________

   ______________________________

# Congratulations!

You've made it! In completing *Serving with CARE*, Part 2 of *People Skills for the Salon Professional*, you have learned how the personality styles you discovered in *Relating with CARE* help you provide the excellent service that keeps clients coming back.

In Unit 5, Service: Introduction, you learned about service and received an introduction to the Service Cycle. Through the Service CARE Profile, you discovered how your own personality style may differ as a consumer of service and a provider of service. Finally, you reviewed the personality styles and how to serve each of them.

In Unit 6, Service Fundamentals, you learned about the two key service skills: understanding values and effective listening. You learned how your values and your clients values are reflected in behavior, and you learned how to listen to clients in ways that make them feel valued.

In Unit 7, The Service Cycle, you learned the details of the six phases of service. You learned how to:

- Greet clients and establish rapport in the Greeting Phase
- Assess their image and needs in the Assessment Phase
- Agree on the services you are going to provide in the Agreement Phase
- Deliver services while maintaining rapport in the Delivery Phase
- Recommend the products and service clients need to maintain their look in the Recommendation Phase
- Complete the visit in a way that ensures clients return in the Completion Phase

In Unit 8, you learned about the relationship between sales and service and how to follow-through with a client. You also completed client review forms and set your own standards of service.

Bon Voyage! In France, that's what they say to wish someone a good journey. We wish you that and more as you begin to develop the "people" part of your career in the salon industry. We hope you thrive in this marvelously varied industry and develop satisfying, lifelong relationships, whether you build a cherished clientele, run a salon, sell beauty products, or teach others salon and people skills.

Be well and remember: Stay in rapport with CARE!

# Glossary

### Active Conversation
A conversational approach in which the salon professional initiates most of the topics and dialogue. This often works well with passive clients.

### Alignment
To be in agreement with another; focused attention of client and designer toward same goals.

### Analyzer
The "A" in CARE. A passive and thinking-oriented personality style.

### Agreement Phase
The third phase of the Service Cycle in which you propose a plan of action, fine-tune the plan, and reach alignment with your client to secure rapport before proceeding with the delivery.

### Assessment Phase
The second phase of the Service Cycle in which you use your listening and consultation skills to understand and accept exactly what the client wants and needs.

### Attention
A basic requirement for effective listening in which you minimize distractions and attend to the needs of your clients to let them know that you are focusing on them.

### CARE
Stands for the four basic personality styles: Cooperator, Analyzer, Regulator and Energizer.

### CARE Profile Questionnaire
A questionnaire that suggests the extent to which an individual possesses each of the four personality styles.

### Client Evaluation Worksheet
A worksheet that allows you to evaluate your performance at each step in the Service Cycle and for each client over multiple visits.

### Client Interaction Plan
A plan for how best to relate to a given client.

### Comfort Zone
The physical, emotional, and mental boundaries or distances we maintain between ourselves and others.

### Completion Phase
The sixth and final phase of the Service Cycle in which you review the service, determine the client's level of satisfaction, acknowledge and correct any problems, and secure the next appointment.

### Consultation
A key component of the Assessment Phase where you ask careful, probing questions and listen to your clients to improve your understanding of them.

### Contingencies
A backup plan discussed during the Agreement Phase that consists of actions your client can take if the service doesn't turn out as expected.

### Cooperator
The "C" in CARE. A passive and feeling personality style that tends to value harmony and wants people to get along.

### Delivery Phase
The fourth phase of the Service Cycle in which technical skills are used to provide the service that you and the client agreed upon, and people skills are used to maintain rapport.

### Emotional Boundaries
The limit of personal sharing and expression between you and your client.

### Energizer
The "E" in CARE. A personality style that is assertive and feeling. This style tends to be more outgoing, expressive, and energetic.

### Entertaining Conversation
A conversational approach in which the salon professional maintains the client's attention with amusing statements or actions. This often works best with feeling-oriented clients.

### Factual Listening (Literal Listening)
Paying attention to the information given by a speaker, such as facts and details, and ignoring context and feeling.

### Feeling Listening (Empathetic Listening)
Paying attention to a speaker's nonverbal messages, body language, and tone of voice to better understand the context and feelings being communicated.

### Greeting Phase
The first phase of the Service Cycle in which you welcome and interact with the client to establish or reestablish rapport.

### Recommendation Phase
The fifth phase of the Service Cycle in which you learn which products your clients are currently using and suggest any products that will help them maintain their new look.

### Hidden Agenda
An unspoken expectation of something we want but do not to discuss openly.

### Interaction
The second part of the Greeting Phase, following the welcome, where you further establish or reestablish rapport with your client before the Assessment.

### Jargon
Technical terms of the salon industry that can confuse the client and reduce alignment, especially during the Agreement Phase.

### Levels of Service
Three different skill levels—Novice, Professional, and Master—used to describe varying degrees of experience and proficiency with the *People Skills* program.

### Lifestyle Values
Values that are reflected in what a person considers important to his or her way of life, including financial security, appearance, comfort, and success.

### Master Level
The highest level of service in which people and relationships are completely understood and strong technical skills come naturally.

### Mental Boundaries
The attitudes, perceptions, and prejudices that divide people, such as religion, class, gender, and race.

### Mirroring
Encouraging the flow of conversation with clients by repeating and paraphrasing what they are saying back to them.

### New Client Assessment Questionnaire
A form used with new clients during the Assessment Phase to obtain information from them and begin discovering their personality styles in order to improve the quality of rapport and service.

### Novice Level
The introductory level of service in which improving technical skills is the primary focus. Novices are just learning to use people skills to build rapport and serve clients.

### Paraphrasing
A technique of mirroring or reflecting speakers back to themselves by using different words to confirm the essence of the original message. This is usually used with feeling listening.

### Passive Conversation
A conversational approach in which the salon professional mostly listens, using occasional responses and encouragement to draw out the client. This often works best with assertive clients.

### People Skills
Skills that give you the ability to relate to a wide variety of people and work well with them.

### Personal Action Plan
A plan for actions you need to take to overcome personality traits that don't serve your success.

### Personality Style
A person's traits and behaviors that reveal something about the way they think and act and feel. The CARE Profile outlines four basic personality styles: Cooperator, Analyzer, Regulator, and Energizer.

### Personality Values
The things that matter to a person, as indicated primarily by their personality style and how they relate to other people.

### Physical Boundaries
The acceptable distance and amount of contact between you and your client.

### Professional Level
The middle level of service in which technical skills are natural but using people skills requires thoughtful planning.

### Rapport
The condition of getting along with people harmoniously. Rapport is an abstraction like a thought or feeling.

### Regulator
The "R" in CARE. A personality style that lends itself to being assertive and thinking tends toward action and direction. Regulators are often leaders.

### Relevant Response
Any type of response to a speaker, including repetition, paraphrasing, a head-nod or a short phrase, that builds rapport and encourages the conversation.

### Repetition
Repeating back to a client exactly what was said to clarify information or to provide a relevant response. This often works well with factual listening.

### Service
The professional assistance and attention you give to your clients.

### Service CARE Profile
A questionnaire to help you understand how your own personality style affects the ways you give and receive service.

### Service Cycle
A six-phase journey that you go on with each client, consisting of the Greeting, Assessment, Agreement, Delivery, Recommendation, and Completion Phases.

### Service Standards Worksheet
A form that provides a review of the Service Cycle and helps you transfer each of the *Serving with CARE* concepts into your daily salon performance.

### Servitude
The condition of slavery or forced labor—often confused with service.

### Standard
The level of performance you intend to be measured against, such as a vision of how you want to act as a salon professional.

### Style Shifting
Shifting from your primary personality pattern to another pattern to temporarily communicate better in a given situation with a particular person.

### Technical Skills
Proficiency at a craft; skill relating to the "nuts and bolts" of a job.

### Value
A quality or standard that is viewed as important, useful, and desirable.

### Welcome
The first part of the Greeting Phase in which you make initial verbal or nonverbal contact with the client.

## Acknowledgements

The author wishes to thank the many people who made this revision of the *People Skills* program possible, particularly the dedicated Pivot Point teachers and students who shared their insights, experience, and feedback.

Following is a list of individuals and organizations who participated in the development of *People Skills for the Salon Professional*.

### Development Team

**Robert Wright**
Author and Originator
School of Exceptional Living

**Collin Canright**
Editor & Project Coordinator
Canright & Paule, Inc.

**Sandy Mauk**
Instructional Development
School of Exceptional Living

**Bruce Kanarek**
Consultant

### Editorial

**Judy Rambert**
Vice President Research
Pivot Point International, Inc.

**Maureen Spurr**
Editor
Pivot Point International, Inc.

**Corrine Passage**
Vice President Publishing
Pivot Point International, Inc.

### Design and Production

**Christina Paule Canright**
Design Principal
Canright & Paule, Inc.

**Rick Russell**
Production
Canright & Paule, Inc.

**Eileen Dubelbeis**
Production
Canright & Paule, Inc.

**David R. Head, Jr.**
Writer
Canright & Paule, Inc.

**Ian Mcintire**
Writer
Canright & Paule, Inc

**Ryan McNew**
Production
Canright & Paule, Inc

### Educational Review

**Anna Fehr**
Pivot Point International, Inc.

**Victoria Anderson**
Pivot Point International, Inc.

**Brian Fallon**
Pivot Point International, Inc.

**Janet Fisher**
Pivot Point International, Inc.

**Sandra Leland**
Pivot Point International, Inc.

**Jean Francois Demars**
Pivot Point France

**Jerry Poer**
Charleston Cosmetology Institute

**Bill Wyer**
Sydney's College of Hairdressing

### Photography, Hair and Makeup

**David Placek**

**Lori Neapolitan**
Makeup

**Victoria Anderson**
Hair

**Frank Campanella**
Hair and Makeup

Historical Photos Courtesy of:
**Tony Kendall**
Wild Hair Museum
French Lick, IN

Esthetic Photos Courtesy of:
**Pivot Point Japan**

Photos shot at:
**Maxine, Ltd.**
Chicago

### Publisher

**Leo Passage**
Chairman
Pivot Point International, Inc.

**Robert Passage**
Vice President, School Division
Pivot Point International, Inc.

**Jan Laan**
Chief Executive Officer
Pivot Point International, Inc.